W9-COR-154

THE Menuchah PRINCIPLE

In Shidduchim, Dating & Engagement

The Pathway to Marriage

Based on the teachings of
Rav Chaim Friedlander, zt"l,
and the wisdom of Chazal

Shaya Ostrov L.C.S.W.

AUTHOR OF *THE INNER CIRCLE: SEVEN GATES TO MARRIAGE*

The Menuchah Principle
In Shidduchim, Dating & Engagement
© 2012 Shaya Ostrov

ISBN: 978-1-60763-077-7

Proofreaders: Tova Salb, Hadassa Goldsmith
Designer: Justine Elliott

THE JUDAICA PRESS, INC.
123 Ditmas Avenue / Brooklyn, NY 11218
718-972-6200 / 800-972-6201
info@judaicapress.com
www.judaicapress.com

Manufactured in the United States of America

YESHIVA OF FAR ROCKAWAY ◆ **DERECH AYSON RABBINICAL SEMINARY**

802 HICKSVILLE ROAD ◆ FAR ROCKAWAY, NEW YORK 11691 ◆ 718.327.7600 ◆ FAX: 718.327.1430

בס״ד

Rabbi Yechiel I. Perr
Rosh HaYeshiva

Rabbi Aaron M. Brafman
Menahel

Rabbi Eli Goldgrab
General Studies Principal

Rabbi Shayeh Kohn
Executive Director

In his The Menuchah Principle in Marriage, Reb Shaya Ostrov shares his own heart and soul with us. A lifetime of experience and a lifetime of wisdom are to be found between the covers of this book. It should surprise us that one only in midlife, as is the author, has distilled much of life's wisdom onto the leaves of this work. But we have already been assured by the ancient Rabi Meir (Avos 4:27) "there are indeed new casks filled with old wine." Reading or rather studying this work, is indeed an educational and maturing experience.

One of the special graces of this work are the many stories and parables with which the author illustrates his teachings. These are culled from our sacred sources and from other places, as well as from the experiences of life. It is sad that our generation suffers a shortage of role models of authentic Torah living. However, properly understood stories of our Torah greats continue to provide us with inspiration and direction even when living examples are absent.

Although this work is primarily directed toward shalom bayis, every person has much to gain from its teachings. The author is to be congratulated for increasing the peace and the welfare of our people.

בתקוה רבה יחיאל מיכל פרר

RABBI NAFTALI JAEGER
ROSH HAYESHIVA

16th of Tammuz 5770

"Deep water is counsel in the heart of man, and the man of understanding will draw it forth" (*Mishlei* 20:5). This is comparable to a deep well of cold, refreshing water that was inaccessible until someone came and fashioned a rope to draw it forth. Then all were able to draw its waters and slake their thirst (*Bereishis Rabbah*).

The S'fas Emes explains that within every one of us there is counsel. To access this counsel, we must turn to the man of understanding, who by means of the Torah can draw it forth.

My dear and wise friend, Reb Shaya Ostrov, נ״י, has devoted many years to guiding and advising others, particularly in family matters. Reb Shaya's previous *sefarim* have been well accepted and now he adds another link to this chain, with his current work, *The Menuchah Principle In Marriage*. Completely based on the teachings of *Chazal* and our teachers, the giants of Mussar and Torah thought, this book enables the reader to attain calmness of spirit and to avoid confusion.

Reb Shaya is a cherished presence in our *beis medrash*. He spends hours each day toiling in Torah, so it is fitting for him to delve into these matters.

I am certain that one who earnestly studies his books with intent to implement the ideas contained within will fulfill the words of Eliyahu *HaNavi*: "If a person has Torah and suffering comes upon him, his heart remains settled, but the heart of a person devoid of Torah will be embittered" (*Tana D'vei Eliyahu*, Ch. 27).

We owe Reb Shaya a debt of gratitude for his insights and advice on how to live a life focused on eternity — a life of Torah and fear of Hashem. Through them, the heart becomes settled, and one merits true happiness.

I humbly bless him that his wellsprings should flow outwards to give ... "to the hungry, bread (there is no bread but Torah), and bring to your home the downtrodden poor (there is no poverty but that of understanding) ... Then your light will break forth like the dawn and your healing will quickly sprout. Your righteousness will precede you, and the glory of Hashem will gather you in" (*Yeshayah* 59:7-8).

In recognition and gratitude for all he does.

With deep endearment,

Naftali HaLevi Jaeger

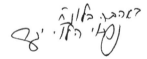

שער ישוב
SH'OR YOSHUV
INSTITUTE

ONE CEDARLAWN AVENUE • LAWRENCE, NEW YORK 11559 • (516) 239-9002 • FAX: (516) 239-9003

PHONE No. 516-239-2444 EXT. 103
E-MAIL: RABBI@SHAARAY-TEFILAH.ORG

FAX No. 516-239-2199

CONGREGATION SHAARAY TEFILA
CENTRAL AND LORD AVENUES
LAWRENCE, N.Y. 11559

DAVID WEINBERGER
RABBI

בס״ד

I read with great pleasure the most recent work of my dear friend, Rabbi Shaya Ostrov "The Menuchah Principle in Marriage." As in his previous works Rabbi Ostrov has based his ideas and concepts on Chazal in addition to effectively using the chochma b'goyim for practical tips.

We are living in an unprecedented difficult time in preparing our children for marriage and ultimately their sustaining a life l'shalom bayis. Many books have been written and many seminars held to deal with the new complexities of our challenging society. Shaya Ostrov is making a difference in the lives of the many that he counsels but will be most effective to the broader Jewish community through the very practical and usable work that he has presently authored.

We are all frazzled and living under a myriad of stresses and tensions that undoubtedly affects our Sholom Bayis. Learning how to have menuchas hanefesh during these trying times will have a major impact in improving ourselves and our families.

I wish him continuous hatzlacha in all of his endeavors in helping to create healthy marriages and homes in Klal Yisroel.

Sincerely,

Rabbi Dovid Weinberger

Haskamah reprinted from the author's previous book with Rav Brafman's consent

YESHIVA OF FAR ROCKAWAY ◆ DERECH AYSON RABBINICAL SEMINARY
802 HICKSVILLE ROAD ◆ FAR ROCKAWAY, NEW YORK 11691 ◆ 718.327.7600 ◆ FAX: 718.327.1430

בס״ד

Rabbi Yechiel I. Perr
Rosh HaYeshiva

Rabbi Aaron M. Brafman
Menahel

Rabbi Eli Goldgrab
General Studies Principal

Rabbi Shayeh Kohn
Executive Director

The name Kelm – or the Alter of Kelm evokes an image of one of the main mussar Yeshivas founded by R' Yisroel Salanter's greatest talmid. Kelm cultivated menuchas hanefesh – calmness of spirit – as the most prized and most necessary quality to achieve spiritual greatness.

This gives the individual the ability to be organized, to concentrate, not to be easily distracted and remain free of anger. Some of the greatest Gedolim and baalei mussar were a product of Kelm: the Alter of Slabodka, R' Yechezkel Levenstein, R' Elya Lopian, Rav Elchonon Wasserman, Rav Yeruchem Levovitz, Rav Eliyahu Dessler, Rav Nossan Wachtfogel, among others.

If one wants to get an idea of what it was and try to achieve this prized state – this is the book for you. It is not easy reading, as are many of the self help Jewish books on the market. It is very deep and makes a very profound analysis of the human nature and the connection of mind, soul and body. But it does not stop at the theoretical, but rather walks you through the difficult work of attaining the goal as one would if he were part of a mussar vaad at Kelm or Slabodka or the Mir.

If one could take these lessons to heart it would go a long way to solve so many problem areas of life. In the world of frenzied, out of control living today, menuchas hanefesh would be a true blessing for all of us.

with sincere wishes
for success in helping
others
Aaron M. Brafman

YAAKOV AND ILANA MELOHN BUILDING IN MEMORY OF REB YOSEF MELOHN
ישיבה דרך איתן ע״ש מרן רבי אברהם יפהן זצ״ל

*T*his book is dedicated to …

The memory of my beloved chavrusa, teacher and friend, Reb Yisroel Bloom, zt"l. Our dream and dedication was to help many Jewish neshamos discover their bashert. With Hashem's assistance, this book will bring us closer to realizing this dream.

A cherished friend whose generosity has provided me with the funding and encouragement to create this work and enabled me to remain focused on its completion. May Hashem grant him and his entire family countless brachos for fullness of Torah life.

The generations of Jewish neshamos yearning to be born as two lives are brought together and loving Torah homes and families unfold.

The courageous and inspiring couples I have come to know, love and respect as they have journeyed together to discover Hashem's true gifts of life.

The loving memory of R'Yitzchok ben R' Aharon Ze'ev Hakohain and R' Yosef ben R' Avrohom Pinchus.

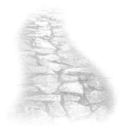

Contents

THE PURPOSE OF
THIS BOOK

This book is meant to successfully guide you through the experience of dating and engagement. I have endeavored to write it in a style and format that lends itself to being read as you are preparing for or progressing through these stages of a relationship that will, *b'ezras* Hashem, lead to marriage. However, for couples ready to enter into a very meaningful shared learning experience, I have also written this book to actually be read aloud and together by dating and engaged couples. My goal is to provide the dating experience with a much-needed dimension of purpose and depth. So, whether you are reading alone or as a couple, you will discover that each word, thought and principle guides you through a very enlightening and meaningful learning experience that brings you closer to understanding how to achieve your goal of a lifetime of marital fulfillment.

The book is also designed to inform and enlighten everyone interested in better understanding the crucial issues related to *shidduchim*, dating and engagement. This means parents, *shadchanim*, rabbis, teachers, siblings and friends. Through reading it alone or with a *chavrusa* (study partner) you will discover that your ability to be more enlightened, insightful and effective with singles who are dating or with engaged couples will be greatly enhanced. Your informed efforts are essential, as the phrase, "it takes a village," is certainly true regarding getting to the *chupah*.

◇ Our Shared Challenge

Today there is a new and daunting challenge involved in dating. It is that all dating and even engaged couples have to remain focused on that one special person in order to be successful and create a meaningful close and loving marriage. However, to achieve this they need to learn to be undistracted, emotionally intact, connected, secure and quiet within the deepest dimension of self as they take the journey toward building a relationship together. The reason is that one soul can recognize its destined life partner only when our deeper self learns to connect to another deeper self.

Now, however, an ever-increasing number of Jewish souls are experiencing great frustration in identifying and learning to develop a relationship with their *bashert* (designated life partner). This is why I feel compelled to present these concepts, which can help couples recognize and connect to each other's true soul partner.

◇ The Goal and Focus of this Book

The intended benefit of this book is to teach you to acquire the ability to be a balanced, caring and sensitive individual throughout the dating and engagement process. It will repeatedly guide you to discover how to reach your goal without distractions while overcoming negative thoughts, feelings — and even habits — that have deprived you of life's greatest treasure — the ability to share your life with that one person designated to be your *bashert*.

I have divided this book into four sections, to teach the concepts and provide a comprehensive overview of how to transform relationships into meaningful shared experiences:

+ *Menuchas Hanefesh* as the Foundation of Relationship Building in Dating and Engagement (Chapter III)

+ Five Dimensions of Experiencing *Menuchas Hanefesh* (Chapter IV)

+ Transforming *Pizur Hanefesh* into *Menuchas Hanefesh* (Chapters V–VII)

+ The EMBERS Program for Cultivating Commitment and Closeness (Chapter VIII)

Each of these sections will become a shared learning experience as you progress on your journey toward *menuchas hanefesh*, which is the foundation for building and enriching your growing relationship. By the time you have completed reading this book, you will have deepened your capacity for the personal qualities of clarity, inner peace and a healthy and focused state of mind so essential to cultivating a mutually fulfilling relationship with the one person designated to be your *bashert*.

It is my deepest wish that each of you who will read this book — whether together with a dating partner, your *chassan* or *kallah*, friend or *chavrusa*, or by yourself — will achieve the understanding and personal experience of *menuchas hanefesh* that Hashem wishes for us all. Beyond this, it is my heartfelt *tefillah* (prayer) that each of you who are searching for your life partner or are engaged will be able to use Chazal's precious tools to build a relationship that will last a lifetime. And if you are a *shadchan*, friend, parent or anyone who desires to help those searching for that singular *neshamah* (soul) destined as a life partner and life builder, may Hashem grant you the wisdom to successfully guide others, and achieve great success in your special and very sacred undertaking.

◇ **Anecdotal and Case Histories**

Throughout this book, I have incorporated many anecdotes and case histories from my practice. In each of these examples, I have attempted to maintain two overarching guidelines. The first is to clearly demonstrate how the application of these principles has the ability to impact in a positive manner on relationship building and overcoming the challenges that all couples need to surmount to reach this goal. The second is to preserve the anonymity of the couples I am describing. I achieve this by changing gender, altering quotable phrases and the description of symptoms. However, the goal of providing the reader with clear examples is never compromised. Throughout this book you will find frequent quotations I have cited from singles and couples. These quotes are used to emphasize the communication of personal experiences and feelings and may not accurately represent the precise wording originally expressed. However, they are all true to the experience that I am attempting to convey.

◇ Overcoming Sima's Helplessness

Let's begin our journey toward this union with a description of a young woman experiencing great distress. It is a tale that I can tell many times over with a different gender, age or symptoms. Yet, each version and description will be true, because these distressing experiences have become so familiar to each of you dedicated to discovering your *bashert*.

> Sima was a teacher in her late twenties who had been dating for many years. Over the past three months, she and Avi had shared numerous dates where they learned to feel very trusting and comfortable with each other. This growing feeling surprised Sima, as recently, she had been experiencing a growing sense of hopelessness of ever finding someone who had the qualities she felt were necessary for her life partner. And now, she was actually learning to feel comfortable with Avi. She was beginning to experience a renewed sense of hope and promise. He was everything she had hoped to discover in a young man.

However, as dating continued and the couple began to discuss the possibility of engagement, her positive feelings began to be overshadowed by a critical voice within her. She found herself irritated by qualities that didn't seem to bother her until now, and she began to hesitate and pull back. She was now rethinking the future of the relationship.

Then she recalled an earlier dating experience she had with a young man she liked very much and wanted to marry. Yet, when he raised the idea of marriage, Sima began to feel an uncontrollable need to delay and put him off. She could not quiet an insistent sense of discomfort over the thought of engagement to him. She felt assaulted by her inner questions. Perhaps he was not as mature and developed as she felt she needed? Perhaps she was being too hasty when there was someone else more suitable? Was he motivated enough in his learning or his plans for a career?

Her questions were relentless and her uncertainty kept him hanging, until he finally told her he could not continue. She tried to pull herself together and told him she was ready. Yet, he sensed she wasn't and moved on. He was engaged within a year, and she had since wondered what would have been had she been able to move ahead with him.

Now, after almost seven years of drought, with no one who seemed appropriate for her, she finally met Avi. And after three months of learning to feel secure with him, the same process was unfolding. First, she began to realize that she could like him. Then, as before, she felt herself creating distance and pulling away. She saw fault with his dress, his moments of indecision, his expressions and his appearance. On one hand, it was clear to her that she would never come across another Avi. Nevertheless, here she was again, feeling critical and wondering whether there could be someone better. She was acutely aware of her anxiety in her thoughts, her feelings and even her body.

As Sima and I met, she began to honestly express her fears that history was about to repeat itself. In her mind, there was no possibility that she could bring her thoughts and feelings under control. "How can I consider marrying someone if I can't stop feeling this way?" However, she was also aware that after seven years of dating, it was unlikely she would be able to meet someone else she felt she could marry. Now, with her and Avi at this critical point, there was a forlorn feeling that she could not proceed, and she was helpless to prevent herself from walking away. "The last time this happened was seven years ago. I made a mistake then, and I'm making a bigger mistake now. But I don't feel like I can prevent myself from falling into the same trap. Am I supposed to remain unmarried for the rest of my life?"

I listened and empathized as Sima expressed her deep despair. However, I was aware that was she was not alone. Many others, both men and women, some younger and some older, continuously struggle with these confusing feelings of uncertainty, irritability, fear, anxiety and countless other negative thoughts and emotions that imprison them in patterns of frustration, failure and disappointment. And it's true that they may function very well in all the other crucial areas of their lives. They may have professions that require complex skills and higher than average intelligence. They may have many friends and love their nieces and nephews. They may even be considered Torah scholars or gifted in the area of religious outreach or *chessed* (kindness). However, in this area of relationship building with a potential life partner, where it matters most, they are entrapped in these repetitive patterns that lock them into their aloneness.

Over the years, Sima has probably been in therapy

where she was told that her behavior was "sabotaging" her relationships. However, this revelation is rarely enough to lift her or anyone else above these self-destructive patterns. Sima learned a far more important and effective truth. Her changing perceptions are the result of entering into a negative state of mind. Even more important, she is never deprived of the ability to transform her state of mind where she can remember those moments when she and Avi were building their relationship, based on caring moments of mutual respect and understanding. Only as she learns that she is never deprived of her freedom to enter her healthier state of mind will she be able to cultivate this relationship that may very well lead to a fulfilling and loving marriage.

Over the next few weeks, Sima learned to see Avi and their relationship from a quieter, more secure and clearer perspective. Sima learned to quiet the critical voices within and complete her journey of discovery toward marriage. Sima learned what each of us needs to grasp. We are never locked into a negative state of mind. Hashem always gives each of us the ability to transform our thoughts and feelings to reflect who we are deep within, and to realize our longing for the union that will enable us to discover completion and fulfillment with our *bashert*. All of these principles are grounded in what Chazal have defined as *menuchas hanefesh*.

Within a few weeks of our meeting, Sima became a *kallah*. She learned many skills related to the art of centering, meditative walking and the three principles of thought that enabled her to regain her sense of balance. Recently, she and Avi celebrated the birth of their first son.

In many ways, Sima's dilemma embodies many of the challenges facing *frum* singles of all ages and backgrounds. You may be a young woman or man returning from a year in Eretz Yisrael and planning to spend the first year or two in *kollel*. You may be a professional living in the Upper West Side or Katamon. You may have begun dating a few months ago, or, painfully, decades ago. You may have even been previously engaged or married. The phenomenon of being caught up in the endless confusion, anxiety and negative thoughts and feelings affects each of us in our lives and especially those of you who are dating. It is not necessarily a sign of pathology or illness, and certainly not a sign of bad *middos* (attributes) or of being punished. Each one of us needs to learn that at each moment of our lives, we have far more choices for self-fulfillment than we were ever aware of. Teaching you how to take advantage of what Hashem gives us all and desires that each of us learn is the true contribution I hope this book will make in your lives.

This book, therefore, has been written as an ongoing relationship building experience that enables dating and engaged couples to utilize valuable time together to carefully share and internalize each concept that lays the foundation of a bond that can continuously blossom and ripen over a lifetime. You can read it together in a restaurant, park, hotel lobby or even over the phone.

During the time spent on each session, you will experience a quieter, gentler and more meaningful bond. And as you progress and complete this work together, its wisdom and mood become the essence of what you have learned to share with each other. In the end, it enables two people to become best friends — the real foundation for engagement and marriage. And, of course, if you are not dating, you can read it alone or with a reading partner. It makes little difference. You will discover that these golden thoughts of Chazal are life-transforming.

So permit me to take you on this personal and shared journey that may very well determine your destiny, as it has for so many.

CHAPTER I
From a Historical Perspective

The desire to discover our soul partner is embedded in a longing that has resided within our deepest selves, and it reaches back through the ages — to our earliest roots, beginning with Adam and Chavah. It is a yearning that has continued unabated through every generation since — until our very own. It is an integral dimension of our humanity. Our search for our life partner exists within each of us, because Hashem has planted this desire within the essence of our very beings, and it has never been, nor will ever be, extinguished. And throughout our long history, there has never been any war or tragedy strong enough to silence this deep, persistent need to share our lives with our destined life partner. Even following the horrors of the Holocaust, couples rediscovered each other, or found new partners with whom to rebuild shattered lives.

However, in our generation, this most human of all dreams has been muffled and even silenced for thousands of young men and women. The noise, distractions and faux illusions of the modern Western society in which we all live have taken a devastating toll. For the first time in history, there are countless single individuals, both men and women, whose search for a life partner may be unceasing, yet unproductive. Each day, I encounter an increasing number of both younger and more mature singles who are dating endlessly and going nowhere. At the same time, I encounter a steady stream of engaged couples who count the approaching days to their *chupah*, filled with a never-ending chorus of dread, continuously obsessing, "Did I make the wrong decision?" and "Perhaps there was someone better?"

So, on one hand, there is a growing number of singles who fear that they will lead their lives alone and will leave this world without having discovered and shared a life with their *bashert* or the opportunity to build a family. And on the other, there are a growing number of engaged couples who, although their dream of engagement and marriage may have finally been realized, are filled with unsettling and even frightening feelings that they may have made the wrong decision.

Just to provide you with a real time perspective, during the very day I was writing these words, I was contacted by three engaged individuals whose weddings were approaching, who are filled with the very thoughts and fears I just mentioned. One young woman told me, "I'm getting married next week and I'm frightened that I have made the worst mistake of my life." Another young man said, "All I know is that I look around and find other girls livelier and more attractive than my *kallah*, and I tell myself I made a big mistake."

It is also important to be aware that of the countless such calls I receive, only a very small number have ever been based on issues that deserve such concern. One young man I spoke to for the entire two-month period before his marriage was determined to break the engagement for reasons that he felt "everyone could see." This same young man called me just a few days earlier and told me that they had just celebrated their first anniversary, and how grateful he was that I never bought into his insistence that he has no choice but to end the engagement.

It is abundantly clear that no previous generation has ever

experienced such irrational and destructive fears regarding dating and engagement on such a staggering scale as ours.

In every generation, the journey of discovery has never been easy, neither for us nor for Hashem. Even in previous generations, Chazal described the difficulties of finding a *bashert* as "*kasheh k'kriyas Yam Suf*, as difficult as the splitting of the Reed Sea." It was as if two *neshamos* had to miraculously be brought together from disparate ends of the universe to discover a shared destiny that was declared even before their births.

However, it wasn't very long ago when two people were able to meet and a delicate and loving bond evolved without the endless fears, anxieties and distractions we are faced with today. Permit me to share a personal memory about a *chassan* and a *kallah* very dear to me — my mother and father, *a"h*.

> An important dimension of my parents' relationship was unearthed with my mother's passing, just six years ago, when we discovered a timeless treasure in an old shoebox. My mother was born and raised in Boston. And since there were very few, if any, young *frum* single men in Boston, about once a month on *motza'ei Shabbos*, she would travel to New York on the Yankee Clipper, arriving at Grand Central Station early Sunday morning. She would then take the subway to the Lower East Side and make her rounds to visit a number of women who had befriended her.
>
> It was at the apartment of Rabbi and Rebbetzin Dworkis, which served as a shul on Shabbos, that she first saw my father on a Sunday morning, as he was spending a few hours learning in the Dworkis' living room before he began his work week at the family dry goods store on Broome Street.
>
> In Boston, she had never seen a young man learning on a Sunday morning and was a bit startled at the sight. When she returned home to Boston that evening, she told

my grandfather about the young man she had seen that morning. She lived alone with him, as her mother had died in an auto accident when local teens had hurled ice chunks at my grandfather's car during an ice storm, causing him to lose control of the vehicle. She wistfully mentioned to her father that she noticed the young man learning that morning in New York, but he had not seen her. However, by the end of the week, a letter arrived from the young man, who had indeed seen her, inviting her to stop by the family store when she would return to New York.

On her next trip, she passed by the store and, as if he sensed her imminent arrival, he was waiting for her. They had never been formally introduced but recognized each other from the *rebbetzin*'s apartment. They greeted each other, went for a walk and began a relationship that ended in 1954, with my father's untimely death at the young age of forty-six.

The treasure we discovered after my mother's death was the shoebox of letters written from November 1939 to March 1940, up until the wedding. These were letters of deep warmth, love and affection. Now, more than seventy years later, they were yellowed and fragile, written in blue Waterman's fountain pen ink. My father's handwriting flowed over the page with smoothness and clarity, *"My dearest Sally,"* and after the engagement, *"My dearest kallah ..."*

My mother was twenty-seven when they met and my father was thirty-one. They had both spent years searching for their *bashert*. Unlike today, in 1939, finding a *shomer* Shabbos person to date was very difficult. At last they had found each other, and the winter of their search was over. And as Shlomo Hamelech wrote almost 3,000 years ago in *Shir Hashirim*, the winter had past and their time of song arrived. Each letter was a carefully prepared testimony to their song; it was abundantly clear that these two individuals, whose loneliness had finally ended, would never permit anything to prevent them from building their lives together. Their *kriyas Yam Suf* was discovering each other.

Today, the deep need and even loneliness is no less than in 1939, or 1239. Yet, each person who is looking for that one special person with whom to build a life faces a very different kind of *kriyas Yam Suf*. It is no longer that difficult for many singles to find a date. Many have met countless dating partners. Still, they go from one partner and one disappointment to the next, in an ongoing ritual of great frustration we call dating.

Each day, I am witness to this painful phenomenon as I meet with both young and more mature singles, all struggling to discover their life partners. What they all have in common is their inability to wrestle with the limitless issues that seem to always get in the way.

On any given day, I will hear countless statements following the same pattern of thinking and feeling. Although all of these individuals want to get married, they still issue claims such as:

- ✦ "I know we are getting married in a week, but I can't seem to stop thinking about the last girl I went out with before we were engaged."

- ✦ "She seemed to be pretty when we first met, but now ... I am not sure."

- ✦ "I liked him for the first three dates, but now I just feel down around him."

- ✦ "I don't want to lose her, but I'm just not feeling anything."

- ✦ "I've been dating for fifteen years and don't know what I'm doing wrong."

- ✦ "I didn't feel like calling him for a few days, and I didn't miss him. It must mean that he's not the one."

- "It's true he's a very special fellow, but I can't see myself being supported by his salary."

- "Each time we get closer, I start feeling anxiety and fear, so how can I possibly continue?"

- "I know we've been dating for a while and it seems serious, but there is this other person I have wanted to meet for a long time and I now have the opportunity."

- "It's true that a certain facial feature didn't really bother me until now, but now I just can't seem to stop feeling bothered by it."

- "Every time I think of engagement, I feel anxious and queasy."

These are just a few of the expressions of the *kriyas Yam Suf* of today. What they all have in common is that they are all firmly stuck within the struggle to reach their goal of marriage. Each moment is filled with questions and challenges that leave dating and engaged couples wondering whether this will be the last date, or whether they will make it to their own wedding. It doesn't even matter whether the couple is dating for a week, a month or six months, or their wedding is scheduled in a week. At any moment, we are aware of the pervasive fear that any wrong word, thought, act, impulse or pressure will bring the closest of relationships to an end.

The clear and unequivocal goal of this book is to diminish this chaos of confusion, frustration and even the tragedies that have become so commonplace in our world of *shidduchim*. Each thought and phrase has been written to empower you with the understanding that Hashem continuously endows you with the ability to build and strengthen your relationship, and the relationship you are building has the potential to bring you and your *bashert* together for a lifetime. At the end of this chapter

I have taken the liberty of including a non-binding agreement that couples can use as a basis for reading this book together.

◇ How This Book Developed

From Seven Gates to the Menuchah Principle

More than ten years ago, I published *The Inner Circle: Seven Gates to Marriage*, which has been very well received. While I feel a great sense of satisfaction over the book's success, I have come to understand that the Seven Gates represented a roadmap for building relationships that lead to marriage. While many valued its clear guidelines, many others felt they lacked the ability to follow this roadmap approach to dating. I felt that dating couples needed to be more focused on the "here and now" of the dating experience. Instead of looking at the dating process from 30,000 feet, this book would examine it at ground level, in the moment, and as a moment-to-moment experience of life.

The Uniqueness of the Menuchah Principle in Dating

I realize that there are countless books and *sefarim* devoted to relationship skills, communications and how to feel and behave in meaningful ways that deepen the growing bonds between two people. And many are quite excellent and well thought out. And if I were to ask a couple what brings them closer together, I would get many possible answers. Some would hope to develop better communications skills; others feel they need to be more open about their personal lives and expressive of their emotions. Many feel it is that ability to mirror each other's *hashkafos* (outlooks) and values related to creating a home and family. Undoubtedly, all of these would contribute to the enhancement of any marriage.

Nevertheless, I have come to understand that there exists an underlying dynamic that enables couples to create lives of deep closeness and fulfillment, that has the depth and strength to enable couples to overcome the negative influences that affect all our lives. This underlying strength is the ability to deal with all of life's challenges, both large and small, while maintaining a sense of personal belief, security and balance. Chazal call this secure and strong sense of equanimity *menuchas hanefesh*.

As I learned and understood more about *menuchas hanefesh*, I began to comprehend that this experience emerges from the depth of our souls and is therefore generated from within. Hashem endows us all with this strength. And once we are aware of its power and come to understand the efforts we need to undertake to acquire it, we can see its effect almost immediately, in every area of our lives — particularly in the way we feel about our own lives and our ability to cultivate a gentle and deep relationship that can lead to marriage and a stronger relationship with Hashem.

When dating and engaged couples acquire this understanding, they begin to discover the pathways to emotional closeness, comfort and security in their shared future. For along with *menuchas hanefesh*, they also develop an inner strength and resiliency to overcome all the challenges to the strength, stability and integrity of their growing relationship.

I also came to understand that this ability to maintain a steady course together, whether at the earliest stages or as a wedding approaches, is the true goal for each of you. For this inner strength needs to remain intact through the moment-to-moment experiences of building your shared understanding and experiences. In addition, when *menuchas hanefesh* is not at the heart of this period of learning to become closer in thoughts, feelings and understanding — the relationship is as shaky as the next feeling of insecurity, hurt, impulsivity and every other challenge, even though the bond may seem secure to the external eye.

As we explore this underlying principle that lies at the heart of personal security and creating a relationship that can truly lead to marriage, we will discover this power of *menuchas hanefesh* to bring positive feelings of understanding and closeness into our lives. The absence of *menuchas hanefesh* creates an alternate universe of experience, and leaves us feeling fragmented, troubled, hurt and vacuous. Chazal call this state of mind *pizur hanefesh*. In the presence of *pizur hanefesh*, a couple's shared experience of dating and engagement is negative and superficial, and always leads to thoughts and feelings of:

+ "There is just no feeling of any excitement."

+ "I look at other couples and they seem to be so happy."

+ "I'm just not attracted."

+ "If only he/she would open up."

+ "On paper it looks perfect, but I'm just not into him/her."

+ "I can't help but feel nervous and tense; it must be wrong."

These all sound like reasonable statements. Yet, we will discover that beneath them all is a *pizur hanefesh* state of mind that can never be trusted. The goal of this program is to teach you how to recognize this negative state of mind and how to transform it to positive experiences and perceptions, so you can achieve the shared lives you deserve. And I will do this by guiding you to the source that Chazal have offered for many centuries. This is the ability to deepen your own sense of *menuchas hanefesh*. I am *mispallel* (pray) that you will all discover the unlimited power of this inner road to bring each of you to the marriage of caring and fulfillment you deserve, which is Hashem's gift for all of Am Yisrael.

Discovering a Treasure in my Own Backyard

How did I arrive at this understanding, about the meaning of *menuchas hanefesh* as a method to acquire *shalom bayis*? Permit me to share the events of the past three years.

There is a well-known story about a man who had a dream that he would discover a treasure if he would go to a certain bridge in a faraway town. Following the dream, he went to the bridge where he met a man who redirected him back to his own home. Arriving back at his home after the long journey, he dug out the treasure that had always been awaiting him right under his own feet.

In many ways, this story rings true for me with bell-like clarity. For many years in my work with dating, engaged and married couples, I had continuously searched for an approach that would enable these couples to create and protect the delicate relationships that Hashem desires for each of us. In my search, I was determined to remain close to my professional training and experience, while understanding that I would always need to return to the Torah perspective on marriage and relationships. It was always obvious that Chazal had a very clear understanding of relationships that lead to a fulfilling marriage based on how we express our feelings, our needs, our definition of love and closeness, enjoyment and the meaning of *tznius* (modesty) in marriage. And throughout my search, I was also painfully aware of the ever-rising divorce rate, as well as the growing number of young people unable to successfully build relationships that lead to marriage. Professionally, I was being inundated with couples on the brink of divorce, while also receiving a steadily growing number of calls from engaged couples ready to break their engagements and dating couples desperate to keep their relationship alive. It became so intense that I began to view my office and study where I saw these couples as an emergency room.

About three years ago, I became aware of the innovative approach of George Pransky, PhD. He and Roger Mills, both psychologists, had spearheaded the development of a revolutionary approach to treating personal and relational dysfunctions. It was based on the core principles that each individual carries a transcendent capacity for emotional and physical well-being that is ever present, regardless of background or life experiences. They called their new treatment methodology Health Realization. The Health Realization approach taught individuals and couples how to access this innately healthy dimension of self. And when this understanding was applied and the obstructions removed, then a deeper sense of personal strength, wisdom and security would naturally emerge as a fishing float that finds its way to the surface of the water.

Pransky and Mills had acquired this understanding and philosophy of health and well-being through the teachings of Sidney Banks, a poet and philosopher living in Canada. Pransky would eventually offer his programs and approaches to individuals, couples, businessmen, corporations, communities and even prisons at the institute he founded, located in LaConner, Washington, a small town about forty miles from Seattle.

While my initial exposure to this approach was through my readings of Dr. Pransky, Sidney Banks, Mills and others, as well as audio and video presentations, my first face-to-face exposure with Health Realization came through Rabbi Michel Twerski, *shlit"a*, of Milwaukee. Rabbi Twerski had been introduced to Pransky's work by Rabbi Chaim Levine, who had founded the Center for Living Judaism in Seattle. Rabbi Levine had studied with Pransky for over a decade and had presented his ideas to Rabbi Twerski, who brought a group of professional and lay leaders to participate in a number of training programs in LaConner at the Pransky Institute. In February of 2006, Rabbi Twerski and Rabbi Levine organized a three-day conference in Milwaukee to open the Torah world to these concepts and introduce a fresh vision that would impact on our ability to reverse the processes that were undermining our marital and family lives.

I was privileged to attend the conference, which featured Judith Sedgemen, who had been a central member of the Pransky

Institute staff in LaConner for over twenty years, and was presently teaching this approach at the University of South Carolina.

I came away from the conference filled with a sense of great excitement for the possibilities that this approach held for our community, especially with its apparent congruity to Torah *hashkafos*. Energized by the conference and my growing commitment, I was also actively seeking parallel ideas and approaches that directly emerged from Chazal's writings.

I discussed my ideas with my son Dovid, in Eretz Yisrael, with whom I conduct a daily learning *seder* (session). And about six months after the Milwaukee conference he shared that he had discovered a *sefer* that recorded *mussar vaadim* (small, interactive study groups) based on the concept of *menuchas hanefesh*, which seemed similar to the Health Realization program but had been solidly entrenched in Torah life and the writings of Chazal. The author of the *sefer* was the late Rabbi Chaim Friedlander, *zt"l*, the Mashgiach of the Ponovezh Yeshivah in Bnei Brak. Rabbi Friedlander had published a series of his works on the *yamim tovim* and *hashkafah*, under the name *Sifsei Chaim*. The volume referred to was titled *Middos and Avodas Hashem* and related to the acquisition of personal attributes and *middos* to bring us closer to Hashem. The volume contained two rather large chapters on the concepts of *menuchas hanefesh* and *machshavah* (thought).

Dovid and I began our explorations by integrating the *sefer* into our daily learning schedule. The more we learned, the clearer it became that what Pransky, Mills and Banks were teaching had been addressed by Chazal, and particularly the *Mussar* Movement over many centuries — on a level that truly led to acquiring the *middos* that Hashem has always desired us to aspire to. Gradually, I discovered that the concept of *menuchas hanefesh* was the underlying emotional state that enabled us to become close to Hashem, our spouses, our families and everything else that made life meaningful and significant. And the beauty and irony of it all was that it was always buried, waiting to be discovered in my own backyard.

Our daily *seder* of studying the works of the *Sifsei Chaim*, coupled with applying a growing understanding of *menuchas hanefesh* to my work with couples and singles, have enabled many couples to experience a significant enhancement in their *shalom bayis* and personal sense of balance and well-being. The result was the evolution of an approach that directly integrated Chazal's value on *menuchas hanefesh* as a significant and highly effective tool to enhance the quality of married and family life.

Because all that I am presenting is a direct result of the insights of Chazal, I am particularly pleased to say that very little in this book is original. Perhaps I may have applied the wisdom and concepts in a manner that may have not been so apparent in the past; however, I proudly proclaim that none of these teachings are mine.

All that you will be reading is a rudimentary distillation of the wisdom of great voices and luminaries of our past. They include Rav Chaim Friedlander, *zt"l*; Rav Eliyahu Dessler, *zt"l*, the author of *Michtav M'Eliyahu*; the *Sfas Emes*, Rav Yehudah Aryeh Leib Alter, *zt"l*, the towering leader of the Ger Dynasty; the Alter of Kelm, Rav Simcha Zissel Ziv, *zt"l*; Rav Shlomo Volbe, *zt"l*, known for decades simply as the Mashgiach, who left a legacy of wisdom that will always be the source of our approaches to *chinuch* (education), personal *middos* and relationships; Rav Avigdor Miller, *zt"l*; Rav Yeruchem Levovitz, *zt"l*, the Mashgiach of the Mir in Europe; Rav Levi Yitzchak MiBerditchev, *zt"l*, and others. I have attempted to weave my limited understanding of their teachings into this approach and offer my sincere apologies for assuming any grasp of their vast and overpowering genius. However, even in my own very apparent limitations, the effects of teaching what I have learned to both married and singles has enabled many individuals to feel a sense of hope and mastery over the quality of their *shalom bayis* and relationships.

I have also incorporated a number of concepts that I respected and valued from the Pransky model. I was particularly impressed by his method of teaching his principles in a very coherent manner and ensuring that clients were able to understand them and integrate them into their lives. However the principles that Chazal teach are significantly different. The primary difference was that where Pransky taught the principles of Thought, Consciousness and Mind as the foundation stones of Health Realization, I had discovered Chazal's principles of *Chiddush* (renewal), *Tzomet* (Crossroads) and the *Mishkan* (the mind as a sanctuary) as the principles governing this approach. All these principles will be discussed later in depth.

In this journey, I have discovered that *menuchas hanefesh* is essential to every Jew, whether related to *shalom bayis*, how we experience Shabbos, our *tefillos* to Hashem and the quality of our lives. Without cultivating this quality of personal security and trust in Hashem, our lives are always rocked by a sense of unpredictability and uncertainty.

◇ My Gratitude and Acknowledgments

There is great clarity that every step in the writing of this book is the result of the loving guidance and *chessed* of Hashem. After many years of attempting to guide singles toward discovering their *bashert*, Hashem led me to an understanding that it is only through *menuchas hanefesh* and spiritual development that each can discern the soul of a destined life partner.

Each step along the way Hashem has literally "spoon-fed" me one discovery after the next within the teachings of Chazal. Therefore, my first words are to express my deepest gratitude to Hashem for His loving guidance in every area of my life and in particular for helping me present these sublime concepts.

In writing this book on *shidduchim*, dating and engagement, there can be no deeper feelings of gratitude than I have for my beloved wife Vivian, who has been a continuous source of devotion, encouragement and support throughout all my efforts to help singles discover their true life partners. No one can ever appreciate the sacrifices she has made to enable me to continue in this *avodas hakodesh*.

I must express a special and loving *hakaras hatov* to my learning *chavrusa* R' Dovid, who is also my son. As part of our daily learning *seder*, R' Dovid introduced me to the writings of the *Sifsei Chaim*, which enabled me to discover what I had been searching for throughout my entire professional career, and which serve as the central focus of this book. Studying these works has deeply enriched my understanding about our inner spiritual lives and marriage. May Hashem bless our *"chavrusashaft"* with many more productive years of shared Torah study.

While these concepts were introduced by and studied together with Dovid, it was in the *bais medrash* of Yeshivah Derech Ayson, under its Rosh HaYeshivah, Rabbi Yechiel Yitzchok Perr, *shlit"a*, and the Menahel, Rabbi Aharon Brafman, *shlit"a*, where my deeper understanding of *menuchas hanefesh* matured. Participating daily in the Yeshivah environment enabled me to deeply comprehend how one's inner life can be cultivated through a close proximity to an *adam gadol* such as the Rosh HaYeshivah, a living embodiment of Torah, wisdom and unfathomable kindness. In such an environment, every *tefillah*, every learning *seder*, every Shabbos, *Yamim Nora'im* and all the Chagim have served to deepen my comprehension of *menuchas hanefesh*.

The very beginnings of this and the previous book on marriage actually germinated in another *bais medrash*, that of Yeshivah Sh'or Yoshuv. That is where I had the honor and privilege of presenting my initial thoughts in a series of *motza'ei*

Shabbos lectures on *shalom bayis*. The Rosh HaYeshivah, Rabbi Naftali Jaeger, *shlit"a*, and his Rebbetzin had asked me to present some of my thoughts as part of a community service program in memory of their late daughter Ruchama, *a"h*. I am grateful to the Rosh HaYeshivah for offering me the opportunity to present these workshops, which served as an important catalyst that led to the writing of this series of books.

Throughout the years there I have had the honor of knowing, working with and developing profoundly close personal friendships with individuals who have devoted their lives to being Hashem's partners in the *shidduch* process. There are far more than I can possibly mention. Yet a number of these individuals must be mentioned including our dearest friends, Mendel and Zissy Zilberberg, along with Fruma Schiffenbauer, Yati Weinreb and all those who work so closely with them at Binyan Adei Ad to bring hope and *simchah* into the lives of *frum* singles. I also want to recognize the lifelong dedication to this *avodas hakodesh* of my two sisters, Mrs. Peshie Schreiber and Mrs. Risha Kaufman, and their families, who live and breathe the challenges and joys of bringing Yiddishe *neshamos* together. I am continuously inspired by the selflessness and ability of these and so many others who devote their lives to helping sacred *neshamos* find their life partners.

I am deeply appreciative to Mrs. Tova Salb, Mrs. Hadassa Goldsmith, Risa Shulman and Gigi Biton, who reviewed this manuscript multiple times, particularly from the perspective of guiding couples through the process of relationship building. Through their efforts, I believe this book can now be used as an accompaniment to the dating process, where couples can actually share in each other's growth from date to date.

As I mentioned in the first volume on marriage, Aryeh Mezei and Nachum Shapiro of Judaica Press have been a great source of friendship and *chizuk* for me and have enabled me to present this second volume in this series on *menuchas hanefesh.*

Once again, as before, Justine Elliott has created a design that maintains the tranquility of the first design, yet offers subtle nuances that make this design unique in its own way.

To all these individuals and countless others, I offer "thank you" from the wellsprings of my heart.

◇ Reading Together

If you as a couple would like to study this book together, you can use the following guidelines to structure your reading schedule and define your level of mutual commitment to this shared learning experience.

As a dating couple, we appreciate the value of bringing *menuchas hanefesh* into our personal lives and into our growing relationship. The following non-binding conditions will help achieve this goal.

1. We will attempt to devote _____ times a week to reading *The Menuchah Principle in Shidduchim, Dating & Engagement*

2. The times we plan to read are:

    _____

3. The amount of time we are allotting to read is:

    _____

4. How and where we plan to read, and who reads is:

    _____

5. We agree to notify each other of any change in plans.

6. We agree to read slowly, respectfully and thoughtfully.

7. We agree to use the readings to create a positive shared experience.

8. We agree not to use the material in an accusing, critical or blaming manner.

9. We agree not to date or seek dates with anyone else while we are learning these principles together.

10. (*Optional, but recommended*) We agree to follow each session by completing the following questions (refer to the Personal Journal on the next page):

    a. My thoughts and insights about today's reading
    b. One concept I learned
    c. A thought I would like to share with you

PERSONAL JOURNAL
Menuchah Principle

Date _____

My thoughts and insights about today's reading:

_____

_____

_____

_____

_____

One concept I learned:

_____

_____

_____

_____

A thought I would like to share with you:

_____

_____

_____

Date _____

My thoughts and insights about today's reading:

_____

_____

_____

_____

_____

One concept I learned:

_____

_____

_____

_____

A thought I would like to share with you:

_____

_____

_____

_____

_____

CHAPTER II

Creating Union from the Center of Self

Relationships emerge from the deepest essence of our "selves." Still, it can be very difficult to focus on this deeper aspect of who we are. I believe the crisis that Shira experienced just a few days before her wedding illustrates this very well.

Shira and I met just five days before her wedding. Until two months before, she'd thought her wedding was to be the most memorable day of her life. Now, though, as the day approached, she was filled with dread and anxiety. She was not even sure she could carry herself to the *chupah*. As she put it, "Right now, it's the last place on earth I want to be."

Shira had been dating for over three years and met many young men. Since her childhood, she had been told that her *chassan* would be extraordinary in every way. The promise was based on her family's status and wealth, her attractiveness and her personal qualities. When she finished seminary in Eretz Yisrael, she was pursued relentlessly by *shadchanim*. The young men she dated came from the very best homes and yeshivas. Yet in Shira's eyes, each had his flaws and was rejected. She was determined to meet and marry the person she had been assured over the years would be her true *bashert*.

Then she met Yussie, who came from a very different background than Shira's. His father was a second grade *rebbi* in a girls' school, and his mother ran a nursery for neighborhood children. The family of nine children lived in a modest house, not nearly large enough for them. Nonetheless, Shira was attracted to Yussie's *middos*, intelligence and gentleness. She had never met such a caring and sensitive person. So while his family status, finances and even his height did not conform to the image she thought she would marry, she found herself wanting to continue the relationship. Then one day, he surprised her and proposed. Although she accepted, the next day she began to feel anxiety over her decision. That was two months ago.

Since her engagement, she had been tormented over her decision. She obsessed over Yussie's family, his lack of clarity about a career and his ability to provide her the lifestyle she had become accustomed to. Her fears grew from day to day. More than her fears was the effect of being repeatedly asked by well-wishers whether she was feeling as excited as everyone expected her to be. She was caught in the quicksand of self-doubt and anxiety. Every question of her excitement and happiness deepened her anxiety and caused her to doubt her decision even more.

When we met, just days before the wedding, she had already been to see a number of therapists, rabbis and mentors she had trusted over the years. As we spoke, she shared with me the following: "It is clear to me that Yussie is the most special boy I have ever met. Still, my doubts and fears refuse to go away." By now it was clear to everyone, including Yussie, that Shira was having very serious second thoughts.

Over the next few days, Shira began to understand the principles of *menuchas hanefesh* and *pizur hanefesh* and learn that she had the ability to quiet herself. For Shira, the clear conflict was her ability to focus on the very special relationship she had developed with Yussie that was rooted in her deeper sensitivities of her self, as opposed to being focused on the externals of the "look" and status that she had always expected her *chassan* to possess.

Learning to discover her own "center of gravity" and quiet herself enabled her to move away from her fantasies about the "image" of her *chassan* she had always harbored. She was now able to remain focused on the special moments they had shared and on his qualities that had become so important to her.

The night before the wedding, she called me to say, "I'm very proud of myself. And I now feel a lot better about my decision. My cousin called me to ask me if I was excited. At first I started to feel the old sick feeling of doubt coming back. Then I realized what I really wanted to say. I told her that I did not feel excitement, but I did have a deep sense of gratitude that I was marrying a wonderful young man." The next day, a very grateful Shira was married.

We all experience the true essence of life from the depth of our "selves," which is that dimension of our being that understands the quality of how close or distant, safe or unsafe, secure or insecure we feel with another person. The excitement that everyone, including Shira, wanted to know about is closer to the downhill plunge on the roller coaster or any adrenaline pumping experience where we lose our sense of our "selves," which has oddly become proof-positive that we are indeed "in love." And if excitement has come to mean love, then perhaps this is why the orchestra leader invariably screams out, "Ladies and gentlemen, now for the very first time …" So, if anyone had any doubt about the rock solid foundation of this marriage, the heart-stopping theatrics are enough to convince everyone present that this marriage really is absolutely, positively, without any question, the real thing. But we all know the truth. It's all canned showbiz and very superficial. We may even find a negative correlation between the ear-piercing level of the announcement and the couple's true sense of shared closeness and security. Otherwise, they would have told the bandleader, "Please don't go overboard. We find it doesn't really reflect our deeper feelings for each other."

All this has become a part of our dating and wedding ritual; in our search for that union, we have erroneously come to use external indicators as a foolproof method of feeling secure. This is why I continually hear statements along the lines of, "I'm looking for a guy who takes charge," or "I need a girl who makes me feel attracted to her." The reality is that it actually reflects insecurity. It's like asking someone, "Why are you biting your nails?" He answers, "Because I'm nervous and it helps calm me down." We all know that this is an absurd thing to say, as the nail-biting generates even more tension.

In spite of this, we have come to believe that when we find someone with the right external qualities, it will inevitably mean that we will share a meaningful inner life together. Our focus on the external causes so many to rely on instant judgments, where an increasing number of people believe they have the ability to make a snap decision on the very first date, and even in the first few moments of the first date, about whether this person would make a suitable marriage partner. This is why many of these individuals will use phrases such as, "one and done," or "dead on arrival." Not only are these phrases dehumanizing descriptions, but they also make a strong statement that declares absolute trust in using these external qualities to determine whether this person and I can spend the rest of our lives together. I have found that the same individuals who use these phrases will invariably have dated many times and remain unsuccessful in their search for their life partner. And when they do finally marry the person who "fits the dream," it never is the dream, and may even become a nightmare.

There is a deeper truth that lies quietly beneath the surface. The true union is always between two *neshamos*, and relationships only succeed through a gradual emergence of the deeper selves of two people, as they create an environment of acceptance and understanding. *Neshamah* and our deeper self are very much intertwined.

I am reminded of this when I walk along the shoreline of the Rockaway Peninsula and look out toward the horizon, where sky and water meet. To the naked eye, there seems to be a continuum between the two, where the two seem to merge as one. It's impossible to know where one begins and the other ends. It brings to mind that the horizon, where the spirituality of the heavens meets the earth and its water, is perhaps similar to that place where the spirituality of the soul meets the self within each of us. It's almost impossible to know where one begins and the other ends. And we all possess a unique self and soul that longs to connect with one special person. This is how Hashem created us.

Allowing the Self to Emerge and Create Union

Developing a relationship that leads to a meaningful and fulfilling marriage is all about two people learning how they can enable each other's self to safely emerge. This is where true trust and security are experienced. And when this dimension of two selves is continuously shared over time, then a relationship develops that enables each to recognize the other as that *neshamah* that was announced on high many years earlier, even before birth. This bond between these two *neshamos* transcends all others in its depth and meaning to each of us. This is the self that longs for the union with another *neshamah*.

In this world, we are always attempting to experience our deeper and truer self. Some of us confuse this deeper self with our professions, our hobbies and cultural interests; others confuse it with our possessions such as cars, homes and clothing. There are a myriad of ways that society has taught us to erroneously express and experience this deeper self. Most of these expressions are external.

In previous generations, there was always a clear hierarchy of expressions of self. I could be a doctor, a lawyer, an accountant, an amateur photographer or a grocery store owner. Each would be a significant dimension of my self. Yet there would never be any doubts as to where the deepest and most authentic expression of my self could occur. This would only be achieved in marriage and family, or in the relationship I attempted to achieve with Hashem.

It could be because this is the one relationship where two lives are inexorably brought closer together, where two people share life's deeper moments — where children are brought into the world and cared for. There are countless reasons why marriage has always been the relationship that was understood to be at the very heart of self. In marriage, our selves merge, while we maintain our own uniqueness.

Two stories will help to illustrate the expression of union in the deepest possible way.

◇ At the Height of a Career

Michael was a young man in his mid-thirties, who was a researcher for a well-known financial firm. I had been working with him while he was single and had been guiding him as he was dating Sarah. Over a period of about six months, he and Sarah had developed a close relationship. And while marriage had been discussed, Michael was also a man on the fast track of life and felt he had places to go. Since his position kept him very busy, he was conflicted about committing to marriage. For him, marriage was desirable, but also very frightening. I had my doubts whether he would able to take the next step. Then, without any explanation, Michael told me that he was ready to get engaged. I wondered what had propelled him forward, but did not receive an answer at that time.

A few years later, Michael, Sarah and their son joined us for a Shabbos meal. When he and I were alone, he asked me whether I ever understood why he had decided to marry Sarah. I admitted that it was always somewhat of a mystery to me, realizing how conflicted and frightened he was about marriage. So at the Shabbos *seudah*, he shared with me the following memory:

Michael had been invited to give an important presentation at a conference attended by America's leading financial firms. He considered this invitation to be one of the most important developments of his career, a tremendous honor that recognized his achievements. He packed his bags and went off to the conference with a great sense of personal satisfaction.

His presentation went extremely well. After receiving effusive praise, he returned victoriously to his hotel room to bask in the glory of his personal and professional triumph. What more could he ask for? But as he entered his hotel room, he was seized by a powerful sadness such as he had never encountered before — a deep sense of emptiness and aloneness. Michael had reached a milestone in his life, one he had worked so hard to achieve — yet here he was in a hotel room, alone, with no one to share his big moment.

Beyond this feeling was an even more powerful one. His aloneness extended past this moment of personal triumph. It went past the present and stretched eternally into the future. He had no one with whom to share his life. The professional efforts that had been at the center of his life for so long were now satisfied. Yet, along with achievement came awareness of a deeper yearning.

For years, Michael's pursuit of success had blunted his ability to hear the gentle voice within that recognizes Hashem's words, *"Lo tov heyos ha'adam levado* – It is not good for man to be alone."* Now, with a deep and unexpected force, this awareness rang within him like a bell suddenly pealing out and breaking the absolute stillness of night. In that moment, it had become so undeniably clear that all this was of no real significance – neither the success nor the recognition. A life without someone to share it with would never bring him the fulfillment he deeply longed for.

Suddenly, he had clarity, and he made the decision that had until now seemed impossible. The time for living life alone needed to come to an end. Instinctively, he picked up the phone to call Sarah. He heard her voice. He was reassured. He knew he would no longer be alone.

Shortly after returning home, Michael and Sarah were engaged. Their marriage has proven to be a blessing for them and their growing family; they recently celebrated the birth of their second child.

I remember Michael and Sarah when I am working with couples because, despite alienation and hurt, this voice within is always just a discovery away. This is especially so when I'm attempting to help couples whose relationship is slipping away as struggles arise. My question is always, "What do I need to say or do to facilitate the awareness of this deeper truth that Hashem has planted in each of us?"

◇ Seeking Solace in the Night

Now we move on from Michael and Sarah, early in life when the voice is heard, to life at the other end. This story occurred in

Boston in 1976 at a conference I attended for Jewish Communal Service Workers. At the time, I was presenting a paper I had written on marital therapy with Orthodox families. While most of the presentations were given by mental health and communal service professionals, a keynote address was given by the late Rav Yoshe Ber Soloveitchik, *zt"l*, Rosh Yeshivah of Yeshiva University, who resided in Boston for many years. I want to share with you what has never left my memory about that speech.

The *Rav*, as he was known, spoke to an overflow audience of conference attendees. He was describing the overwhelming power of loneliness that is part of our human condition, and how Hashem places within us the need for human closeness. I found it difficult to spot other yarmulkes in the audience. Perhaps ten percent were Orthodox. But the *Rav* was mesmerizing in his description of how Hashem has created us all with a need for a true life partner.

All of his previous eloquence paled, however, when he shared an episode from his own life that has left a life-altering impact on me and, I'm certain, on so many others who heard him. He was disclosing details about the final days of the illness of his late wife, Tanya. He vividly described the pain of sleeping alone in their bedroom, while his frail wife was downstairs in the enclosed porch being cared for by an attending nurse.

It was in the middle of the night when the *Rav* thought he heard his wife groaning in fear and pain. Fearing that the sounds of her agony indicated the end was near, he was filled with an overwhelming sense of vulnerability. At any moment, the woman with whom he had shared his life would be snatched away from him! He needed to see his beloved wife once again, perhaps to say goodbye for the last time, or just to make certain that she was as comfortable as possible.

He put on his robe and made his way down the darkened stairs. However, as he got closer, she was silent and the porch was unusually dark. He entered the room, anticipating the feelings of relief he would feel at being with his wife of so many years on this dark and frightening night. But when he stepped closer, he suddenly became painfully aware that the bed she had been sleeping on was empty and there was no nurse. He then realized what he had forgotten. She had died three nights ago.

A frail and elderly *talmid chacham* (Torah scholar) had transmitted to a mostly secular audience of perhaps a thousand, in the most personal and intimate way, how Hashem has planted in our hearts the overwhelming human need to share our lives with one person. And when that person is no longer a part of our world, part of us is gone, as well.

The *Rav's* message was poignant and penetrating. Hashem has created us to share our lives. The audience and the *Rav* may have been from dissimilar backgrounds, and few may have had any notion of what his understanding of life represented. Yet every person there was suddenly faced with the stark reality of his or her own mortality and need for companionship, love and closeness throughout life with one special life partner. Suddenly, the reality that Hashem has placed at our core a profoundly deep and human yearning for a life partner made every person in that large room so poignantly aware of life's vulnerability and mortality. And at the heart of it all was the voice of "*Lo tov heyos ha'adam levado.*"

◇ **Losing Half of Himself**

Many years ago, I came across a brief yet very poignant Chassidic gem about the Baal Shem Tov, the founder of the Chassidic movement, which has stayed with me over the years.

> Shortly after the death of his wife, the Baal Shem Tov lamented that he always believed that when he died he would rise toward the heavens in a fiery chariot like Eliyahu Hanavi. But now that his wife was missing from his life, he came to accept that this would never occur, because, in losing her, he had become half a person. He was telling his followers that when he lost his wife, he lost half of himself.

The powerful reflections of the Baal Shem Tov are neither unique nor original. At the beginning of *Bereishis* (2:18), the Torah tells us that Hashem never intended for Adam or any of his descendants to live alone, separated and apart: *"Lo tov heyos ha'adam levado."* But the clear message from Hashem is this: Not only is it not a good thing for man to be alone, but the very design of how we were created promotes sharing and building our lives with one special person. And mankind has always recognized this, as well. "No man is an island" are the well-known words of the poet John Donne.

Because Hashem creates us all with this deeper need, discovering a life partner is not simply an option, but as necessary as the air we breathe. Its absence causes us to experience an internal pain that is deep and relentless, an inner condition of profound emotional confusion and chaos. It's not just that something is missing in our lives, like a new car or a vacation home. Sharing, growing and building our lives together are inherent to how we have been created, and in their absence we cannot feel whole and intact. This is because within the essence of our deeper selves, we all harbor the need for this close, safe and loving relationship. In its presence we are fulfilled; in its absence we have failed to develop our deepest expression of self.

◇ The Empty Substitutes of Western Society

In the contemporary society that is now our present and prolonged *galus* (exile), we have learned to internalize other dimensions of our self that are experienced as more authentic and true to who we really are. In a sense, we have learned to be married to other perceived life partners, including our professions, our gym, jogging, our iPhones and Blackberries, our social network of digital "friends" and countless other expressions of our newly discovered "deeper selves."

Another pitfall is the willingness to pursue a lifestyle that is focused on fulfilling one's individuality through the relentless chase after money, power, fame, excitement and the fulfillment of sensory needs. Yet none of this allows the development or the emergence of the deeper self. Along the way toward these illusory goals, the seekers will make attempts to bring another person into their lives, but only if no one dares to interfere with their pursuits and life plans. As a result, couples date, but constantly struggle with the conflicts between developing a relationship that creates a union between two *neshamos* and maintaining a relationship where each remains ensconced in his or her single lifestyle. The outcome is that these relationships are always in conflict with friends, professional interests and the ideal image of a partner that must be filled. These conflicts inevitably create negative states of mind such as tension, anger, depression and moodiness. In the end, dating more often than not ends in failure, while an increasing number of engagements are called off. This is why the refrain I hear so frequently is, "I just don't feel anything deep in this relationship." This eventually leads to the inevitable breakup.

It is very understandable that many will seek other solutions to fill the vacuum in the absence of being with their life partner. Nevertheless, the awareness of being alone resurfaces in countless forms and there is no real escape, for there is no substitute for a life partner.

◇ When the Truth Comes to the Surface

In truth, while many singles have learned to make the necessary adjustment to not yet having discovered their *bashert*, underneath the surface lies a personal sense of disappointment, confusion and frequently even hurt. On the surface, many are leading lives of purpose, personal meaning and valued personal relationships. Then again, within the *neshamos* of their being, there is an awareness of a deeper need to be met. In the language of our present experience, we have come to define personal success and stability through the achievement of daily life. Deeper within, there is that yearning for that one special lifelong relationship between man and woman that is shared in a manner in which no other relationship can ever be.

Once we get to the deeper level of awareness, we become profoundly conscious of how Hashem has designed and created us to discover this union with our *bashert*; even though we are all unique and separate, our destiny is to become one. This need — to share a loving and secure life with one special individual — is at the very heart of our deepest calling and the center of all our life's experiences. It literally defines the only true definition of our real self and who we are. While our society has placed so much emphasis on personal agendas based on the pursuit of pleasure, achievement and acquisitions as the nucleus of life, the true experiences of our lives emerge from the *neshamos* within us.

To open the door a bit on this deeper need, I would like to share an experience with you.

◇ One Self Seeking Another: Creating Spiritual and Emotional Foundations

When we were born, the very first words of *brachah* that our parents received when the news was shared of our births were "... *L'Torah, l'chupah ul'maasim tovim* — [may you be worthy of raising him] to Torah, to marriage and to good deeds." As a people of Hashem, we have always understood that only a life shared with a *chassan* or *kallah* is at the center of our existence. It is only through the marital and family relationships that we are able to feel complete and connected in deep and secure ways. For Hashem has inscribed within our physical and spiritual DNA the awareness of this need for human completion, and has made it as essential to our souls as water and air are to our bodies.

Yet, when a couple is first getting to know each other, or even when they are engaged and feel the need to deepen the bond, what are the principles that govern the building of this relationship? I will relate to the many dimensions of this relationship later in this book, especially in the chapter on EMBERS. At this early stage, there are a number of significant concepts that serve as the foundation of everything else you will be learning about how two *neshamos* and two unique selves develop a sense of comfort, trust, security and closeness required in this special union.

Dating and Relationship Building from a Different Perspective

If you are a couple who is dating or engaged and reading this book together, there may be people in your vicinity who are aware that you are on a date. They may not know anything about you, yet many have their assumptions, visions and many other thoughts about you as a couple. Some of these observers may be so taken by the impression you are creating as a couple, they may have already made the leap for you and can envision you walking down the aisle.

As a couple, however, your experience from within is very different. For the couple, there is a constant shift of moods, thoughts, feelings of comfort and discomfort, security and anxiety. A dating couple experiences an ever-changing dimension of self. Nowhere else in your moment-to-moment experience of life are you so aware of these shifting patterns of thoughts, moods and your experience of self.

I frequently find the metaphor of the jam cam to be very appropriate. Traffic patterns in New York are frequently monitored by video cameras called "jam cams." We can set up one of these jam cams to observe a dating couple in a way that captures their movements during the dating process. We can observe how the young man pulls up in his car, checks the address, straightens out his suit, rings the bell and is greeted by a smiling young woman or one of her parents. We can observe their initial meeting, their walk through the Botanical Garden on a sunny spring day or their sipping cokes in the Marriot Hotel as they engage in thoughtful and serious discussions. We can begin the video at 7 pm and follow them until 11 pm. From the camera's perspective, this couple appears to be relating well to each other.

Judging by an "aerial" view of their dating, they may seem to be the "ideal" couple. Perhaps if a panel of blue ribbon judges were watching the jam cam, they would evaluate the prospect of this couple's success by holding up Olympic-style scoring cards. For most couples, the scores, determined by external impressions, would be a resounding 9.2, 9.3, even 9.8. To the external eye, it all looks like a well-tended country garden with everything neatly in place. All that is missing is the address to show up for the *l'chaim*.

Then again, if these judges were to use a kind of MRI to scan the dating couple's feelings and experience of life from within, we may very well discover that instead of viewing the well-tended and orderly garden that the world sees, we would be looking at a distressed terrain of troubled thoughts and feelings, more reminiscent of the untamed wilderness of Afghanistan. For dating is never solely a function of externals and even external gestures.

If we were to take these "scores" for dating couples as they are observed on the jam cam, we would predict very high success rates for dating couples. On the other hand, when we compare these predictions to the reality of how many of these couples continue on to marriage, the discrepancy is staggering. The difficulty is that in our culture we confuse the inner selves of a couple with our outer selves. We may sit in a busy Manhattan or Yerushalayim restaurant, filled with dating couples. Each looks better than the next. There is a feeling of "being in the right place." The feeling is electric and actually enhances the sense of "looking like a great couple."

Still, the illusion is short-lived. In the end, each couple must spend time alone, away from the crowd, where they will need to gain a greater sense of trust, comfort and security with each other. They will learn that looking good and being in the right place adds nothing to the relationship.

There is only one consistent dimension that matters in a relationship that can bring two lives together. It is learning to create an environment where two unique selves can emerge and feel safe, special and deeply valued by the other. This is the environment where one can sense an ability to recognize that *neshamah* designated to be a life partner. No hotel lobby, museum, garden, restaurant or any place else on earth can evoke this phenomenon. It needs to come from the quiet, gentle and tranquil resonance in each of us.

Imagine planning a trip to Eretz Yisrael and feeling a deep yearning to stand by the Kosel, to express your many *tefillos* for yourself and loved ones. When you get there, you find a nice, quiet place away from the crowd, close your eyes and begin to express the stirrings of your heart. But a young man or woman stands next to you wearing earphones connected to an MP3 player, and you can hear the sounds and beat of rap music. It disturbs your concentration and bond with Hashem and this special place. You look around and find there is no place else to stand. You traveled seven thousand miles, spent a fortune to be able to commune with Hashem at this holy site and now you cannot focus on your inner feelings that you have waited so long to express. Finally, you turn to your neighbor and ask, "Can you please make the music lower? It is disturbing my *tefillos.*" His response is, "The music shouldn't disturb you. I have my way of communing with G-d and you have yours." Yet you know in your heart this is not so. The *neshamah* is repelled by rap music, with its beats and rhythms of the street culture. It goes into hiding by anything but life's most delicate and modest gestures and words. Dovid Hamelech says in *Tehillim* (45:14): "*Kol kevudah bas melech penimah* — All the glory of the princess is within." The soul is gentle, modest and delicate.

Imagine that my neighbor standing next to me tried to engage me in a discussion to consider that the reason I traveled across the globe to stand at the Kosel was so I could hear his music, as a way of enabling me to seriously communicate with my deepest inner self. My response would be to gently pat him on the head and say, "Young man, you are delusional. There is nothing to discuss." How else could I respond to such an absurd claim? Everything I have learned about life, and that Chazal teach, is that the stirrings of the heart and soul are never a function of adrenaline. One is quiet, personal, gentle and very safe. The other is raucous and emotionally and spiritually chaotic.

The metaphor becomes particularly significant when I meet with singles who are in a dating relationship and even engaged individuals who tell me, "I think he/she is a very nice person. He/she is sweet, kind and thoughtful, but I'm just not feeling any excitement. I should be feeling swept off my feet." I cannot count the number of occasions when I have heard, "We've been going out for four, five, six, etc., dates and nothing is happening." The reality is that they are confusing the electric chaos of rap music with the gentle stirrings of the soul. The source of the confusion is that we don't understand that true closeness evolves from the emergence of two deeper selves experiencing their own and each other's delicate souls. Instead, our focus is on the appearances of the jam cam and all of life's superficialities.

◇ The Key Elements: Trust, Gentleness and Balance

The truth is that two *neshamos* can only emerge and recognize each other in an atmosphere of deep trust and quiet security. Everything else is superficial and empty of any meaning or depth. And there are three experiences of self that enable the self of two people to emerge and recognize the deep bonds waiting to be created. These are trust, gentleness and balance. These three shared experiences become the only emotional environment that brings two lives together in a meaningful way.

Trust: For Life

Consider an infant comfortably snuggled in its mother's arms. The warmth and protection it experiences enables it to develop internally. The infant experiences a sense of quiet safety that is essential for this stage of life. Dovid Hamelech recognizes this inner feeling of quiet trust between mother and child as the bond that most resembles the relationship that his soul has with Hashem. In *Tehillim* (131:2), he expresses, "I swear that I silenced my soul like a suckling child at the side of its mother, like a suckling child is to me my soul."

How does this relate to the emerging relationship between a dating or engaged couple? For the self to truly emerge, each aspires to experience a sense of trust and safety with the other.

Nothing should ever be done or said that creates a sense of discomfort and insecurity.

> One young woman told me of her experience with the young man she was about to get engaged to. "I sit next to him in the car and I ask him not to speed or weave in and out of traffic. I feel so scared when he drives that way. Yet, he's oblivious to my fears. I'm wondering whether this is a warning that he is unable to be sensitive to my need to feel safe?" Clearly, the young *chassan* is being driven by his impulsivity and is unaware of his own need for security and certainly his *kallah*'s. His behavior does not bode well for their future.

There are many ways to make someone feel unsafe, whether it's driving recklessly, using language and gestures that are perceived as aggressive, being in a place where you may meet an old dating partner, coming late without notifying your partner, dropping someone off without a proper escort, keeping someone waiting for an unnecessarily long time between dates or any other indication of being insensitive to engendering a sense of trust.

With this in mind, there are two concepts I teach couples that tell them they are ready for engagement and marriage. For a young woman to feel she is ready to consider committing herself to a young man, she should be able to say to herself, "I trust him with my life." This means that the *chupah* she will enter under is his trusted and secure canopy of protection. She should be able to feel that every area of her life is safe and sheltered under his loving protection — whether physical, financial, emotional or spiritual. In addition, she should feel secure with his unshakable loyalty, his concept of honesty and his relationship and loyalty to all those close to him.

And the young man should feel that this young woman understands him more deeply than anyone he has ever met. She grasps his essence, his aspirations and his deeper self. He, too, experiences a sense of profound trust. It is a trust that whispers to him that here is a person who will enable him to fulfill his most cherished life goals through a deep sense of respect, understanding and caring. This is the meaning of why he needs to see her as a best friend — for life.

Gentleness: *The Soul of Silk*

When we try to understand why a self and a soul emerge through feelings of gentleness, safety and security, the answer I have come to embrace comes from what Rav Yeruchem Levovitz, *zt"l*, the Mashgiach of the Mir Yeshivah, describes as the "soul of silk."

A soul of silk means that we have a delicate inner sense of any gesture or word that our soul or self finds abrasive or hurtful. This is how Hashem created us. And while we can be appropriately aggressive, "in your face" and assertive in other relationships, this bond where two *neshamos* are on a journey to recognize each other can only grow and thrive with someone who understands the silken nature of who we are deep within. And if there is a moment in which we are unaware of our own inherent gentleness because of our silken souls, then we also forget that it exists in the person we are attempting to recognize. We can only be aware of this quality in others if we are aware of it within ourselves. This is where it begins. And even when it is forgotten, it's always there. This is how Hashem has created each of us. Yet, because we are unaware of its presence, it's a gift we are unable to use at this particular moment.

Permit me to cite an experience from my work with married couples. A number of years ago, I was giving a presentation to married couples in Los Angeles. The workshop on marital sensitivity included an experiential exercise during which couples would focus on their feelings as they entered the door of their homes. Couples did a guided imagery exercise, wrote down their thoughts and feelings and then shared them with each other.

After the workshop was over, a woman approached me. "The experience I just had," she confided, "answered a question I have been asking myself for almost a decade. For many years, as I walked up the steps of my house and turned the knob to open the door, I had a slight sense of anxiety and could even feel myself tremble. I was always aware that something at home was bothering me, but this exercise drew my attention to the symptoms. And even more than being aware of the feeling, through this experience I was able to remember the moment when it began."

She went on to describe a difficult experience earlier in their marriage when she and her husband were very tense. The conflict quickly spun out of control, and for a very brief moment she was the target of an outburst of unbridled anger from her husband. He said things she had never heard him say before, and his shouting frightened her. He soon brought himself back under control, but she had never known he had this anger inside him. Then she said to me, "As I was doing the exercise, I realized that the fear I felt at that moment ten years ago was still inside me today. It's as if I'm afraid that such an explosion could happen at any moment again, without warning. Just now, as we were doing the exercise, I realized that this is the feeling I still have when I'm approaching my front door."

Hashem created us all with very delicate and silken feelings. Every abrasion, no matter how slight, can reverberate endlessly. On a date or during engagement, each moment of emotional discomfort and insecurity is picked up by the delicate antennae of the soul. While we maintain our outer demeanor, we experience the hurt caused by insensitivity, rejection, abruptness, inconsideration and impatience to the very depths of our being.

And each such moment creates its own impression that drives a wedge between two people. It does not take too many of these difficult experiences to feel that a relationship has no future. In the section on EMBERS, we will explore in great detail which behaviors bring a couple closer together or further apart.

Because Hashem creates us all with this "soul of silk gentleness," it is not an option or an upgrade, but a necessary part of our very essence. When it is lacking, we experience an inner pain that is deep and relentless, an inner condition of profound emotional confusion and chaos. It's not just that something is missing in our lives. Within our DNA, we all harbor the need for a gentle, emotional environment. With it, we are fulfilled; without it, we experience a sense of loss and isolation. As a result of a lack of this gentleness, we may sense that we are out of sync, as if our body temperature jumped three points and just "doesn't feel right." We can tolerate abrasiveness from people whom we know only casually, because the distance has no deep meaning for us. Conversely, we can never truly tolerate this from someone with whom a relationship is developing, because Hashem never intended the self to emerge without appreciating that our souls are silk.

Balance: Life on the High Wire

The third condition necessary for two souls to emerge is balance, for the secret in cultivating healthy and fulfilling relationships and protecting the delicate fabric of emotional bonds is learning the art of balance. There are two dimensions of balance. The first is internal, which is experienced within us, like an inner balancing ear that guides us to walk erect. But in this case, we are referring to feeling emotionally secure, caring and whole. The second dimension is using this inner equilibrium to help your life partner maintain his or her balance, as well. I find it helpful to illustrate these two aspects of balance through this *mashal* (parable) that has helped couples understand the dynamic balance that needs to exist between a dating couple or a *chassan* and *kallah*.

> When I was a young boy attending yeshivah on the Lower East Side, the arrival of Nissan and spring also meant that we would start seeing the subway and billboard ads for the Ringling Brothers and Barnum and Bailey Circus at the old Madison Square Garden. And since the arrival of the circus in New York always coincided with the spring recess, it was frequently in town on Chol Hamoed Pesach. So we would pack our hard-boiled eggs and our matzos and head to Madison Square Garden. We would sit as high up as imaginable and munch away, mesmerized by the spectacle far below us in the three rings.
>
> Of all the attractions, I found the high-wire act to be one of the most fascinating. To a naïve child, it was incomprehensible that two high-wire artists could be standing motionless on a thin wire high atop the Garden — even higher than we were. How was it possible, I wondered?
>
> As I looked up, I saw two "perfectly" balanced artists, each firmly holding a long, arched pole, high above us. We were locked in to their every move! After a drum roll, they would begin moving toward each other as they somehow managed to maintain their balance and not fall.

When I was older, I realized that both my perceptions were neither complete nor accurate. First, to the child looking at the artists, it seemed that they were actually standing still. This, I learned later in life, was only an illusion. I came to understand that balance, whether on a high wire or in life, is a perpetual challenge. The more they appeared to be standing still, the more they had to keep balancing their muscles and their poles, continuously shifting their feet and posture ever so slightly. There were probably thousands of different balancing adjustments that had become unconscious and second nature. To my fascinated eyes, all these adjustments were not perceived. To me they were "standing still." Nevertheless, for the artists, staying balanced was a very delicate and dynamic process that left no room for even a moment of casual relaxation. To remain on the high wire, each needed to monitor and adjust his or her inner sense of balance on a moment-to-moment basis.

My second perception — that of two independent people moving closer together — was also inaccurate. These two artists must have been very focused, not only on their own inner balance, but also on each other's balance. At any given moment, each could notice even the slightest tremor on the wire or any sign of tension in the other. They needed to be able to communicate with each other so that each could help the other maintain this balance. And when there was any sign of shakiness, each had the ability to deliver the message in just the right way. Perhaps the message was to "straighten your shoulders, bend your knees, take a deep breath and quiet down," or many other similar reassuring messages. Whatever the message, the ability to help the other could only emerge from the inner balance each had achieved within his or her own experience of life. This is what enabled them both to remain stable on the high wire. It is this same wisdom that serves as an internal frame of reference that enables two spouses to help each other at every moment of their shared lives.

Therefore, when someone asks me, "What is the most important quality a couple needs to enable each other to feel trusting, safe and growing?" I am able to answer, "The ability to help each other feel balanced, cared for and secure." Without these qualities, a sense of trust and security can never be experienced.

Thus, the dynamic we have been looking for is a dating couple's ability to be truly balanced and to protect each other as they move their relationship forward, helping each other grow through each stage of mutual understanding and trust so necessary in feeling the possibilities of their future together. It's the satisfaction in knowing that they will constantly help each other stay balanced and even learn to thrive while on this high wire of life.

◇ The Emerging Bond of Closeness

Hashem created us to build our connection to Him in this closeness. Twice daily we recite "*Shema Yisrael*," followed by "*V'ahavta es Hashem Elokecha* ...." Chazal guide us to cover our eyes to fully concentrate on the bond between Hashem and us. Ever since we were small children, we marveled at the heroism of Rabbi Akiva and so many countless Jews before and after him who were able to experience life's ultimate closeness to Hashem. It is with this undistracted focus of love that Hashem wants us to relate to Him, in a way that is unwavering and unequivocal. And in the desire to experience this love, we attempt to utter the final word, "*Echad* — One," with a readiness to accept Hashem's Oneness. It is this personal encounter with Hashem's "*Echad*" that enables us to realize the deeper essence of our spiritual selves.

We are so profoundly aware of the need for this experience, particularly at times in our lives that call to us to pierce through the barriers of separation — such as on Yom Kippur at Ne'ilah, or when we are standing by the Kosel and feel the stirrings of the *Shechinah* in our midst. At these moments, the veils of separation are lifted, and, just as an infant experiences trust and breathes so effortlessly in its mother's arms, we, too, feel close to Hashem and realize that life and love are continuously emerging from Him.

For me, there is a distinct parallel between the closeness that we attempt to experience with Hashem and the connection that Hashem wants us to experience with the individual who is destined to be our life partner. The discovery process is one that evolves through learning to create a continuous flow of trust, emotional openness and personal security, along with the ability to appropriately share at every stage throughout the relationship building process. It begins during dating and extends for a lifetime — to the *chasunah* and *sheva brachos*, through *shanah rishonah*, with the building of a family, throughout the years of raising children and into life's twilight years.

Therefore, when we sense and experience this relationship in the course of our lives, shared through emotional fulfillment of *shalom bayis*, then in its loss we understand the pained expressions of the holy Baal Shem Tov or the revealed sense of human aloneness shared by the late Rav Soloveitchik in Boston more than thirty years ago. And since this need is so innate to the DNA of our inner lives, we can also understand how a young man like Michael, in returning to an empty hotel room, can become aware of a truth that suddenly emerged in his consciousness, a truth that had never before been formulated.

All couples, whether at the beginning of their union, in the prime of their marriage or in their later years, need to acquire the understanding and skills to continuously create an environment of security and comfort where each can feel emotionally safe and respected. And this experience emerges as couples acquire the understanding required to ensconce them in the experience of *menuchas hanefesh* so their deepest selves can emerge from behind the veil to be understood, respected and cared for. It is the ability of a couple to create an emotionally safe environment that allows each other to feel secure, while enabling children to grow emotionally, physically and spiritually whole, and to appreciate the true wonder of growing in a loving Torah environment. This is the suitable setting for the *Shechinah* to dwell in.

◇ The Bas Kol

Perhaps this is why Chazal tell us that forty days before a child is born, a *bas kol* announces the future life partner of this soul. The reason, in my mind, is that the nature of this bond between husband and wife has to be so exquisitely tuned. These two *neshamos* will one day meet and begin to share a life together, and it is only through the delicate fine-tuning of their emotional and spiritual selves that they can guide each other and create an environment where Torah life thrives for both parents and children alike. For this couple to fulfill their roles in the long and unbroken chain of Jewish history, these two personalities need to be prepared in every way, beginning before birth. Then, as they grow, Hashem places each in an environment that prepares them for the task of weaving their lives lovingly together. Every moment is all in Hashem's hands. Nothing is accidental or without meaning.

This long period of growth and preparation that enables us to be ready to meet and become acquainted with our *bashert* is why, when we reach the age to discover this relationship and do not, the hurt is so penetrating and inescapable. I liken it to a little girl on the day of her birthday. No one has informed her of a party, but she has "a feeling" that a surprise is being planned by her best friends. Then the invitation to play in her friend's house arrives, and she's now sure that she was right. As she enters, she is expecting to be greeted by "Surprise!!!" Instead, when she enters, she finds no party, just a family going about business as usual in the home. No one is even aware that she's there, nor seems to care. Who can describe her disappointment and pain? Yet this is the disappointment and hurt that dating *bachurim* and *bachuros* (young men and women) experience on an ongoing basis as dating experiences become disappointing experiences.

We are raised and prepared from the very moment of our conception for the time when we will meet our *bashert*. We are promised that our lives will be fulfilling, inspiring and loving. Similarly, when marriage comes and it is filled with hurt, there are no words for the poignancy of the pain.

◇ Developing the Deeper Dynamic of the Dating Relationship

There are many factors that contribute to healthy relationship building that leads to a fulfilling marriage. These include conveying feelings of respect, attentiveness, emotional stability and an ongoing sense of appreciation. Each of these essential *middos*, qualities and skills will always contribute to a slow and gradual development of trust in a dating relationship.

Yet, we also need to become aware of a deeper personal dynamic that must be present, just beneath the surface. This is the ability for a young man and woman to discover a firm and stable sense of inner security, personal fulfillment and inner calm as they move from each stage of their relationship to the next.

This dimension of self that Chazal call *menuchas hanefesh* serves as a personal gyroscope. It helps each maintain his or her sense of balance through the challenges of mutual understanding that each partner is attempting to develop.

CHAPTER III

The Link Between *Menuchas Hanefesh* and Relationship Building

◇ I Bought You a *Chassan*

Dating is a very recent phenomenon in our long history and bears no resemblance to how *shidduchim* were made in the past, neither in how parents agreed to marry their children nor the way a young couple developed their relationship. To demonstrate the vast gap between our experience today and a century ago, I am retelling a brief and humorous story I came across while in Eretz Yisrael and then contrasting this *shidduch* with an approach we are more familiar with. The first is about a young woman who was married perhaps 150 years ago, and the other is a young man who began dating about seven years ago and has not yet discovered his *bashert*.

Perel was a young Chassidish girl who lived in Europe. She recalled how she asked her grandmother, *Bubby* Chanah, to share how she and *Zaidy* met and were married. Her grandmother told her the following amusing story about her engagement.

"When I was about six years old, my father went shopping on erev Shabbos. While he was at the marketplace, he was approached by a *shadchan* who suggested a *shidduch* for me. My father heard the proposal and it made sense to him. So before he came home, he was introduced to the father of the boy. They spoke for a few minutes and came to an agreement that his son and I would be married in about ten years, when we would both be ready. A financial settlement was agreed upon and then he went home.

> When my father returned from the marketplace, he was carrying all the Shabbos food he had purchased and happily exclaimed, "Chanala, I have a surprise for you. I bought you a *chassan* today." I had heard all about being a *kallah* before and was very excited that he had bought me a *chassan*. So I started to look through the packages with great excitement. Thinking I was looking for some special food he bought for Shabbos, he asked me, "Chanala, what are you looking for?" "I'm looking for my *chassan* that you bought me."

We are perhaps 150 years away from this tale. And it is clear to us that *Bubby* Chanah was very amused as she retold the story of her engagement to her granddaughter. Chanah appreciated how looking through the bags of Shabbos food for her *chassan* made great sense to a six-year-old girl. Now, however, as she looks back, having gone through decades of marriage and telling the story to a third generation, she also understands the comical absurdity of her childhood impressions about finding her *chassan* in a bag of Shabbos food. And as Chanah finished the story, about ten years did in fact pass while she eagerly waited to meet her *chassan*. When they did meet, she liked him and they were married.

What I find so poignant about the story is not that she thought of her *chassan* as similar to a Shabbos cake or challah, but that all through the years, she was aware that someone was waiting to marry her. And when they finally met a decade later, she was pleased with and even liked the young man she met.

As I thought about this story, which I am sure has been

successfully repeated countless times over our history of more than three thousand years, Chanah maintained a state of mind that was fully receptive to engagement and marriage and she was just a positive nod away from moving on toward the next step of meeting her *chassan* and proceeding on to the *chupah*. So when she and her *chassan* finally met, barring any unexpected surprises such as an extremely disturbing physical or personal blemish, she was emotionally ready to say yes. If all went as planned, everything she would see and hear would be perceived in a positive manner. From the age of six, Chanah was ready and determined to move forward.

From our Western perspective, we have no concept of what this was like. However, it was the way *shidduchim* were negotiated for millennia, and chances are pretty good that each of us is here today because an arrangement was made between two sets of parents that brought the lives of their children together.

Let's jump in time and space to a very different perspective about *shidduchim* and relationship building. Shlomo is a young financial executive for a New York bank, who has shared his frustration and difficulties in finding a young woman who fits all his criteria. He has dated well over a hundred young women over a seven year period. A hundred plus girls is quite a number. And if we stacked all his ancestors over the past thousand years on each other's shoulders, he has probably gone out with more young women than all of them combined.

When we explored the reasons for his difficulties with moving ahead, he openly shared how he usually felt little attraction, and even when there initially was, after a few dates he took a closer look and invariably found flaws. There were times when he began to feel comfortable, but then began comparing them to other girls he had dated in the past. And when he got past these hurdles, he began asking himself whether he had strong emotional feelings or a sense of excitement. Whatever the questions, intrusive thoughts, fears or doubts, invariably, he would always pull away and move on to the next girl on the list.

It's not that Shlomo is cruel or an Achashverosh, or suffers from any mental illness. I know that he deeply wants to discover his life partner. However, when he is in a dating relationship, he does not know how to release himself from the quicksand of the endless assault of distraction, uncertainty and negativism. He may be showing up for the date in a new car, or wearing a really great suit, and may have even invested the time and money to plan a creative and even pleasant evening together. However, what he consistently leaves outside the relationship is his ability to see the young woman from a positive state of mind. He may even be able to get past the first few meetings feeling that it has possibilities. However, as the dating continues, he inevitably falls back into the same repetitive pattern that he's been stuck in for many years. In essence, he is paralyzed.

The thought of him surveying a young woman for the flaws and blemishes he will eventually pick up reminds me of a high tech airport scanner capable of picking up even the minutest metal object. So, over the years, when it comes to finding reasons not to continue, Shlomo can be merciless.

Now, let's do some creative exploring of two diverse worlds from the lenses of two jam cams — the video cameras used to monitor traffic. Imagine a split screen where we can somehow fold time so that we can observe *Bubby* Chanah and Shlomo meeting their prospective partners for the first time. On the surface, from the jam cam we are seeing many differences in dress, age, behavior, facial expressions, the comfort or discomfort each feels as they communicate with their partners, and the settings where the respective meetings occur. Two worlds cannot be further apart.

However there is an even greater division. The jam cam only shows us the story from the outside. However, what if we focus within the minds of both *Bubby* Chanah and Shlomo? We would observe Chanah, now a young woman in mid-adolescence, awaiting the first meeting between her and her *chassan*, probably with great trepidation because she knows she will probably be marrying this young man, regardless of who he is. Yet internally she also experiences a sense of trust that her life with him will unfold over time and together they will walk to a *chupah* where she will hear the seventh *brachah* expressing wishes of *gilah, rinah, ditzah v'chedvah, ahavah v'achvah v'shalom v'reius* — all expressions of human joy and love befitting a *chassan* and *kallah*. This is the expectation of each *kallah* over our many generations. Many years later, as Chanah related the story to her granddaughter Perel, she gave personal testimony that this life did actually unfold, that her life of personal and shared fulfillment was achieved.

Shlomo on the other hand is going through the motions, and would like to *be* married. He has no idea how he will ever *get* married. He is hoping for a life-transforming epiphany that will literally carry him above all his fears, doubts and anxieties to the *chupah* and beyond. For Chanah, the transformation is a natural and smooth progression from her not yet married and private self to a shared and married self. However, this transformation seems impossible for Shlomo. Everywhere he turns he feels unable to move forward. Asking him why will not help because he has been analyzing the reasons for years, and the more he analyzes, the deeper he's caught in his own web. As someone once wisely said, it's like asking a centipede how it walks. Once it has to stop and figure out how it once moved a hundred legs so effortlessly, it can never walk again. Shlomo can never keep track of all the issues, and while he is making every external effort to find his *bashert*, deep within he fully expects to discover countless reasons why each candidate just won't work.

While Chanah once lived and Shlomo is with us today, beyond being themselves, they also represent prototypes of two states of mind. Chanah may have trepidations and fears, yet she is clear, calm, focused and quite secure in her purpose. She will meet her *chassan* and get married. Shlomo is fragmented, fearful, distracted and quite insecure. He is paralyzed.

Shlomo is just one person struggling to discover his *bashert*. In my daily experience with this phenomenon, I come across many others facing similar frustrations in the world of *shidduchim*. Here are just a few:

Shana is a social worker in her late twenties and has dated many young men. She invariably stops a relationship after a first or second meeting, feeling she can not compromise on the quality of who she needs to marry. Her focus is on core issues including: personal attraction, income, family, *middos* and religious commitment. These are all very important standards. However, she realizes that as the years pass by, she is dating less frequently and feels the quality of men she is dating has also fallen. She is determined, however, to remain true to these standards. "You may think I sound very demanding, but what choice do I have? I will have to spend the rest of my life with this person, and I can't compromise on my life."

Benzion is twenty-five and has been dating for two years. On two previous occasions, he felt he found the girl with whom he wanted to spend his life. In both relationships he told me, "When it came to thinking more seriously about engagement, I became very nervous and felt as if I was walking on the third rail (electrified). I was tense, my heart was beating wildly and my breath was shallow. In both situations I asked myself, how can this be right if I'm feeling this way? Now I'm asking myself whether it was them or will I be this way with everyone I try to marry?"

Bracha is a teacher who is engaged, and is scheduled to be married in a month. Throughout her life she has waited to be a *kallah*. Yet now she is feeling uncertain, nervous and wondering whether her *chassan*, Shimon, is the right person for her. She feels she is more mature than he is, perhaps even smarter, and has picked up on some of his mannerisms about which she feels critical. She has been considering calling off the wedding.

Danny is almost thirty and is dreading reaching his birthday while still single. He has dated many girls in the past but has consistently experienced the same pattern. "I can't figure myself out. When I feel I finally found someone who I believe is the right one, I begin to pick apart every aspect of her personality. Suddenly everything I thought I could live with begins to bother and irritate me."

Suri was engaged to be married in a few weeks. As the wedding approached, she began to feel increasingly worried and tense. Finally she began to experience physical symptoms of nausea and weakness. No medical basis was discovered. Although she respected and even liked her *chassan*, she was fearful that her physical symptoms were giving her a message that she was making a mistake by going ahead with the wedding.

All these individuals have one experience in common. These troubling and even painful experiences in the search for a life partner are all accompanied by a negative state of mind. It may be experienced in a variety of forms. These include disappointment, anxiety, irritation, obsessive thinking, abdominal discomfort or other physical symptoms.

All these individuals function well in every area of their lives. In any previous generation, they would have been married early in their lives and led lives filled with all the joys and challenges that have always been an integral dimension of leading *frum* Torah lives. However, Shlomo, Bracha, Suri and all those many more I cannot possibly enumerate are caught in the webs preventing them from the freedom they need to discover their *bashert* and move their lives forward, as a couple.

Everything you will read, experience and discuss in this

book is designed to bring you to the realization that there really is nothing holding Shlomo or anyone else back from marriage. This generation is no different than any other. Each of us has the ability to transform all of these negative and troubling experiences of self, whether cognitive, emotional or even physical, and to deeply understand how Chanah, and the countless like her, were able to transition so effortlessly from being an "I" to becoming a "we."

◇ ## Understanding *Menuchas Hanefesh* and *Pizur Hanefesh*: Two States of Mind

To begin our journey, we must first understand that the Torah has a very different way of understanding the phenomenon of human experience. While Shlomo and others who share his inability to move forward can be characterized in very descriptive psychological terms such as commitment-phobic, anxiety-prone, or OCD, the approach I take here will be closer to the perceptions of Chazal and how they have interpreted human behavior over the millennia. Therefore the difference between Chanah and Shlomo is that they are really metaphors for two states of mind, which Chazal describe as *menuchas hanefesh* and *pizur hanefesh*. The significance of using these definitions to describe our state of mind is that it approaches the world of dating, engagement and all significant relationships as an opportunity for personal transformation and growth.

I do not mean to say that there are never situations that require effective and competent professional intervention, whether through psychotherapy or medication. However, over the years I have dedicated to working with singles and married couples, my experience has demonstrated that the vast majority of individuals have the ability to cultivate and maintain a healthy caring and loving state of mind, so vital in building a relationship that lasts for a lifetime.

Therefore, to further refine our path, everything you will read in this book is focused on a single goal, which is to teach you that each of you always has the ability to transform a *pizur hanefesh* state of mind to a *menuchas hanefesh* state of mind. This ability to transform ourselves is the primary condition for experiencing life's gifts to their fullest and for developing all meaningful relationships.

Defining Menuchas Hanefesh

I have referred to the concept of *menuchas hanefesh* many times, but have yet to provide a clear and workable definition. For many of us, the concept of *menuchas hanefesh* conjures up visions of relaxation and being "chilled out." However, Chazal's definition of *menuchas hanefesh* involves our learning to coordinate all the powers that Hashem has granted us toward achieving our life's mission. For Chazal, the concept relates more to an ability to maintain a sense of focus, clarity and meaning, which, in turn, produces the healthy and positive state of mind with which Hashem intended us to experience life. It is an awareness that regardless of life's challenges, we are able to maintain a quality of consciousness that continuously addresses life's deeper and eternal priorities. Therefore, concepts such as being *dan l'chaf z'chus* (judging others favorably) or *hakaras hatov* (feeling gratitude) are states associated with *menuchas hanefesh*, because they enable us to see life closer to Hashem's perspective.

However, the ability to maintain our *menuchas hanefesh* does not come naturally. It must be continuously strengthened. Its acquisition can even be compared to developing a muscle. Through learning how to cultivate our *menuchas hanefesh*, we are enhancing an awareness of the power that Chazal call *rikuz* (concentration on a goal), to help us maintain a state of mind that enables us to experience purpose, well being, meaning, caring, humility and everything else that brings us closer to Hashem and those we care for.

Consider this brief vignette that occurred almost a century ago:

> A commandant from the Bolshevik regime walked confidently and boldly into the *bais medrash* of the yeshivah in Kelm, fully expecting to be accorded the overt gestures of honor and respect due a representative of the revolutionary government. However, to his annoyance and anger, his entrance into the Kelm *bais medrash* caused not a stir. Not a single head was raised; no one even noticed him.
>
> With his pride sorely wounded, the commandant approached the *talmidim*, demanding to know the meaning of the disrespect shown a representative of the ruling government. The response was clear and reassuring. He was told, "This is certainly not a sign of disrespect. You see, here in our Talmudic academy, our students are taught the value of focusing only on what they are studying at that moment in time. Everything else is a distraction. They are taught that one never looks up from the Talmudic tractate during the study session for any reason, not even for a moment. You were not noticed because we have trained our students not to notice anything but the folio in front of them."
>
> Little did the commandant realize that he was being taught the value of achieving *menuchas hanefesh*.

The Gra's Definition of Menuchas Hanefesh

An even clearer idea of the centrality of *menuchas hanefesh* in Torah study and personal development is derived from Rav Eliyahu Dessler, *zt"l* — a student of the Alter of Kelm, *zt"l* — who shared how the Vilna Gaon described the focus required in Torah study to achieve *menuchas hanefesh*. Rav Dessler said that the Gaon made three suggestions to cultivate this quality of *menuchas hanefesh*. First, a student should imagine that the page or *daf* of the Torah he is presently studying is the only page or *daf* in existence; there is none that precedes or follows it. Second, he is the only individual in the world who has been given the Divine responsibility to master this piece of Torah. Third and last, this is the only opportunity he will ever have to grasp it. Either he will master it now or the opportunity will be lost forever.

This is how the Gaon describes achieving the focus required for *menuchas hanefesh*. There are no distractions of the past, no worries about the future. There is only this very moment that carries echoes of eternity. The acquisition of *menuchas hanefesh* is acquiring the art of "living in the moment." As an *adam gadol* once told me, this is the essence of the prayer that we say in Maariv in the *tefillah* of *Hashkiveinu*: "*V'haseir satan mil'faneinu umei'achareinu* — May Hashem remove the *satan* from in front of us and from behind us." We are praying for *menuchas hanefesh* and the ability to remain focused in the moment.

This concept of "living in the moment" defines a state of being wherein all is focused on being in the present as the key to achieving the goal at hand. We can be distracted neither by the past nor the future as we apply ourselves to the task of fulfilling our lives. There can only be the here and now. Worries and anxieties about the past and future play no role in the development of our ability to be focused and in the moment. They are actually impediments and distractions. Perhaps this is what Chazal mean when we are told, "*Dai tzarah beshaato* — Worry about the problem later, if and when it arises, not now."

Menuchas Hanefesh *as the Mayor*

The *sefer Sifsei Chaim*, by Rabbi Chaim Friedlander, *zt"l*, which has been my primary source for many of the concepts in this work, describes the development of *menuchas hanefesh* as similar to serving as the mayor of a city with its many commissioners and services. Each department head has his own domain, sphere of influence and budget. Each commissioner has his own operation to run successfully in order to keep the municipality capable of meeting the needs of the residents. The role of the mayor is to ensure that each executive does what he is supposed to do, without infringing on the boundaries or power of others. When all are working together under the guidance of the mayor, then the city is functioning well.

This is the same for a corporation, a government or any organized entity where all parts of the entity have to work together to achieve maximum results. And it is certainly true regarding the concept of *menuchas hanefesh*. *Nefesh* is a life force that Hashem places within each of us that enables us to fulfill our life tasks as Jews in this world. It has many dimensions, powers and drives, all of which were intended to work together to achieve life's most precious goals in the service of Hashem. And when all of these forces place themselves under the direction of a unifying force — our Torah-inspired vision and aspirations — then all aspects of our cognitive, emotional and biological selves work together to achieve the ultimate purpose for which Hashem gave us life. The harmonization of these powers, guided by a clear and lofty focus, is what Chazal call *menuchas hanefesh*. It is the synergistic blending of emotional, physical and spiritual forces within us that gives us a sense of profound security and well-being, all of which contribute toward achieving the goal at hand.

Menuchas hanefesh means that we have the perspective to handle the challenges that confront us, as depicted in the following scenario:

You are holding a multi-million-dollar lottery ticket, but you could only win if you travel cross-country in a hurry. However, that would mean taking a very uncomfortable seat on a very uncomfortable plane to get from California to New York in time to cash in the ticket. During the trip, you may look a bit foolish to the other passengers, but your sense of security while on that journey would be very intact. It may very well be that on another occasion you would be bothered by the color of the seat upholstery or a slightly recognizable odor that you didn't care for. But in this situation, you are very capable of dealing with great physical and even emotional discomfort to get to your desired goal to cash in this ticket. Through *menuchas hanefesh*, you learn to keep distractions at bay while pursuing your goal.

◇ A Lifetime of Desserts

There are many who have learned that *menuchas hanefesh* is an inner power that can help quiet the discomfort for much longer than just a few hours. It may even last over a period of decades. While our focus is on dating, I want to relate this story about a married couple, which far exceeds any expectations I have for myself, yet emphasizes what some are able to achieve through *menuchas hanefesh*.

A number of years ago, while I was waiting to *daven* Maariv in Yeshiva Derech Ayson, also known as the Yeshiva of Far Rockaway, a *rav* from Eretz Yisrael arrived early and sat to learn. He was recognized by one of the *rebbeim* as a well-known *talmid* of Rav Shach, *zt"l*; in fact, he was waiting to *daven* before leaving for nearby JFK and his return flight to Eretz Yisrael. In appreciation of the significance of his presence, the *rav* was asked if he would speak for a few minutes before Maariv. Hesitantly, he agreed. As this was the week preceding Shabbos *Parashas Vayechi*, when the last *parashah* of *Sefer Bereishis* would be read, the rav chose to speak about the *sefer* that was about to be completed.

Sefer Bereishis, he explained, is also known as *Sefer Hamiddos* because of the *middos* of the *Avos* and *Imahos* that are mentioned throughout each *parashah*. And with the closing of this *sefer,* he felt it was important for us to be left with the essence of what Hashem wants us to understand about the truly deeper strength of the *Avos* and *Imahos* that are described throughout *Bereishis.*

In his discussion of *middos,* he told a story of a *rosh yeshivah* he was close to, but whose name he did not reveal.

While enjoying a Shabbos *seudah* at the home of this *rosh yeshivah,* a young *bachur* sat through the meal and ate the rather bland food of the *rosh yeshivah* and the *rebbetzin.* They spoke in Torah, and the young man appreciated the opportunity to experience every moment in the presence of this great man and his wife.

At the end of the meal, the *rebbetzin* served stewed fruits, also known as "compote." The dessert promised to be a positive finish to a rather plain menu, so, with the expectation of ending the meal on a tastier note, the young guest swallowed a heaping spoonful of the dessert. However, to the *bachur,* the fruits tasted intolerably sour and nearly inedible. He had to force himself to swallow them and make sure that he suppressed his instinct to vomit.

As soon as the *rebbetzin* left the room, the *rosh yeshivah* gently took the *bachur's* bowl of compote and pulled it over to him. As he did so, the *rosh yeshivah* said in a whisper, "I know, the compote can be a little difficult to eat. Let me finish it for you so the *rebbetzin* doesn't feel slighted. You see, I've been eating it this way for almost fifty years."

For the *rav,* this mundane story about cooked fruits portrayed the essence of the *middos* he was attempting to convey. For fifty years a man whose greatness was known to the world of Torah had managed never once to complain about his wife's compote, even though he would have preferred it another way. Shabbos after Shabbos, there was never the slightest hint or gesture that he was displeased with her dessert.

What enables a man of great personal wisdom and pro-found depth and faith to be so vigilant over his wife's sense of dignity and self-esteem? Some may even call him foolish for not letting her know. I can just hear them offering the well-known advice that is so rampant among marital counselors: "Why not be honest with her?"

We can say he was patient, self-denying, humble, self-effac-ing or any number of descriptions that point toward his consid-eration for her dignity and self-respect. Actually, I once shared this story with a chef. He was mortified. "How could he subject his guests to such terrible food? And why would he want to fool his wife into thinking that it actually tasted good?" My answer to him was that for this *rav*, his *shalom bayis* came first.

To my mind there is only one description that encompasses his ability to literally swallow her dessert unflinchingly for half a century. It is the strength of his *menuchas hanefesh* that enabled him to subdue his need for a sweet dessert and focus instead on his love and respect for her as a person. *Menuchas hanefesh* gives us the clarity and strength to make these choices over and over — even for fifty years. And if we survey in our minds the countless stories of heroism on a giant scale such as the behav-ior of the Bluzhever Rebbe, *zt"l*, in the Nazi death camps, to the Brisker Rav, *zt"l*, walking through enemy lines, to stories about the gentleness of Rav Moshe Feinstein, *zt"l*, the courage and determination of Rav Aharon Kotler, *zt"l*, and countless other individuals who have come to represent how mortals can acquire Hashem's strengths and *middos* in this world, we will always discover the acquisition of *menuchas hanefesh* at the cen-ter of this development.

I know of a couple that was engaged to be married. They had developed a very close and special relationship. However, just two weeks before the marriage, the young woman learned that she had a malignancy in her abdomen. Both were in shock.

The relationship that had become so important and special to each was suddenly in jeopardy. The couple consulted with many *gedolim*, yet none could tell them whether to continue with the wedding plans. In the end, they decided to marry, and through their shared feelings of *menuchas hanefesh* they were able to transcend their challenge and create a warm and loving marriage.

Acquiring Menuchas Hanefesh

The acquisition of *menuchas hanefesh* is a prerequisite for *avodas Hashem*. It therefore cannot be the sole domain of *gedolim*. Consider the *tefillah* for Shabbos Minchah and you will become aware of how *menuchah* is at the heart of the *ruach* of Shabbos. The word *menuchah* is mentioned no less than ten times in a single *brachah* in the Shemoneh Esrei for Minchah. And along with each mention of *menuchah*, there are a total of nine separate descriptions of *menuchah*. If the Eskimos have multiple words to describe snow because of its centrality in their lives, than consider how significant the experience of *menuchah* is to Shabbos and the Torah experience of self. Later in this book, we will take a closer look at the inherent connection between *menuchas hanefesh* and Shabbos.

Menuchas hanefesh is not achieved through a passive process. While Hashem endows us with a *neshamah* that guides us when we are in state of *menuchas hanefesh*, its acquisition and integration into our moment-to-moment experience of life is only the result of a determined and focused effort that permeates our existence. There are times when we discover ourselves feeling this sense of completeness and mastery. The challenge is that when we are not in this state, how we can be aware of its absence? Once we are aware of its absence, we then need to understand how we can access this healthier state of mind and return to a personal experience of self that brings us closer to how Hashem intended us to experience life and those around us.

In summary, our challenge is to know when we are experiencing it, when we are not and how to return to it. We may feel very comfortable one moment with ourselves and others, and the very next moment we are feeling critical and hurt. The question is how to organize our lives so that we always have a portal that gives us access to this dimension of ourselves where the gift of life and *shalom bayis* truly lies.

◇ ## Returning to the Yerushalayim within Us

This brings to mind a moving and memorable short story I read many years ago by the Nobel Prize laureate, S.Y. Agnon. He writes of a young shepherd boy tending his father's sheep in the Carpathian Mountains. As he grows up, he hears his father's tales of the wondrous city of Yerushalayim where the *Bais Hamikdash* once stood and where the *kedushah* of Hashem's *Shechinah* still hovers. He dreams of reaching this Promised Land.

> One day, a small lamb runs off into a cave. He runs after the lamb, which eludes him as it scampers through the labyrinthine trails in the cave. Finally, after a long and exhausting chase, the lamb leads him to an opening in the cave. He emerges to find the golden city of Yerushalayim. He cannot believe his eyes. He grabs the lamb and runs back into the cave to find his way back to where he began, to the grazing pastures of the mountainside. Breathless, he races home to inform his father that he has discovered the golden city of Yerushalayim. He grabs his father's hand and pulls him to the pasture and into the cave. However, when he enters the cave, sadly, he cannot retrace his steps. He knows it's there. He smelled its pine-scented air, saw its beauty and experienced its holiness. If only he would have left a trail to follow! Now he cannot find his way back.

The story is a metaphor for the Yerushalayim within us. Hashem places the golden beauty of Yerushalayim within us when we are brought into this world. It is an experience of life that enables us to feel whole, deep and secure within ourselves, close to Hashem and all those we care for. It never leaves us. It's always there. We experience it when we are with people we love, when we are standing at the Kosel and when we are enjoying Shabbos *zemiros*, the joy of *yamim tovim* and the *smachos* that fill our lives. And even when we don't experience this elevated dimension of our lives, it never leaves us. It's always waiting to be rediscovered beneath the surface of our consciousness. And it's there even in our unstable moments. It's waiting for us to find our way back through the cave. But we need to leave signs along the trail, to drop pebbles and markers that remind us of the circuitous path we need to follow to retrace our steps to the *menuchas hanefesh* that Hashem has provided for us as a gift of life.

◇ A Portrait of Rav Chatzkel, *zt"l*

In our true selves that Hashem has placed within us, the sense of *menuchas hanefesh* brings us closer to Hashem, ourselves and those to whom we dedicate ourselves, such as our spouses and children. *Menuchas hanefesh* allows us to experience a sense of security, trust, humility and *hakaras hatov*. We are aware of life's many miracles. In this state we understand the meaning and experience of human love and closeness to others. In it we can study Torah, think clearly, make wise decisions and participate in every phase of life that is uniquely related to Hashem's world.

It is crucial to understand that *menuchas hanefesh* is not a state that is dependent on our physical, financial or social conditions. I remember so clearly visiting my close friend and *chavrusa* who was lying in a hospital bed during a long and torturous illness. Although he was wracked by unspeakable pain, none of this affected his ability to find meaning in every moment. There he lay, hopeful and filled with a gentle calmness, facing a portrait of his late *rosh yeshivah*, Rav Chatzkel Levenstein, *zt"l*, the former Mashgiach of Ponovezh, whose *talmid* he had been more than forty years ago. He gazed at the picture and said, "He taught me to be prepared for all that I am experiencing." As he spoke to me, I realized that despite his condition and pain, he was in a state of *menuchas hanefesh* that was the result of a life lived — and still being lived — to its fullest.

Gratefully, the majority of us are not faced with such a great test of faith. Yet the need to acquire *menuchas hanefesh* is even more significant for the well-being of our lives and those we care for. Our focus is to use this state to discover our *bashert* and create a fulfilling marriage. This is where *menuchas hanefesh* plays its most important role.

◇ *The Power of* Pizur Hanefesh

On the other side of our spiritual universe is *pizur hanefesh*, which is characterized by emotional states of mind that could be described as confused, insecure, fragmented and impulsive. These states of experience contribute to emotional imbalance that undermines our ability to build relationships. In short, they are the multitude of negative thought patterns that prevent individuals from recognizing their *bashert*.

The word *pizur* means to be spread out, scattered and unfocused. There is an aphorism that a ship without a port is always in a storm. This is why *pizur hanefesh* is usually accompanied by a sense of internal chaos. The world we live in today invites *pizur hanefesh* through its constant bombardment of distractions that invade our lives on a multitude of levels. It is a world that thrives economically and culturally on promoting *pizur hanefesh*, filled with electronic gadgetry, an array of addictive distractions that we call leisure, and the incessant and empty online and text-based chatter. What characterizes *pizur hanefesh* is that once we are in these negative states of experience, we are essentially imprisoned and frequently rationalize our right to feel insecure, worried, unstable, fidgety and depressed, and to wallow in many other similar states of negative personal experience. Over time, we learn to cultivate *pizur hanefesh* as an acceptable — and even preferred — state of mind.

◇ A Precious Gift

I frequently use a metaphor that many have found helpful in describing the difference between *pizur hanefesh* and *menuchas hanefesh*. Let's say I have a very close and beloved friend to whom I want to express my great esteem for him and our friendship. So I buy him a gift of a luxury Lexus automobile with all the options, for a price tag of well over $100,000, and park it in front of his house. A few days later I walk past his house and notice that the car is filled with bags of trash. I'm quite puzzled and dismayed and ask him, "Why did you fill the Lexus with all this smelly trash?

His answer to me is, "I certainly appreciate the value of the car and what a special gift it is. However, the sanitation department has been on strike for a few days and garbage has been accumulating in my house. So I decided to put it in the car."

My response would be, "Don't you realize it's a luxury automobile with rare leathers, fine woods and hi tech and delicate instrumentation? Its purpose is to help you feel how important you are to me as you ride in style and grace. It's certainly not a suitable place for trash."

The *nimshal* (meaning) is that Hashem has given us many exquisite gifts in our lives. Perhaps the most precious is our mind, and how we use it to discover our *bashert* and create relationships of love and closeness. The "Lexus" of our mind is never intended to be a receptacle for trash. The "trash" I am referring to consists of the troubled thoughts of criticism, feelings of annoyance, jealousies, hurt, sadness and anger that so frequently fill our mind and hearts and prevent us from experiencing Hashem's precious gifts of life to their fullest and sweetest. This trash is what Chazal refer to as *pizur hanefesh*.

So when a couple such as Chaim and Sandy are sitting together in a car, without any reason Chaim feels "annoyed" by the way she articulates a particular word. He not only feels annoyed but accepts his annoyance as reality. Chaim's mind has become a receptacle for *pizur hanefesh*-trash. Or when Sandy is sitting in the front seat and gazing at another car, wishing they were driving the newer or more luxurious model, and wondering whether Chaim and she are suited for each other because he may never be able to afford the Lexus, this too is *pizur hanefesh*. When the relationship is diverted by a random and unexamined thought or feeling, we have come to make peace with the trash in our minds. It is only when we are able to quiet these negative thoughts and feelings and learn to maintain a state of mind and heart that enables us to appreciate Hashem's gifts that we achieve *menuchas hanefesh*. Only then can Chaim or Sandy have the freedom to determine the truthfulness of the thought, or whether it's just more "noise" from a troubled state of mind.

◇ ## Quieting *Pizur Hanefesh* at the Eleventh Hour

I distinctly remember Yaakov, who was about to become a *chassan* and was standing outside of Pearl's house holding the engagement ring. However, as he prepared himself to walk up the steps, he felt paralyzed by a sense of fear welling up within. He began to obsess over a facial feature. He couldn't bring himself to ring the bell. After a few minutes he called me. "Shaya, I can't do it. I know to you it's a minor thing," he said, "but it has bothered me since the first date." As they came to know each other, this feature had faded into the background. However, at the very moment when he was ready to give her the ring, his thoughts began to run wild. Once again he began to focus on this feature and obsess over it. "How can I live with this for the rest of my life?"

On one hand, we can certainly say he was feeling anxiety, "commitment phobia" or emotional distress, and offer many other similar terms. But whatever we call it, he was in a state of *pizur hanefesh*, where every moment of personal closeness that had led both of them up to this moment was no longer accessible. He was trapped in a perception influenced by a state of emotional chaos and insecurity that was wiping out his "emotional hard drive." At that moment, he was truly feeling the need to walk away from the young woman who, he had said many times over, was the "best person I have ever met to spend the rest of my life with." He was accepting this momentary fear as reality and permitting it to determine the rest of his life. For a brief yet critical period of time, he was telling himself, "I have the right to find a *kallah* without this feature that I'm not comfortable with. I'm entitled to have it better. And I'm even ready to walk away and wait for the right one." In this state, every moment of sharing and closeness between them had suddenly fallen out of sight.

Hearing his anxiety, I understood that my role was to help him regain his sense of *menuchas hanefesh* and to remember some of the moments they shared that brought them to this stage of their relationship. After following my advice, he was able to pull himself back to a clearer perception of *menuchas hanefesh* and retake control over the ship of his life. I can share that last year he, his wife, and their first child stopped by on *Purim* with *mishloach manos*.

◇ **The Nature of the Crossroads**

One concept I taught this young man was that we should never make the mistake of thinking that we <u>are</u> the negative state we are in. We have been created with the potential to experience the dimension of *menuchas hanefesh* or *pizur hanefesh* at any given moment. In effect, at each moment of our lives we stand at a crossroads of our selves, where we are given the option of thriving in one state of personal experience associated with *menuchas hanefesh* or another state of personal experience that entraps us in the quicksand of *pizur hanefesh*. As the Alter of Kelm describes our options, we are always standing at the crossroads between these two states of being. Our perception and personal experience offer many different ways for us to define our present concept of reality.

This potential for either state of being is always in front of us. It's similar to how Rabbi Naftali Tzvi Berlin, known through his writings as the Netziv, *zt"l*, understands the opening *pasuk* of *R'eih*, in which Hashem says, "See that I place in front of you today a blessing and a curse." The Netziv says that we should be able to see both potentials as clearly as two distinctive mountain peaks standing in front of our eyes. The Alter of Kelm describes how there exists a continuous flow of conflicting and contradictory thoughts and feelings that fill our minds and hearts. Even when we may be in a seemingly quiet state, our thoughts and feelings are never at rest. At any given moment, our continuous flow of ideas and emotions can move us either toward or away from *menuchas hanefesh*.

◇ The Eternal Struggle between the Two States of Mind

This challenge is one that has accompanied every soul that has ever walked the earth and accompanies us at each moment of our lives, dividing two extraordinarily different states of personal experience. One brings us closer to a sense of wholeness and an ever-present appreciation of Hashem's countless gifts of life, while the other force takes us away from the sense of wholeness and covers our awareness of Hashem's gifts of life. In one we are closer to *Echad* (One-ness), and the other pulls us into the abyss of *pizur hanefesh* — the troubling experience of fragmentation. One brings us closer to the union we are always searching for deep within, while the other creates fear, anxiety and isolation.

The Glass is Always Half Full and Half Empty

Consider being offered a glass of water that is filled to the half-way mark. At one moment you may feel that the offer is for a half-full glass, and that gives you a feeling of satisfaction and gratitude. However, the next moment your perception changes and you now see the glass as half empty. Along with your perception, your feelings about the offer change, as well. There has been no change in the quantity, only in the way you view it.

The reality is that both potentials exist simultaneously within us. They reflect the two mountains or the two states of *pizur hanefesh* and *menuchas hanefesh*. We always have the capacity to see the glass from the two very different perspectives. We are never trapped in any negative state, as Hashem gives us the power of free will, or *bechirah*, to determine how we will view the contents of the glass. One perception contributes to a feeling of *menuchas hanefesh*, while the other perception leads to a very different experience of self.

It is crucial to understand that the choices are not simply, "If you want to, you have a right to see the glass as half empty." That would be comparing it to which of two ties will be a better color match for your new suit. In the case of color preference, either could do very well. However, when it comes to a sense of wholeness and satisfaction, the choice is at the very heart of existence. For in our lives, Hashem is constantly challenging us to choose between two forces within. One choice brings us closer to Him. The other choice creates dark emotions that separate us from Him.

The Shifting Sands of Perception

A young couple, Malka and Ellie, asked to see me. They were engaged with a wedding planned in just a month. However, Malka had been feeling increasingly critical of Ellie. As soon as they became engaged, she began to see him as too heavy and unmotivated. She was now wondering whether she had made the right decision to get engaged. Ellie began to feel Malka's misgivings. When I met with them, the confusion and uncertainty filled the air. They were having disagreements over the menu, the seating plan, where to live. The wedding itself seemed to be in jeopardy.

Both were frightened at the enormity of change in their lives and the fear that the responsibilities of marriage would be too great. After learning the principles of *menuchas hanefesh*, I could feel their perceptions and moods shift. They became easier with each other, friendlier, more relaxed and positive about their future. We might say that they changed, but this is not true. We do not change so fast, yet our perceptions are continuously changing. Our understanding changes as we stand at the crossroads between *menuchas hanefesh* and *pizur hanefesh* and we continuously process the myriad of possible ways we can experience reality. If we choose one direction, it will bring us closer to our true selves, to Hashem and to those we care for. If we choose another direction, we will become more distant from all that is precious in our lives.

There is a crucial understanding that resides at the very heart of this dynamic: At every moment, Hashem gives us the choice and the ability to escape the quicksand of emotions and perceptions that seemingly imprison us. And at every moment we can transform ourselves to move from one state and experience to another. It is crucial for us as *baalei emunah*, who deeply believe in reward and punishment, that we truly believe we have this choice and ability. For if we really were trapped and imprisoned, then there would be no free will, no responsibility and no freedom. We are all very aware that Hashem never deprives us of our freedom.

CHAPTER IV

The Five Dimensions of our Experience of Life

To introduce the five dimensions of our experience of life, we first need a brief review of what we've covered until now.

The ability of a couple to develop a relationship during dating and to maintain a stable and growing relationship during engagement is not based on any external bond or attraction, but on how each as an individual enables the other to continuously experience an inner sense of trust, security and balance. Chazal define this inner road to personal security and balance as *menuchas hanefesh*. With it, we can gain a sense of security that we can achieve everything that contributes to our deepest needs — this is what tells us we have discovered our *bashert*. Without *menuchas hanefesh*, we live in a chaotic world of runaway and negative thoughts, feelings and countless other reactions that will lead us to feel isolated, emotionally alone and in conflict with ourselves and each other.

In our own lives, many of us have known couples who have created marriages and families based on their ability to cultivate this inner state of *menuchas hanefesh*. When we are in their presence, we can sense this closeness and the harmonious way their lives are interwoven. This quality is never a function of financial security, family size, age, health or attractiveness. It emerges from the inner security that is achieved by two people who have developed this inner capacity for *menuchas hanefesh* and are then able to use this strength to being close and loving with each other.

However, this state is not exclusive to great people. Each of us has experienced this state within ourselves many times. Perhaps as we sit comfortably around a Shabbos table with our family, friends and all those we care for, we experience the calmness and tranquility of Shabbos. We can experience this *menuchas hanefesh* when we are walking in the woods or along the shore. We can be intensely focused on a project at work, davening in shul, or sharing a quiet and enjoyable moment with someone. We can even experience it during a moment of crisis, when we call upon reserves of wisdom and clear-headedness to make the correct decision in a defining moment of truth. The common denominator of *menuchas hanefesh* is that whenever and wherever we experience it, the feeling is always accompanied by a sense of security, inner focus and clarity.

On the other side of our emotional and cognitive universe, we also experience times when we are in a more troubled and distressed state of mind, when we are unfocused, insecure and frequently confused. We call this state of mind *pizur hanefesh*. It makes no difference whether we are at work, at home, driving a Lexus, on vacation or elsewhere. When we are in a state of *pizur hanefesh*, we are always alienated and emotionally isolated from each other and ourselves. We can observe its effects through agitation, anger, confusion, hurt, conflicts and long periods of uncomfortable and mutual silence when we feel insecure, alone and many other negative experiences in dating and engagement. In short, *pizur hanefesh* always locks us into a negative state of mind and deprives us of our ability to remember the experiences that have brought us together.

In summary, the primary reason that couples date, develop a close relationship, become engaged and have loving and close marriages is because they have learned to cultivate their own and shared states of *menuchas hanefesh*. And the primary reason that couples date without success, continuously experiencing irritation, dissatisfaction, annoyance, hurt, criticism and all the other negative thoughts and emotions toward each other is due to *pizur hanefesh*. One moment we are clear thinking, rational, caring and related, and the next moment we may feel impatient, angry and critical. In dating and engagement, a couple can feel very close and understanding, and suddenly — seemingly without warning — an argument erupts. No one wanted it, yet here it is, filled with hurts and abrasiveness between two people who just a few moments ago may have felt close and seen great promise in their future. And suddenly, regardless of everything they have shared, the relationship is in jeopardy.

◇ **Defining the Dimensions of *Menuchas Hanefesh* and *Pizur Hanefesh***

What are the criteria by which we define the presence of *menuchas hanefesh* and *pizur hanefesh* in developing the delicate bonds of growing relationshps? While it may be possible to objectively look at a couple from the outside and judge whether they are secure and close, I believe that most of us would find that the externals are not a reliable litmus test. They never really tell us what's going on inside. You can be sitting in a restaurant and notice a couple entering. On the surface they look smiling, well groomed, with an aura of competence and success. From an external perspective, everything looks very much like the ideal couple, ready to become the ideal engaged couple, ready to experience a memorable wedding. However, as we look at the deeper dimension of their thoughts and feelings, the picture may be very different. Internally, most dating couples are challenged by recurring feelings of tension, uncertainty, thoughts about ending the relationship and moving on to the next person on the list. This is the ever-present impact of *pizur hanefesh.*

Therefore, our measuring device of how a couple truly feels about each other will be through the five dimensions that determine whether we are in a state of *menuchas hanefesh* or *pizur hanefesh.* These five dimensions comprise the tools through which we are aware of our experience of life. Before we introduce them, permit me to give five examples that I have heard from dating and engaged couples, and see if you can define the five dimensions from them.

1. Shmuel is twenty-eight. He is a successful mortgage broker and has dated far too many young women. He tells me, "When I am sitting with someone on a date, my mind keeps on wandering, comparing her to other girls I have dated. It's not that I want to. I just can't seem to focus my thoughts on the person opposite me. They are always revisiting other relationships that I dropped for the same reason."

2. Brenda is a psychologist in her thirties. She has been dating for almost ten years. She shared the following: "I am a person who shares too much too soon. I can't help it. This is who I am. And when I am with a date that I feel has potential, I feel a need to share who I am inside, what I have been through in life and how I would like to grow. However, I am always left feeling that I am not being heard, and walk away feeling empty and disappointed."

3. Sheindel is a twenty-one-year-old *kallah*, just two weeks away from her wedding. This is what she told me: "My *chassan* is a *m'tzuyan* (exceptional) *talmid chacham.* He is

everything I always dreamt of in a young man. However, the thought of marriage makes me feel literally sick to my stomach. I can't eat or sleep; I'm shaking like a leaf. I don't know whether I can make it to my own *chupah*."

4. Mark is a twenty-five-year-old lawyer. He wants very much to get married but goes from date to date, either rejecting or being rejected. "There are a lot of girls I like and would certainly pursue marriage with. However, those that I like can't seem to tolerate my lifestyle. I'm always on the phone, spend long hours in the office and usually am running late. This is who I am and these are the demands of my firm. I don't believe I have a choice."

5. Yechiel is thirty-two. He is a thoughtful, caring and very sensitive individual. When I asked him why he thinks he's not married, he shared this: "I love people. That's who I am. Most of the girls I date are very fine and I would have been able to try to marry many of them. However, every time I get close to someone, I begin to experience fears and anxieties about being hurt and abandoned. It's as if I can be very sociable during the early stages of a relationship, but when it gets close I feel threatened, insecure and scared."

These illustrations, all based on individuals I have met and worked with, are expressing one of the five different dimensions of *menuchas hanefesh* or *pizur hanefesh*. They are:

1. Shmuel's Thoughts,
2. Brenda's Feelings,
3. Sheindel's Physiology,
4. Mark's Behavior, and
5. Yechiel's Self in Transition

Now we can take a closer look at each of these five areas from the perspective of how each of these dimensions moves us toward our *bashert* or away from each other. Then, after we take a closer look at these dimensions, we can begin to consider approaches and strategies that help us transform each of these areas of our personal experience of life in a manner that brings us closer to *menuchas hanefesh* and discovering the person with whom we can share our lives.

THOUGHTS

The first dimension of our experience of life is the power of thought. Dating and engaged couples continuously think about each other and the relationship in both positive and negative ways. When the thoughts are calm or positive, they feel like they are ready to spend every day of their lives with this person. And when the thoughts are not quite so positive, then they wonder, "What am I doing in this relationship?" We tend to take each thought as an undeniable reality that will last forever. The truth is that we are always thinking and we do define our reality by our thoughts. The philosopher Descartes said, "I think, therefore I am." Whether positive or negative, thinking is as natural as breathing or the beating of our heart.

But what *is* thought? Is it a physical entity? Does it have a size, a footprint, a molecular weight, a quantum of energy? Where does it come from as we are aware of its presence and influence on our consciousness? And where do our thoughts go after they leave our field of awareness?

Chazal tell us that the power of thought is the gift from Hashem that makes us unique in the entire Creation. In Shemoneh Esrei we say, "*Atah chonein la'adam da'as* — Hashem bestows on us the power of thought, wisdom and insight." Even beyond this, it is the power of thought that is actually the closest experience we have as human beings to emulating Hashem. For thought is, in essence, spiritual in nature. It is beyond the tangible and concrete, yet it has the power to define our reality. Consider where it exists as we are aware of its presence, as it passes through our consciousness — at the very height of our physical selves, in our brains.

Thoughts are also our primary tools for defining reality. When we have a thought, we have a tendency to accept it as if it is the very essence of the world we live in. And in our lives we come to accept these thoughts as the reliable guide to define our reality. However, we also need to understand that, as the Alter of Kelm tells us, many thoughts are flowing through our minds all the time. Some will bring us closer to *menuchas hanefesh* and others will bring us closer to *pizur hanefesh*. Some bring us closer to our *bashert* and others distance us. We cannot blindly accept our thoughts as reliable and trustworthy.

◇ Unwanted and Runaway Thoughts

Our thoughts have a way of challenging us in our moment-to-moment experience of life. They simply invade our consciousness like a swarm of mosquitoes on a summer night. One young man asked me what he could do when he is davening Shemoneh Esrei and his mind seems to be roaming all over.

The question about mastery over our thoughts is not a new one. We *daven* three times a day, and Chazal appreciate the difficulty of maintaining our focus. They suggest that, since many of us are not able to go through all nineteen *brachos* with *kavanah* (full focus and intention), at a minimum we should attempt to stay focused during the first *brachah*, which contains only forty-two words. This sounds easy enough. Yet, when many people attempt to get through these forty-two words while maintaining their focus on the simple meaning of the concepts, they are invariably pulled toward countless distractions. Their thoughts are flying all over the place without any association to the meaning of the words. Regardless of their determination at the outset, before they realize it, they have finished the first *brachah*, and once again their minds have wandered far and wide.

But what is even more important for us to understand is that not only are the thoughts distracting us from the focus of our *tefillos*, but they actually cause us to experience a sense of distress and disappointment over another missed opportunity to speak clearly to Hashem. We may even want to define the struggle by saying that when we are focused on each word and its meaning and feel a sense of clarity and accomplishment, we are in a state of *menuchas hanefesh*. And when we are distracted, unfocused and feeling disappointed with ourselves, we are in a state of *pizur hanefesh*.

The difference between dating, engagement and davening is that in davening we all attempt to maintain our focus, and are disappointed when we discover once again that somehow we "lost our way." However, in these relationships so crucial to our future, we may experience very troubled *pizur hanefesh* thoughts about our dating partner, yet claim that the criticism is an "objective truth."

A young man is sitting in a restaurant with his *kallah*. Within a few minutes the tables are filled with other dating couples. He finds himself looking at other women and automatically thinks to himself, "That girl over there is so outgoing. Did I make a mistake by picking such a quiet *kallah*?"

The *kallah*, meanwhile, may be looking at a couple and observing their lively interaction and say to herself, "That couple looks so connected, so thrilled to be with each other. I don't really feel that way with my *chassan*. Did I make the wrong choice?"

These thoughts occur without any desire to have them. However, once they have entered either of their minds, they are embedded as very powerful arbiters of reality. They have taken the high ground and will not relent so easily. Even though they are untested and unchallenged, they have become the truth. While this engaged or dating couple may have invested much time and effort into getting to know each other, and have no idea what the real experience of the other couple is, the effect is still the same. From an external perspective this new couple is endowed with magical and ideal features, which enable runaway thoughts in the observer's mind.

Our couple may be feeling the pressures of an upcoming decision about an engagement or a wedding just weeks away. They may be under the pressures of their workplace, family, even health issues, all of which can affect their thoughts. Yet, what is important is that they accept these troubled thoughts that idealize the other couple as "better candidates to be engaged to" as the only possible interpretation of their reality. They will then permit this unquestioned reality to determine their attitude and behavior toward each other.

Each may insist that there is no other way of reading this situation. In both of their minds, their perception is justified by the belief that there is no other choice but to think this way, even if it leads to a state of *pizur hanefesh*. The claim is simply, "I may not be happy with my thoughts, but there's no doubt that I'm thinking them, so they must have some validity."

However, whether neither of their thoughts are an accurate perception of the reality of their relationship or the relationship they would have if they would suddenly switch tables, both are insisting that they are correct in accepting this negative state of mind, almost as if it is both an indisputable reality and a responsibility. "I believe in accepting my thoughts as a reflection of who I am." The reality is that if this or any meaningful relationship is to be maintained, they will need to somehow assess the appropriateness of their fantasies and emerge from the entrapment of their negative thoughts, regardless of how accurate or inaccurate they may seem.

A young man from a well-respected yeshivah once told me, "I just can't figure this out. When I am at a wedding, I try to see if they are any girls on the other side of the *chupah* who I would be interested in dating. If I spot someone, then I try to find a *shadchan* at the *chupah* to get us together. It always turns out that when I'm looking at this girl from the other side of the aisle she looks so ideal. And when we date, I'm thinking of other girls."

When we fall into this pattern of believing that our negative thoughts are justified, we become locked into negative thinking that becomes the norm. In other words, it becomes the "wall-paper" of our thinking. Just as we no longer consciously look at the wallpaper in our homes — we just assume it's always been there — we no longer see our thoughts as negative. "He's just a stingy guy" or "There's no getting away from it; I used to find her attractive, but not any more" are typical kinds of negative thoughts that we come to assume are objective reality.

◇ Stuck in a Thought

There is nothing in life that is static and unchanging, especially our thoughts. They are always in motion. And there are moments when we are actually aware of our changing thoughts. Here is an experience that led to a proposal shortly after our meeting.

> A young couple, Mordechai and Shoshana, came to see me to explore why they were stuck on a dating tread-mill going nowhere. After speaking to Mordechai alone, I understood that he was considering proposing; however, there was something about the way Shoshana spoke that "irked" him. He had forgotten about this during the earlier stages of their dating. Now that they were in a more

serious stage of their relationship, the thought of her almost imperceptible lisp kept popping up in his head, especially now when they were approaching engagement. He saw his exaggerated focus on it as a "sign" that they were not meant for each other and had made up his mind not to continue.

My meeting with Mordechai was followed by a meeting between the three of us. We began to relate to a personal challenge he had been dealing with for many years. During our meeting he began to grasp that Shoshana had a keen insight and empathy for what he been struggling with since his childhood. No one had ever articulated this understanding quite so well before. After the session, he confided in me that "as we were talking, I actually saw how my perception of her changed. My obsession with the lisp disappeared. Somehow, I began to feel closer to her and all my fears seemed to melt away."

◇ Our Ever-Active Minds

To have a better understanding of our choices, we must also realize that the thoughts we are aware of are not the only ones traveling through our minds. The *Alter* of Kelm tells us that even when we are sitting quietly and under the impression that our thoughts are at rest, our minds are filled with many varied thoughts. A number of years ago, I came across a psychological study that claimed there are about seventy different possibilities that our mind sifts through before we make a decision about our reality. Even if the number is a fraction of this, our minds are similar to a fiber-optic cable, with many thoughts simultaneously running through it. Our awareness can only process one thought at a time. This means that I may be walking in the street, while deciding whether to cross the road. My mind automatically sorts through countless possible options until I make my decision and act. Yet all the while I am unaware of most of the considerations that I have internally processed.

Whether we have seventy different thoughts to choose from or just a few, it is clear that the thought we are aware of at any given moment in time is not the only one that the mind is considering. Some of these thoughts have the potential to evoke a state of clarity and *menuchas hanefesh*, while others will lead us to confusion and *pizur hanefesh*. Both are always within us. Therefore, when Chazal tell us to accept each person "*b'seiver panim yafos* — with a favorable countenance and a pleasant disposition," it makes sense that within us at this very moment we have the potential, and therefore the choice, to view that person either positively or negatively. Hashem always gives each of us the choice as to which perspective we wish to embrace. However, we need to be clear as to which perception brings us closer to Hashem, and which creates distance and alienation.

I may walk into a very lavish home, filled with the most exclusive possessions, and immediately focus on all that I see that I don't possess. I may see a couple walking together on a Shabbos afternoon and think to myself how they must be so happy. Seeing them causes me to idealize their lives and assume that my thoughts are true, and then to think of all the problems I may be having in my dating or engagement. What may begin with an invitation into someone's home or a pleasant walk on Shabbos afternoon suddenly places me at the crossroads between experiencing thoughts that are associated with *pizur hanefesh* or others that elevate me to a higher level of perception.

When Mordechai's perception of Shoshana changed, it was not a new thought or perception. The very meaningful dialogue enabled him to get "unstuck" from his focus on an almost imperceptible speech flaw. Their connection over Mordechai's personal challenge enabled *menuchas hanefesh* thoughts to emerge to the surface — and *menuchas hanefesh* thoughts always unite couples. However, when Mordechai was pulled toward focusing on the way she spoke that he found "irksome," this was a *pizur hanefesh* thought that determined his perception of her and separated them. Just a few moments later, he was aware of thoughts that were emerging from the other dimension of himself. A few days after our meeting they were engaged.

Therefore, when Chazal tell us to *"dan l'chaf z'chus* — judge someone favorably," it is not only for the other person that we are exercising this effort to reframe our perception and assumptions. Achieving this positive perception has an immediate effect on our own sense of *menuchas hanefesh*. We begin to appreciate the preciousness of a healthy and positive thought, which is the way Hashem intended our minds and hearts to function. The shift in perception has an immediate impact on our sense of self. It is not as if we pulled another thought out of the air. The *"dan l'chaf z'chus"* thought was there all the time and it emerges because that's how Hashem intended us to perceive others. In a *pizur hanefesh* state, we either assume that the negative thought was the "truer" one, or we're aware that it's not — but can't seem to shake off its iron claws.

In no way am I suggesting that inappropriate or negative behavior that leads to hurt and conflict be overlooked by viewing it from a rosy perspective that denies its impact. Each of us has an internal sense of wisdom that can determine how to evaluate the behavior of someone we are dating or engaged to. But this wisdom can only be accessed when we are in a state of *menuchas hanefesh*. When Mordechai begins obsessing over Shoshana's speech, it is a clear indication that he has entered into a *pizur hanefesh* state of mind. And these thoughts only lead to the deterioration of a relationship. They limit his options and paralyze creative thinking and approaches toward improving their relationship. For this reason, my goal is to help you become aware that you are not your thoughts, especially when they emerge from a *pizur hanefesh* state of mind.

◇ Five Principles about Thoughts

Here are a few important principles to summarize our discussion on thoughts:

1. Many thoughts flow through our minds at the same time. Some will cause us to feel secure, and others will cause us to feel insecure.

2. The positive thoughts enable us to experience *menuchas hanefesh*, and the negative thoughts create a state of *pizur hanefesh*.

3. There are many possible reasons why we are aware of our *pizur hanefesh* thoughts; many are unrelated to our present situation.

4. Hashem always gives us the ability to drop our negative thoughts and become aware of our positive ones.

5. *Menuchas hanefesh* thoughts bring us closer together. When we learn to drop negative thoughts, we set the stage for bringing two lives closer together.

EXERCISE 1. Defining your *Menuchas Hanefesh* and *Pizur Hanefesh* Thoughts

We each carry within us thoughts that bring us closer in our dating relationships and in engagement and thoughts that drive a wedge between us as couples. Take a few minutes to write down some of these thoughts in the space provided. I have included an initial example as a starter.

My *Menuchas Hanefesh* Thoughts

+ I am able to remember meaningful moments that enable me to want to build a relationship with you.

+ _____

+ _____

+ _____

The Impact on my Perception

When I remember these *menuchas hanefesh* impressions and thoughts, how does my perception of you change?

_____

My *Pizur Hanefesh* Thoughts

+ I keep thinking about how much money you made me spend at the restaurant. I wonder whether I want to see you again.

+ _____

+ _____

+ _____

_____

_____

_____

✦ _____

_____

_____

The Impact on my Perception

When I experience these *pizur hanefesh* thoughts, how does my perception of you change?

_____

_____

_____

_____

FEELINGS AND MOODS

Our thoughts frequently trigger our feelings. However, our feelings are a more intense and persuasive way of defining our experience of self and the quality of our relationships. I can say "I feel love and joy," or I can say, "I feel low, alone and sad," and at that moment I define my life in just this way. My feelings tell me this is reality and there is no other possibility for defining myself at this moment. Moods are similar to feelings, but tend to last much longer. Our feelings and moods are the second dimension that defines where we stand on the *menuchas hanefesh* and *pizur hanefesh* spectrum so central to building and cultivating a relationship.

Feelings are at the heart of our *avodas* Hashem and define the quality of our spiritual connection to Hashem. Each day we repeat *Shema Yisrael*, where we declare the *mitzvah* of "*v'ahavta*"— to love Hashem "with all our soul and all our heart." *Ahavah* is love, which represents the quintessential positive human emotion that we experience from deep within. We are told by the Torah to cultivate this and many other feelings in our desire to feel close to Hashem. Just as these feelings define our spiritual state of being, they also define the quality of our relationships. I frequently hear complaints such as, "I just don't have the right feelings in this relationship." On the other hand, I may hear, "I deeply care for my *chassan/kallah*." The principle is quite fundamental. Just as feelings connect us to — or, *chas v'shalom*, isolate us from — Hashem, they also determine whether we experience our relationships as fulfilling and meaningful or as empty and even unsafe.

◇ Defining Our Feelings

What are feelings? When thoughts become more intense, they trigger feelings. The difference between our thoughts and our feelings is this: Thoughts are word or picture messages we make to ourselves and experience as living in our minds, while feelings tend to flow from every cell of our beings and are experienced as all-consuming. My self can see a thought. My self can be overwhelmed by a feeling. We know that a thought is taking place at the top of our heads. However, we cannot pinpoint any special place in our body where we experience feelings or emotions, unless they take on a physiological dimension, like a queasy feeling in our stomach. How many times have you heard, "I have this feeling in my gut"? And because they are so enveloping, feelings can be experienced as powerful, and even overwhelming, to our sense of self.

In dating and engagement, and in all our meaningful and

important relationships, our range of feelings is vast. We can feel close and secure, or distant and insecure. We can feel angry, content, jealous, sad, depleted, lonely, hurt, resentful or happy. The list can go on with countless emotions that define our self and our relationships.

Our relationship suffers when either of us carries a feeling that is troubled or negative, and that feeling can hang on for an interminable length of time. I recently met with a couple that had been married for almost twenty years. In the very first interview, the husband told me, "During the first week of our marriage she hurt my feelings by telling me that she really didn't know whether she felt love for me. I was very hurt and never forgot what she said. After that, she never really told me anything that would make me feel more secure about our marriage."

This husband was expressing a feeling that had been hovering for two decades and had deprived them and their children of the benefits of *shalom bayis*. Although the couple managed to raise five children, their home was rocky and emotionally fragile the whole time. Was it all the result of her statement? Obviously not, but he had held on to the memory of this feeling as if it were a rare coin that he wouldn't let go of.

Hurt and negative feelings, regardless of where they are coming from, have the power to sever a relationship, even just before a wedding.

One afternoon I received a call from a catering hall located somewhere in the Midwest. It was from a *chassan*, Chaim, who was just hours away from his *chupah*. "Shaya, I have a very insecure and frightened feeling about getting married." He began to tell me all the things that worried him about Chava, his *kallah*. He had a long list of issues related to her physical features, her brother, the girls he "almost" married and those he hadn't even met. "I'm not sure I want to go ahead with it." He was feeling scared and trapped. He still had a few hours before the wedding and I urged him to take a walk and remember one moment when he felt connected to Chava. He called me back an hour later to tell me he regained his balance and was able to proceed with the wedding.

Our feelings may seem to be rooted in the present. At the eleventh hour, Chaim's jitters obviously seemed to be the result of an inner voice telling him, "Chaim, you are about to make the worst decision of your life. You are in serious trouble. You'd better start running." As dating and engaged couples get closer to each other and marriage, their feelings are always shifting and it's difficult to know what's triggering the changes. These shifting feelings are frequently expressed in terms of anxiety, fear, sadness, worry and even hurt. When these negative emotions take on a life of their own, they cause the relationship to end.

Therefore, one very basic principle I teach all couples, regardless of where they are on the relationship spectrum, is that feelings do not always come from where we assume they are coming from. *Menuchas hanefesh* requires us to understand that these feelings can emerge without warning and can be overpowering.

◇ **A Midnight Fear**

Consider a young boy who goes to bed feeling safe and sound. Suddenly he awakens at midnight. He sees the closet door open and is seized by the fear that there is a monster in the closet. He cries until his father comes in. His father brings him a glass of water, reads him a story, quiets him down and then, when all is calm, may even offer to open the closet and show his son that there really is no monster there at all.

If the child is relaxed enough, he will allow his father to cautiously approach the closet, shine a flashlight inside and say, "There, now, you see, there is no mean monster in the closet." The child will breathe a great sigh of relief.

When this little boy believes there is a frightening and sinister power lurking behind the closet door, he does not believe it will ever go away. It is there forever. The reason is that the monster exists within his own inability to control his imagination and fears. This is a form of *pizur hanefesh* because one aspect of his self, his imagination, is uncontrolled; he doesn't have the ability to soothe himself back to safety and to sleep. His father can help him, and does. Once he is soothed and safe, he can look inside the closet. In reality, he is looking inside himself and saying, "I'm no longer afraid of the monster within me."

It is the same way with couples. When either one or both experience negative feelings — whether for a short period of time or even years, long after a negative and hurtful experience has occurred — there is a sense that these overwhelming feelings will never subside. Couples believe that their painful feelings and moods are an understandable reaction to their hurt and don't believe they have a choice.

If I should ask someone, "Why are you breathing?" the answer would be, "I need to breathe! What else can I do?" This response is the same as, "Of course I feel this way; how else should I possibly feel?" This is why many couples are convinced they have no choice but to hold on to negative feelings; they cannot forgive.

The truer representation of the problem of feelings and moods is that they follow patterns that have been learned over time. We can call them neural pathways, where the slightest stimulus can trigger a patterned reaction. It may be a word, a look, an association, pressure or anything else that sets off the response. This is why our feelings are frequently so illogical. One man told me that he can get a statement from his bank informing him that his 401k lost a few percentage points — a loss amounting to tens of thousands of dollars — and he'll just shrug it off. However, if he should get a parking ticket for $50, he'll feel deeply upset and carry his negative feelings around for days.

Chazal have always understood that feelings play a powerful and frequently illogical role in life and in our most precious relationships. When they emerge, we are literally overwhelmed and helpless to quiet their impact. This is why they have an even greater impact on our perception of reality than our thoughts.

Let's return to the little boy who feels scared. In the end, his father soothes him. But where did the feelings of fear go? We all know that, of course, there never was a monster in the closet. It was all in the imagination of the child. And when the father comes into the room and quiets him down, the boy is soothed and calmed. But where does the quiet within this little boy come from? Does it come from the father? The father cannot give him anything that is not already there, within his son.

There are two sources of his inner quiet that enable him to fall safely to sleep. The first is that he has been soothed many times in his life; the experience of being calmed down was always within the child, even when he was experiencing his fears. Every moment of being soothed in his mother's loving embrace has become an embedded memory of knowing the meaning of calmness. Later in life he experiences it with his father, *rebbeim*, grandparents and many others. However, lying in bed and frightened, he needed his father's reassurance to teach him that there is a way to access these feelings of safety and security. As he grows, he will learn that he can cultivate the inner strength and skills to soothe himself even without his father's or mother's comforting presence.

The second source of his inner strength is his *neshamah*, the true fount of all inner tranquility and safety. Hashem creates us and renews within us an inner core of calmness and tranquility.

This is our spiritual inheritance, which is never relinquished. So, even when he was frightened, our young warrior carried both feelings — of fear, and of being soothed — simultaneously within himself. The problem is that at the actual moment of fright, he had no access to the other, quieter and more secure side of himself. It took the father's love and wisdom to bring his son back to feeling like a secure and loved little boy.

This same principle applies equally to couples. Even while experiencing a distressed state like Chaim did just before his *chupah*, his ability to feel trusting and safe was present on the inside. It is just that at that moment he had no way of accessing this state of self.

Couples take their feelings very seriously, and for good reason. Emotions are the weathervane that determines the quality of our experience of self and our relationships. This is especially so in our society, in which we pay homage to the unquestionable authority and power of our emotions. In this society, all emotions are sacrosanct. I have since learned the absurdity of this belief and its ruinous consequences for dating, engagement and marriage. I recently heard an NPR broadcast praising the ideals of a woman who was committed to spending the rest of her life single. She proudly exclaimed, "I prefer to live alone. I can do exactly what I feel like doing. I eat what I feel like eating, watch the TV programs I feel like watching, walk when I feel like walking, do whatever I feel like and I just love to live this way." For her it's absolutely fine. For Am Yisrael, the consequences are unspeakable.

In our society, so dependent on the fulfillment of personal needs, the focus is frequently on being aware and expressing *pizur hanefesh* emotions. These include feelings of anger, deprivation, resentment, insecurity, jealousy, fear, inferiority, hurt and countless other negative feelings and moods. One moment I would prefer to forget was when Ken and Rosalyn came to see me after dating for a number of months. Roslyn was feeling they were not going anywhere and we met for a few sessions. Finally Ken told me he would like to try and propose to Rosalyn but first wanted to discuss a few things with her together with me.

When the couple arrived at my office, Rosalyn was as white as a ghost and Ken was silent. On the drive to see me, Ken said he wanted to share his "true feelings" with Rosalyn. So he opened up with all barrels, telling her how sometimes he doesn't find her so attractive and he finds himself looking at other women and wishing he was with them.

Who could have withstood this kind of patent emotional abuse? Rosalyn was devastated. She came in, sat down and was speechless until she burst into tears. Ken, in all his naiveté said, "All I was doing was being truthful. Is there anything wrong with that?"

"Not if you don't mind destroying someone," I answered.

Like our caring and truthful friend Ken, when couples experience these negative emotions and moods, they tend to see the other as the source of the problem. Yet when we take a closer look at these couples and their complaints, it's often clear that many of these negative feelings are rooted in other experiences, such as earlier life experiences, fears of commitment, work pressures, the challenges of daily living and the countless ways we are confronted by the many trials of our lives. And regardless of their source, these same feelings, whether having occurred earlier or recently, are frequently experienced as being a result of their present relationship.

I sat with an engaged couple, Moshe and Rivky, as they discussed each other's family. The conversation was pleasant and clear. Suddenly I heard Rivky choke up, her eyes begin to tear and from nowhere she blurted out, "You always need to talk about my brother and my family that way. You just can't stop being so critical." I was somewhat surprised. I didn't understand where her emotions were coming from. There was little in his statements about her brother and family that appeared to be critical or insensitive.

As I came to understand Rivky's feelings about growing up with a brother who had borderline symptoms of autism, it was clear that she was highly sensitive and conflicted about her relationship to him and to how others viewed him and her family. Somehow, Moshe's comments touched the hornet's nest that had been stirring within her. It reminded me of a tow truck parked on the side of the highway with the driver listening in on the police band for an accident to occur so he could be the first truck on the spot. These feelings are powerful and deep, just waiting to be expressed. And when they do emerge, they pounce out of nowhere with a force that surprises and shocks.

The deep challenge for couples is that when Rivky feels hurt that Moshe is insensitive to her brother's condition and says, "I have a right to feel hurt," her powerful emotions feel like they describe an objective reality. The more a couple comes closer together, the more they touch deep feelings that lie dormant beneath the surface. At that moment, the feelings are very strong and even overwhelming. And neither the little boy with his fears nor Rivky are aware that within each of them lies fuller and healthier emotions that are always alive, just waiting patiently to emerge and give them a truer sense of their real choices in life.

This principle of the power of our feelings resonates within us as a people, as well, throughout our history. As I write this, it is *erev* Shabbos *Parashas Ki Sisa*, when we read the Torah portion related to the *eigel hazahav* (the golden calf). The *midrash* on this event illustrates how feelings of fear and abandonment caused a trauma and a tragedy that has cast its shadow over all our generations. After Moshe Rabbeinu was on Har Sinai for forty days, the *satan* caused *Klal Yisrael* to witness an image in the heavens of Moshe Rabbeinu's funeral procession. The entire nation was gripped by fear and helplessness, alone in a wilderness without a leader. The illusion evoked a feeling of loss and helplessness. This was the desired effect that the *satan* wished to create. It was these compelling feelings that directly led to the building of the *eigel hazahav*. Chazal tell us that each tragedy we face as a people is related to this tragedy.

◇ Living with our Feelings and Moods

Each year on the Ninth of Av we fast to commemorate the tears that Am Yisrael shed through the night after the return of the *meraglim* (spies) with the news that they were powerless to subdue the enemies that awaited them in the Promised Land. Once again, the fears and feelings of hopelessness and powerlessness were overwhelming enough to obliterate any awareness that Hashem had placed within them other feelings that connect them to Him and to their healthier selves. We all are painfully aware of the results, the succeeding events that have plagued our people each year at this time. And in these and many other events, both national and personal, we were unable to overcome the tsunami of our feelings and believe that there was no other choice but to succumb. Yet the message that the Torah continually gives us is that feelings may be a tool to help us define reality, but are never to be accepted as reality.

In dating and engagement and in our nationhood, we are all mortal, yet there is a spark within each of us that exists beyond the realm of nature and mortality. Hashem endows us with a *neshamah* that continuously strives to experience the true blessing and fullness of life. This fullness is achieved through cultivating feelings related to *menuchas hanefesh*, such as trust, joy, security, modesty, love and closeness. These and other experiences are the emotions that enable us to feel whole and complete.

Without the capacity to have these healthy emotions within a relationship, the vacuum will always be filled with either indifference or negative feelings.

◇ How Relationships Die: Not with a Bang, but a Whimper

In our idolization of feelings, we also need to consider the most repeated phrase in the *shidduch*, dating and engagement experience, which is, "I have no feelings, so it's best to move on." In a sense, what is being said is "I have a feeling that my lack of feelings is telling me this is not for me."

Dating relationships do not usually end with negative feelings. I have encountered very few dramatic endings to relationships; the great majority just fade away like old soldiers. The 20th century poet T.S. Eliot wrote in his poem, "The Hollow Men," that life will end "not with a bang but a whimper." It's a depressing poem, but it describes how the end is not very dramatic. It comes with silence.

In dating, the countless failures occur in this same muffled and silent manner. When couples who have been searching for their *bashert* begin dating, there is the hope that this time they will discover him or her. They meet with someone a number of times and wait for that magical "feeling" to occur. The difficulty is that no one really knows what that feeling is. Mostly it is a fantasy that comes from looking at other couples, with our assumptions of what we think they are feeling. Or it comes from remembering feelings of excitement at weddings or *vorts* that we always assumed we would feel that would tell us, "This is the one." Or it may be memories of feeling close with family members or friends at a midnight bonfire, or any other moment when we felt close to others.

However, dating is different, and whatever we assumed our

feelings should be is wrong. The reality is that when we wait for these feelings, we are waiting for excitement and being overtaken by emotions. And when they don't occur, the hope is that the next one will deliver the goods. This disappointment is frequently expressed by individuals who are engaged through statements like, "I thought she would be more into me" or "It can't be right. I'm just not feeling the excitement I always believed I would." A common fear that many engaged couples have is, "I look around and see other couples happy and excited to be with each other. I don't feel that. Something must be wrong."

The crucial message I attempt to give everyone I meet with is that the wildly popular notion about excitement as proof positive of "being in love" is actually more a function of *pizur hanefesh* and plays no productive role in bringing two *neshamos* together. And if there happens to be excitement, it is usually followed by a dramatic dip into disappointment territory, when the couple begins to realize the deeper emotional demands of bringing two lives together in marriage.

◇ The Power of Niagara Falls

A number of years ago my wife and I visited Niagara Falls and took a boat ride to the foot of the falls. The impact was overwhelming. Millions of tons of gushing water assault the senses and create an unforgettable appreciation of the wonder of Creation. When we took the elevator to the reception area I could not help but notice a wall where visitors had placed their notes in wonderment. I looked at the notes that read, "Now I know there is a G-d." Another note said something like, "Suddenly I am a believer." Reading these little *"kvitlach"* (notes) that expressed profound awe at Hashem's wonders reminded me of the notes that fill the crevices of the Kosel, which contain our most heartfelt prayers to Hashem. Indeed, the Falls' overwhelming power and beauty attract millions of visitors each year. The problem for many of us is that we are raised with a corrupt value system that tells us that in dating we need to be overwhelmed in the same manner.

◇ Where Does Love Come From?

The reality is that feelings between two distinct selves need to emerge slowly and gently over time. The self/*neshamah* is delicate and cautious. It exists in the most private domain of our existence, and is never on display for the world to gawk at. Slowly it emerges through feelings of trust, acts of kindness and mutual feelings of balance, respect and understanding.

I had the opportunity to sit in the *sukkah* of Rav Yitzchak Berkowitz, *shlit"a*, in Yerushalayim. One question I asked him was, "Where does the love between a *chassan* and *kallah* come from? Do Chazal view it as innate, or does it emerge from the nature of the relationship?"

His answer was quite simple and direct. He told me, "Just look at the last of the *sheva brachos* (the seven blessings we say at the wedding ceremony). It reads, '*Asher bara sasson v'simchah* ([Hashem] creates joy and happiness),' and then continues to include *ahavah* (love).

"It's simple," he explained. "Hashem creates love and then gives it to the *chassan* and *kallah* as a gift."

I realized that for Rabbi Berkowitz, the answer was that Hashem bestows the experience of love between a *chassan* and *kallah* in order to bring the couple even closer. It seems so logical when we understand that everything comes from Hashem. Yet this idea is so strange to many of us who were brought up on Hollywood and Broadway tales, in which love somehow just happens magically.

I remember, as a young boy, listening to the show tunes of Rodgers and Hammerstein. "Some enchanted evening; you may meet a stranger across a crowded room ...." The song speaks of strangers "falling in love" at the very first moment they see each other. This "love at first sight" idea has corrupted our understanding of the meaning and experience of love. Yet, so many dating and engaged couples have very definitive expectations about needing to feel love in their relationship. The difficulty is that love is not a state of mind that we acquire. It's an experience that is a very precious gift from Hashem, and the result of deep emotional and spiritual maturity.

It's very true that love is at the heart of our lives as Torah Jews. We are commanded to love Hashem with all our heart and all our soul. In the morning davening, between the *brachos* of *Krias Shema* and the end of Shemoneh Esrei, the word *ahavah* is mentioned thirteen times. And it's most prominent and most concentrated in the *brachah* preceding *Krias Shema* and during the *Shema* itself.

The cultivation of our ability to understand and appreciate love is so central to our personal development that Rabbi Elimelech Bar Shaul, *zt"l*, the former chief rabbi of Rechovot, describes it as the basis for the *mitzvah* of *shiluach hakan*. This is the *mitzvah* of chasing away the mother bird from her nest before taking the egg or infant bird in the nest. He explains that the mother bird will give her very life to protect her chicks, even against a towering and powerful enemy. At the moment when her offspring are endangered, her love for them knows no fear or limits. This is the power of love. Each of us needs to deeply respect the self-sacrifice of a bird protecting her young as nature's profound and touching demonstration of the commitment of love. When we attempt to capture a young bird or egg in front of its mother, we show callousness to this love that Hashem has placed in all of Creation and in each of us. And when this most precious of all human bonds — that of mother and child — is not deeply respected, it cannot be respected between man and wife.

We take this concept and incorporate it into our lives on a

daily basis. Even as I put on my *tallis* in the morning, I recite how an eagle hovers over its nest, gently stirring and alighting onto the nest of its young in its loving and protective manner. This is how Hashem hovers over the People he loves, lovingly and gently. This is how a bird and a mother hover over their beloved offspring. And this is how Hashem wants us to care for those with whom we are sharing our lives. Once again, this is compassion, not passion. Love is delicate, soft, sweet and very protecting of those we love and care for.

Love begins at life's earliest moments and progresses until we can share and experience this emotion in marriage and in bearing and raising children. I have always been moved and fascinated by the Torah's description of how Yitzchak Avinu first meets his new bride, the young Matriarch-to-be, Rivkah, and brings her into the tent of his late mother, Sarah. Rivkah's presence consoles Yitzchak for the emptiness in his life that was occasioned by the painful loss of his mother. Once again, in his bride's presence, his life is filled by a woman whose *middos* and *kedushah* create an aura of beauty and kindness that envelops their home and lives. This is the Torah's description of the growing experience of human love. It is the essence of human compassion and emerges when two people are deeply committed to the same inspiring vision of their lives, and when they fill the deep needs for caring, fulfillment and comfort within each other.

These are the conditions necessary for a *chassan* and *kallah* to be receptive to Hashem's gift of love. It can only be received when they are emotionally and spiritually attuned to receiving this gift. And this is when each has learned to cultivate a sense of inner peace and calmness, which we call *menuchas hanefesh*.

Marriage is our opportunity to share experiences of delicate thoughts, feelings and acts of *chessed* toward each other. So as we grow together, we learn to appreciate that throughout this vast universe, Hashem has led us to the only individual destined to be our true life partner. It is under these conditions that we are open to Hashem's gift of love and we can then recognize that we have truly met our *bashert*. And it is with this person, and only this person, that our deeper and truer selves can continue to merge. And this emergence of self only occurs through shared experiences from a *menuchas hanefesh* state of mind.

Therefore, instead of focusing on, "Am I in love or am I excited?," I try to have each individual ask, "Am I doing whatever possible to enable us as a couple to receive and experience this gift of love from Hashem?" For this is where two individuals can stand in each other's presence and comfortably say, "We feel trust and closeness in our relationship." So my role is to help couples learn to appreciate how our true sense of self needs to feel secure and trusting enough to emerge so we can recognize our *bashert*.

For an overwhelming experience of high voltage excitement, perhaps after they are married the couple can take a trip to Niagara Falls and be overwhelmed, not by each other but by the majesty of Hashem's Creation. For now, we must focus on the even greater miracle of bringing two *neshamos* closer together, which is far more subtle and gentle.

EXERCISE 2: Assessing your *Menuchas Hanefesh* and *Pizur Hanefesh* Feelings

We each carry within ourselves feelings that bring us closer to *shalom bayis* and *menuchas hanefesh*, and feelings that destroy our relationship harmony. Take a few minutes to write down some of these feelings in the space provided. I have included an initial example as a starter.

My *Menuchas Hanefesh* Feelings

+ There are times when I feel very grateful that you are in my life.

+ _____

+ _____

+ _____

The Impact on our Relationship

When I am experiencing these m*enuchas hanefesh* feelings, how does my perception of you change?

_____

_____

_____

_____

_____

My *Pizur Hanefesh* Feelings

+ Sometimes I feel very frustrated by your inattentiveness to my needs.

+ _____

_____

_____

+ _____

_____

_____

✦ _____

_____

_____

✦ _____

_____

_____

The Impact on our Relationship

When I am experiencing these *pizur hanefesh* feelings, how does my perception of you change?

_____

_____

_____

_____

_____

PHYSIOLOGY: *Our Physical Selves*

The third dimension of our experience of self that determines our position on the spectrum between *menuchas hanefesh* and *pizur hanefesh* is physiology, the way our experience of physical well-being is affected by our state of mind.

> Cindy was a *kallah*, with her wedding just weeks away. However, she was seriously considering calling off the wedding because while she cared for and respected her *chassan*, whenever she was with him she began to experience tension, abdominal pain and other physical symptoms. "Sometimes, my heart starts beating so fast that I feel like I'm going to pass out. This is no way for a *kallah* to feel.

All this is telling me something. And while I care about him and I have every reason to want to marry him, there is no way I can go ahead while I'm feeling this way."

What contributed to Cindy's physical symptoms? Of course we can say that her stress and anxiety is being expressed through her body and we would certainly be correct. However, from my understanding, the answer lies in that almost mystical area where our physical selves meet our souls. It's almost as if we are looking over a broad ocean vista and see a distant mist hovering over the waters. It appears as if the mist is rising from the waters below. However, if we were closer we would see that the mist is actually rain descending from clouds above, downward toward the water. From a distance it's impossible to discern where the ocean's water begins and the rainy atmosphere above it ends. Unless we are standing in the rain itself and feeling the drops, the water below and the water above all seem like one.

In terms of our physical selves, Hashem has placed a delicate homeostatic mechanism within each of us, where our physical and emotional well-being is delicately balanced and mutually interdependent. This elegant and sensitive system maintains the stability of our physical functioning. It enables our body temperature to hover at around 98.6 degrees, our blood pressure to remain at around 120/80 and our heart rate, breathing rate, blood sugar, digestion, excretion and countless other functions and indicators of our physical well-being to function optimally. From a distance, the human body seems to "operate by itself," with the uncanny ability to know exactly what is required to maintain healthy physical functioning. In contemporary language we relate to these as our immune, respiratory, cardiovascular, digestive, nervous, glandular and other systems. They make up the ongoing miracle of our existence.

However, we understand these functions as being under

the moment-to-moment *hashgachah pratis* (Divine supervision) of Hashem. Through this continuous caring, each of us is a personal recipient of the love and wisdom Hashem has placed in our *neshamah* and in our body. There is nothing accidental or automatic about our ability to function, from being able to move a limb — which we can do with intent and great accuracy — to our autonomic systems that function seemingly on their own. All are part of the miracle of Hashem's ongoing gift of life, lovingly implanted in each of us. And when we are performing optimally, this wisdom within us sends its healing and nurturing powers to every part of our physical selves. We feel alive, we heal quickly, we are resilient and we have stamina, energy and a sense of vitality that makes life so special and precious.

Upsetting the Delicate Balance

Many forces can upset this balance. Some people get more depressed and lethargic in the winter months. Blood pressure can rise during an exciting sporting event. With aging and illness we find that we require medications and other means to maintain the healthy range of our vital signs and functions.

The dynamic is that when we are not functioning well emotionally, the list of aches, pains, weaknesses and other troubling symptoms grow exponentially longer. The Torah itself alludes to this, in the area of our breathing. When Am Yisrael was in Mitzrayim enduring the hardships of slavery, the *Chumash* tells us that they were suffering from *kotzer ruach* (shortness of breath). The great Torah commentator, Rashi, explains that when an individual cannot feel free to be spiritually and emotionally expressive, it leads to the inability to take a deep and natural breath. So while Hashem has lovingly placed the power of vitality and healing in us all, the cardinal principle is that our bodies function in a healthy and healing manner when they are unimpeded. Otherwise they are thrown out of synchronization and harmony.

For example, you may have a paper cut. If you dress the wound before you go to bed at night and keep it protected, you will probably notice that by the next morning the healing process has begun. You will observe a closing, and even a slight scabbing, of the area. This is a sign of the healing process that occurred during the night while you were resting. However, if you leave the small wound open and unprotected, then chances are the healing process will be delayed. The wisdom of the healing process has not been lost. Your body still has the ability to heal the wound. However, in the presence of impediments, such as exposure to the cold or dirt, this healing process is neutralized and cannot perform properly.

In spite of the predominant evidence, many of us tend to view physiology as independent of our emotional and cognitive states. A close friend who is a physician shared with me that when he checks a patient's blood pressure, the initial measurement will frequently be higher than later ones. Physicians understand that the anxiety produced by measuring such an important indicator will frequently drive up the blood pressure, so they repeat the test. After a few minutes, when the patient has had a chance to calm down, the blood pressure will frequently return to its normal level.

Let us return to the continuum of our experience of self. Our thoughts flow into feelings as they intensify, and feelings become moods as they are prolonged. Physiology then flows from feelings and moods as our emotional imbalance triggers us to react physiologically.

When our thoughts, feelings and moods unbalance our sense of physical well-being, the impact on our relationships can be, and usually is, devastating. It is almost impossible to feel secure enough to cultivate a relationship when our delicate physiological balance feels shaky. This is why I frequently hear comments that include: "How can I continue in the relationship when I have a headache that won't go away?" "Every time we are together she makes me feel like I'm walking on the third rail." "Because of him, my nerves are shot." "Sometimes I get so upset with the idea of the wedding that my stomach is out for a week." "We had an argument last week, and I was shaking like a leaf." "My heart was palpitating like a kid banging on a bongo drum. I thought I was having a heart attack." The list is inexhaustible. Here is an incomplete list of the physical symptoms I have encountered in my work with both dating couples and singles.

+ Abdominal cramps and nausea
+ Backaches
+ Shortness of breath
+ Rapid heartbeat and palpitations
+ Dizziness
+ Shakiness and tremors
+ Headaches
+ Muscle aches and tension
+ Twitching eyes or lips
+ Sleeplessness
+ Loss of appetite or overeating

What is important for us to understand is that our physical symptoms should never have voting rights in our decisions. In each of these situations, we have the responsibility and the ability to learn to quiet each of these physiological alarms. The body never knows what's right, only our minds and hearts. Once we learn to quiet the symptoms, we can then have the clarity and freedom to make the best possible decisions for our future.

The security that is inherent in *menuchas hanefesh* will enhance our physical sense of well-being, while *pizur hanefesh* will usually diminish our sense of physical comfort and our ability to tolerate discomfort. The closer our lives move toward *menuchas hanefesh*, the healthier we will feel physically, and this opens the door for two people to help each other maintain their balance on the continuum toward deepening their understanding and level of trust and comfort with each other.

◇ EXERCISE 3: Assessing your *Menuchas Hanefesh* and *Pizur Hanefesh* Physiology

Our body understands the language of our heart. The closer we are to *shalom bayis* and *menuchas hanefesh*, the better and healthier we feel. And the more we move toward *pizur hanefesh*, the greater our sense of physical discomfort and lack of well-being. Take a few minutes to reflect on those physical states that enhance *menuchas hanefesh* and those that create the opposite effect, and then write down some of these feelings in the space provided. I have included an initial example as a starter.

My *Menuchas Hanefesh* Physiology

There are times when I feel physically sound and good about myself and our relationship, like when:

+ We take a quiet walk together and have a chance to share our thoughts.

+ _____

  _____

+ _____

  _____

+ _____

  _____

My *Pizur Hanefesh* Physiology

+ Sometimes I feel physically low, like when we have an argument.

+ _____

_____

+ _____

_____

+ _____

_____

_____

My symptoms may be:

+ An upset stomach

+ _____

+ _____

+ _____

+ _____

+ _____

The Impact on our Relationship

When I am experiencing these *pizur hanefesh* symptoms, how does my perception of you change?

_____

_____

_____

_____

BEHAVIOR

The fourth dimension of our experience of self is how our state of *menuchas hanefesh* or *pizur hanefesh* affects our behavior — the way we act. At one moment we may be able to perform a great *chessed*, set aside our own self-interest and behave in a manner that enriches our own life and the lives of others. This form of inspired behavior is always a result of *menuchas hanefesh*. Then there are other times when our behavior is self-centered, uncaring and impulsive. This is the domain of *pizur hanefesh*. In dating and engagement, our ability to say and do things for each other that enhances well-being and trust always emerges from *menuchas hanefesh*, while our behavior that undermines trust and feelings of closeness always emerges from *pizur hanefesh*.

◇ An Impatient Suitor

I received a call from Miriam who told me that she needed to make an appointment to try and save a relationship.

> Miriam and Shaul had been dating for three months. Both were in their late twenties. Miriam had never been married, while Shaul was married for three years and had a two-year-old daughter. Following his divorce, Shaul began to date. He felt that his first marriage was a disaster and that this time he deserved to find a wife who could be his true life partner.
>
> Miriam was a lawyer who had been dating for about six years and was beginning to give up on marriage. "Every guy I met had no idea that I needed to be heard and respected. Dating became so frustrating that I just wanted to give up and be a recluse in my office.
>
> "Then I met Shaul. He had been married before and knew how to listen. I began to feel I could trust him. However, a few weeks ago he began to push me toward

the idea of marriage. I very much want to get married, but I certainly wasn't ready after just a few months of dating him. He began texting me, wanting to know where I am, and how I'm doing. If he didn't get an answer, he would text me again with messages like, "Why are you making me feel so bad? Just send me a quick answer!" Since then, it's gotten progressively worse. I find his need for control very overwhelming. I feel like I'm suffocating. This was the first person I thought I could possibly marry. Now his behavior has been so impossible that I am ready to walk away."

We can certainly understand Shaul's behavior as controlling, insecure, anxious and intrusive, and we can use many other unflattering descriptions. And we can also understand Miriam's very legitimate fears. However, we can also view his behavior as an expression of his ongoing state of *pizur hanefesh*. His frenetic and frantic texting and his need for constant reassurance are distortions of behavior that have become accepted as the norm to many dating and engaged individuals in our society. Everywhere we look, people are texting and asking each other, "Where R U?" You may say it's how we behave today. I say it's *pizur hanefesh* and it escalates as couples get closer together. Shaul, however, has taken it to an extreme and is in danger of losing the relationship.

I believe the reason this type of behavior develops is that we now live in an economy that thrives on exploiting human needs and insecurities, and this is where *pizur hanefesh*, with all its distractions and impulsive behavior, thrives. These distractions divert us from focusing on our deeper inner life, which is necessary for achieving *menuchas hanefesh*. Instead we come to believe in and rely on more tactile and habitual means — such as smoking, work habits, drinking, addictive texting, reckless driving or whatever the "drug" of the moment is — to feel secure, but in the end these create only more insecurity.

Let's consider smoking, as another example. Craig and Estelle were about to become engaged. However, Estelle was concerned about Craig's smoking habit. I was asked whether I felt this was reason enough to wait. I felt that it was, because throughout my own personal and professional experience, any addiction always places the drug before the person. It diminishes our ability to care, be empathic and be patient. So when someone tells me, "I need a smoke to relax," I understand that he is confusing the false sense of security that comes with smoking for a deeper sense of security that can only emerge from human closeness.

I have a vivid memory of witnessing the following scene on a subway platform that occurred many years ago.

> A young woman was in a panic because she could not find her child. She was running up and down the station calling his name. A police officer approached her and began alerting other officers about the missing child. Suddenly the woman said, "Officer I'm really scared and shook up. You don't mind if I have a smoke, do you?"
>
> She knew it was illegal to smoke on a subway platform. However, she felt the cigarette would give her a sense of security. How could the officer refuse such a request? He agreed and she lit up and took a long deep drag on her cigarette. As I observed her I wondered to myself, "What kind of security is she getting now? She wants her child back. The cigarette makes her feel better but won't produce her child."
>
> The deeper security she was seeking was to achieve some assurance that her child was safe. All she could give herself was the sensation of a column of smoke entering her lungs. Watching her nervously and narcissistically suck in the smoke was a pitiful sight. That's how all addictions fuel our illusions of security. Feeding an addiction calms the panic but never really relaxes. However, in *pizur hanefesh*, we never really understand what true relaxation and

calmness is, so we accept satisfying the deadly addiction as the "real thing."

Therefore, when I am told that cigarettes "calm me down," I always remember that woman on the subway platform and tell the smoker that it's simply not true. It is well documented that they clog arteries and escalate tension and anxiety. Yet the dependency is so great that there is little awareness of the rising sense of inner tension. When this occurs, whether because of an addiction to cigarettes, other harmful substances or an "exciting lifestyle," there is very limited awareness that real security is only experienced within our truer and authentic selves. And this only occurs when we can experience a calmer, deeper and more meaningful experience of self.

Let us consider another situation where a young dating couple is experiencing a crisis in their relationship related to behavioral symptoms of the *pizur hanefesh* lifestyle:

> Shari is a thirty-year-old pediatrician who is very dedicated to the children she cares for. She has been dating for eight years and has experienced deep feelings of loneliness, especially since she spends almost every Shabbos with friends and siblings who are married and have children. Shari began dating Eric, a thirty-seven-year-old law professor, who has been dating for a number of years and felt his life was slipping away.
>
> They began dating and immediately felt a connection that neither had experienced before. For the first time Shari, felt this could be the beginning of the life she had been waiting for. Yet, Eric was becoming increasingly impatient with Shari's inability to separate herself from her work and patients. Dating was becoming more difficult to arrange. She was constantly on the phone or sending texts and emails to colleagues, patients, their families and her own friends. When they arranged to meet, she would

> consistently arrive an hour late. And when Eric would ask
> her to try and devote more attention to the relationship,
> Shari would become upset and say, "I need to be accepted
> for who I am."

On one hand, how well we can understand and even be inspired by Shari's dedication to her young patients. Yet this same dedication was making it impossible for her to separate herself from that dimension of her profession, which could also be a "drug" of total involvement leaving no room for building a close relationship to Eric.

Many years ago, when my family and I were living in Eretz Yisrael, I had been assigned for army duty, where I gave lectures to officers in dealing with trauma. My group was planning a number of scenarios dealing with attacks on the civilian population, *chas v'shalom*. After a couple of days there was a lull in our work and we were given the option to go home to our families. I found it very odd that I had a difficult time pulling myself away from the group to return to Yerushalayim to my family. The intensity of our efforts seemed to have locked me into that place. Whether it's army duty in Eretz Yisrael, a pediatric ward in a hospital, or an accounting or law firm, the effects are the same.

Here is another example of *pizur hanefesh* behavior. Chaya and Shloimy were engaged, and were eagerly looking forward to marriage. However, Chaya felt very tense when Shloimy drove fast and wove through traffic. Shloimy drove a BMW. He waited years to purchase the car and loved the feel of it on the road. It annoyed him that he had to drive the way he drove his old four cylinder Camry. So whenever he was having a great time on the road, Chaya sat next to him feeling frightened, clutching the seat and closing her eyes. Here, too, his *pizur hanefesh* behavior is very acceptable in the society in which we live. However, it was destroying their relationship.

I suggested to Chaya that unless he had the ability to contain himself behind the wheel as an expression of his caring for her, his impulsivity and insensitivity to her fears and well-being would probably take on other forms after the marriage.

The behavior of Chaya, Shloimy, Shaul and others flows inevitably from their troubled thoughts, feelings and even physiology. The primary difference between behavior that is a consequence of *pizur hanefesh* and that which flows from *menuchas hanefesh* is very apparent.

Behavior guided by *menuchas hanefesh* is always directed to the well-being of others. *Menuchas hanefesh* behavior is never "It's you or me." It emerges from a deeper and more secure experience of self. This is the state of mind that enables us to feel centered and intact. And when we experience our stable and integrated selves, then our physiology is under control. Under these conditions, our behavior is always informed by the precious meaning and value of our relationship. This is why in a relationship where there is a greater sense of *menuchas hanefesh* there is always an abundance of thoughtful, caring behavior — the ability to share, be helpful and giving, and enhance the lives of others. The couple that understands this direction of life will always pursue forms of behavior rooted in *menuchas hanefesh*, such as caring, kindness and *chessed* toward each other and others in their lives.

However, when behavior emerges from *pizur hanefesh* — a state in which thoughts, feelings and physiology are fragmented, and life is pulled in different directions — the stage is set for actions that instinctively and impulsively serve our limited and self-centered needs, usually at a cost to others. In this form of behavior, we are driven compulsively to satisfy our needs, even at the most primitive and selfish levels.

◇ Experiencing *Pizur Hanefesh* at a Wedding

I recently had an experience in our world of excess, which helped me understand what it's like to have behavior determined by an "acceptable" form of *pizur hanefesh*.

I arrived at the wedding of a close friend's child. The lavish smorgasbord was in full array. Men with high chef's hats were proudly manning their carving tables, while ever sharpening their gleaming knives. Wannabe samurai warriors were whizzing through their elaborate sushi creations. All the signs were there: What our culture has come to view as a wonderful wedding was about to unfold.

After quickly wishing *mazel tov* to the *chassan, kallah* and their parents, I selected a plate of veal covered with a very delicate sauce. As soon as I sampled the first mouthful, I knew this was the "real stuff." However, before I could take a second bite, my mind was distracted by what I was missing at the other food stations. There I was, standing with my plate of tender veal — yet I couldn't wait to finish it so I could sample whatever else caught my hungry eyes! Even as an old friend approached me, I remained distracted and kept looking around for the next chafing dish to attack. My impatience was palpable. I disappointed myself.

"I'm not enjoying my friend's company," I realized. "I'm not enjoying the veal, and I won't enjoy the next dish any more than this one. And I am certainly not fulfilling any *mitzvah* by being here."

Then it dawned on me. My behavior of running from one food station to the next was pure *pizur hanefesh*. Whereas I should have been more focused on the *mitzvah* of *simchas chassan* (enhance the *chassan's* joy) or some other worthwhile activity, instead, I felt like a kid running frantically through Toys "R" Us with a hundred dollar bill in his hand. Where does he run to next? What can he grab next? This realization helped me understand more deeply how *pizur hanefesh* has become so rampant in our generation.

A short time later, I was reminded of this wedding experience after I came across a *dvar Torah* (Torah insight) by Rav Yeruchem Levovitz, *zt"l*, who suggested that the only purpose for attending a wedding is to be *m'sameach* (to bring joy to) the *chassan* and *kallah*. I wondered what he would have said about my urge to run from one chafing dish to the next.

Our challenge is that we live in a society that has created more opportunities for distracted behavior than ever before. And where it really gets problematic is when our *pizur hanefesh* behavior embeds itself into the core of our *mitzvah* observance.

Recently, I was in shul next to a gentleman who was davening Shemoneh Esrei, apparently quite devoutly. When he finished, he took three steps back, followed by a deep and very long bow. Curiously, I peeked over to see why his head was down for so long. Then I saw the object of his true adulation. As he was ending the *tefillah*, he was receiving and sending emails over his Blackberry! I said to myself, "He is saying *oseh shalom bimromav* (a prayer proclaiming that Hashem makes peace on high). However, for this poor fool, there is no peace on high or down here below — just a lot of distractedness and insecurity."

At a moment of great closeness between him and Hashem, this man was unable to control the urge to *daven* to his Blackberry. (Perhaps that's why it's also known as the "crackberry.") He had incorporated his classic *pizur hanefesh* behavior into his most intimate moments of davening to Hashem. In *pizur hanefesh* behavior there is no peace, just tension, distractedness and insecurity. And for this fellow, the only pacifier that quiets these down is his Blackberry. I have little doubt that this individual is equally distracted when he is communicating with his wife and kids. He is what I call an "equal opportunity distracter." He distracts others and himself and is rarely in *menuchas hanefesh*.

◇ A Plethora of *Pizur*

My own list of what I call *pizur hanefesh* behaviors in our society seems to grow daily. It includes unnecessary consumption, overeating and addictions that include substance abuse, cigarettes, gambling, work, internet, media and the need for couples to have physical contact. Aside from these, there are interpersonal behaviors such as anger, reckless driving, the use of foul language, compulsive habits and many other behavioral expressions of *pizur hanefesh*. All these behaviors are self-perpetuating, because the interactive nature of our thoughts, feelings, physiology and behavior keeps us entrapped in inescapable repetition.

The irony is that *pizur hanefesh* behavior never really satisfies. *Pizur hanefesh* behavior is always directed toward "me," which heightens emotional isolation, alienation and insecurity. And the more we behave this way, the emptier we feel; and the emptier we feel, the more we behave this way to compensate for the hollow feelings. It creates an empty black hole that just grows larger and larger. On the other side of the spectrum, *menuchas hanefesh* behavior is always directed toward the big picture, toward relationship growth, trust, caring and building bridges of closeness and understanding.

The level of overt religious commitment may have very little effect on the inappropriateness of this type of behavior.

> I sat in the conference room of a large financial equity firm waiting for a meeting to begin. The heads of the firm are known throughout the world as generous supporters of worthy Torah causes and *chessed* initiatives. Sitting there, I

understood that the money that flowed from this corporation was in a league far beyond any that I could fathom.

Suddenly, I heard loud noises coming from the inner office. The noises increased in volume, and I began to recognize the sounds of rage punctuated by what may have been the angriest and most profane language I can ever recall hearing. The verbal sewage flowing from the office saturated every square inch of the vast organization. Obviously, someone had "messed up" and was getting "dressed down."

But what became clear to me at that moment was that these sounds were not unusual in this environment. They had to have been a commonplace occurrence. This was a place where *pizur hanefesh* reigned supreme. I understood that this form of outburst was not simply the way these bastions of success and support "stay on top," but they were trapped in their own inability to control themselves. This environment reflected their ongoing state of *pizur hanefesh*. All this was occurring while they were seen as the financial savior of so many worthy Torah institutions.

Chazal point out that if we have a hundred dollars we want two hundred. We are never really satisfied when it comes to acquisitions and fulfilling our needs. Perhaps that's what I was feeling when I had the urge to gather as much food as I possibly could at that wedding. And when we consider the *"askanim"* who are so driven by their compelling need to make lots of money, they can even justify their dehumanizing rage. Neither the food nor the money leads to any deeper satisfaction. Behavior that is driven by spiritually empty compulsion never gives us deeper satisfaction.

When these forms of behavior rooted in insecurity and compulsion occur between a dating or engaged couple, they inevitably get hurt and hurt the other.

◇ **EXERCISE 4: Assessing your *Menuchas Hanefesh* and *Pizur Hanefesh* Behavior**

There are times when we are inspired to behave in ways that are beneficial to our marriage, our family and even *Klal Yisrael*, even if it entails self-sacrifice. This behavior always flows from *menuchas hanefesh*. And there are times when our behavior is not only self-centered, but even more so — uncaring about the well-being of others, even those who are important to us. This form of behavior flows from *pizur hanefesh*.

Take a few minutes to write down some of these forms of your behavior in the following exercise:

My *Menuchas Hanefesh* Behaviors

There are times when I am ready and able to demonstrate my caring for my partner, such as when:

+ You call me just to stay in contact.

+ _____

_____

+ _____

_____

+ _____

_____

The Impact on our Relationship

When I am acting in a manner that is rooted in my *menuchas hanefesh* thoughts, how does our relationship change?

_____

_____

_____

My *Pizur Hanefesh* Behaviors

There are times when I behave in ways that demonstrate my inability to care for my partner, such as when:

+ I tell myself it doesn't make a difference to you whether or not I call.

+ _____

_____

+ _____

_____

+ _____

_____

The Impact on our Relationship

When I am acting in a manner that is rooted in my *pizur hanefesh* thoughts, how does our relationship change?

_____

_____

_____

THE SELF IN TRANSITION — I TO WE

The fifth and perhaps most important dimension in which *menuchas hanefesh* and *pizur hanefesh* impact on our ability to create a relationship that leads to a close and loving marriage is the experience of our *self in transition*, or how we experience growing from an "I" to a "we." This dimension takes on greater meaning as a relationship deepens and begins to bring two lives closer together.

Each of us has developed significant relationships, to our parents, friends, siblings, teachers and many others. Yet no other relationship is similar to our selves in transition from being an individual to becoming a partner in the enterprise of life, which is marriage. In other relationships we know who we are. Our relationships to our parents and siblings have been developed throughout our lives. Friendships take years to cultivate. Yet with all of these we grow independent of them all. We may feel close, but we are separate in our lifestyle.

In dating and engagement, the relationship is still young and undeveloped. We don't know who we are in the same way as in the other relationships. Before this relationship has begun to unfold, we harbor many hopes, dreams and even fantasies about how we would feel when this special person enters our lives. Yet, none of us could have had any realistic notion about how this would be experienced. Everything we thought it would be resided within our limited and distorted conceptions of our own private selves, totally unrelated from the powerful reality of moving from being an I to a we. Even when we observe the marriages of our parents, friends, siblings and others, we are only imagining what each feels like within their relationship. And we are always wrong, because we imagine the experience from a personal and singular perspective.

Our selves are always attempting to understand the nature of this new relationship. From the very first moment we hear the name of a possible *shidduch* date or the very first words of an introductory phone call, and certainly through the experience of being face to face, our inner self is continuously exploring the possibility of what it would be like if …? We have no idea who this person is, yet our self is exploring countless possibilities; some are positive and others are not. Yet, none have any basis in reality. However, as a relationship deepens we begin to experience another person in our lives, and this is when we also experience our selves in transition.

At this time when two selves are bridging the great divide that separates them, we become aware of how we really have no previous experience in understanding just what we should be feeling or thinking about this person. One moment our fantasies can easily overtake us to idealize the relationship and feel it will last forever, and the next moment we are observing other couples and feel we are missing out. This is why we experience intense swings between exhilaration and fear, joy and depression, calmness and agitation, or togetherness and isolation. The result is that for no explainable reason, one or both dating partners or even an engaged couple suddenly experiences frustration, anxiety, boredom, lack of interest and even physiological symptoms. And while all these reactions can be seen in the first four dimensions, until now the *pizur hanefesh* was not based on a relationship, as this other person was merely an acquaintance. Now, when a couple is closer and bonds have been formed, the self is struggling between feelings of comfort, security and trust, which are expressions of *menuchas hanefesh*, and confusion, fear, anxiety and doubt, which are expressions of *pizur hanefesh*.

From this perspective of the self in transition, we can better understand how couples make statements like:

"I didn't mind her birthmark until now, but suddenly it really bothers me."

"Until now the relationship was comfortable and we liked each other, but now we're at a plateau and I feel it's not going anywhere."

"I don't understand why it's just now that I feel so nervous when we're together."

"For some reason I keep on thinking about my former relationships."

"I keep on asking myself, maybe we should take a break to see if I miss being together?"

In all these and countless other similar statements, nothing has changed, aside from the effect of two people coming closer together and sensing the "I" of self being transformed into the "we" of self. It's a very different way of experiencing life and it can be very overwhelming.

◇ The Nucleus of Our Lives

To better understand this phenomenon of our selves in transition, let's take a closer look at this experience of self. There is at the heart of each of us a capacity to experience the essence of our being. We may experience our self while standing at the Kosel, at a wedding, at a *bris*, at Ne'ilah on Yom Kippur, or with loved ones who are special and very trusted. In dating and engagement, as our lives begin to bond we sense that our deeper selves begin to emerge.

However, as couples get closer, on the surface we can see how many "issues" begin to suddenly appear and get in the way of the relationship. They may be issues related to wedding plans, finances, attraction or religious conflicts, and in a great number of these situations these complications escalate as the couple gets closer. It's not that the relationship has been lost, but that we become aware of more and more challenges to our sense of trust and comfort, and our doubts escalate.

◇ The Five Expressions of the Self in Transition

In many ways the turmoil of transition is unavoidable. There is no way two lives can come closer together without doubts, fears and anxieties. The big question is, how can couples who are experiencing this self in transition learn to be comfortable in each other's presence without running in opposite directions? I have found that there are five *menuchas hanefesh* expressions of self that enable a couple to securely remain in each other's lives as they move through this period, and five *pizur hanefesh* expressions of self that jeopardize the relationship.

1. Awareness

We are in *menuchas hanefesh* when we have the ability to be aware that Hashem desires us to discover the one person in the entire universe with whom we can share our lives. We can achieve this by asking:

+ Is this a person I can grow with?

+ Is this someone who has the ability to understand me and my deeper self?

+ Am I able to focus on this person's deeper self?

+ Do I feel we can help each other fulfill our life goals?

Asking these questions enables us to remain focused on the first dimension of awareness.

The *pizur hanefesh* expression of this is to forget to be aware and to drift toward a focus on the external or other superficial thoughts.

2. Tranquility

The second *menuchas hanefesh* expression of self is understanding that at the center of every growing relationship there needs to be a shared sense of tranquility. At the heart of each of us resides a tranquil and gentle soul, able to sense a deep feeling of inner peace, wholeness and personal fulfillment with the right life partner.

The *pizur hanefesh* expression of this expression is impatience, and fantasies about a relationship based on overwhelming and exciting emotions.

3. Our Secure Selves

The third *menuchas hanefesh* expression of self is our ability to be aware of our fears, anxieties and criticisms and to acquire the skills that permit us to let them drift gently away, like the receding tide disappearing from the shore. This is what enables us to create an atmosphere of mutual comfort, respect and security as the relationship is developing.

The *pizur hanefesh* expression is to tenaciously hold on to and justify our fears, anxieties and criticisms.

4. Focus on a Life Partner

The fourth *menuchas hanefesh* experience of self is to remain focused on the person we are cultivating a relationship with, to the exclusion of everyone else. This occurs when we resist distractions that deprive us of the ability to move ahead.

The *pizur hanefesh* expression is to be unfocused and easily distracted from the relationship, whether these distractions are familial, professional, or memories of old relationships that suddenly feel "right" again.

5. Freedom

The fifth *menuchas hanefesh* experience of self occurs when we learn that we discover we have the freedom to consistently rise above our limitations, personal entrapments, painful habits and everything else that prevents us from being able to take the next and most important step of our life — commitment to another person for a lifetime. This is the ultimate self that Hashem wants us to experience in life — in its fullest and most precious sense.

The *pizur hanefesh* expression is when we are in a state of ongoing fear that we do not possess this ability to be free enough to move ahead.

◇ **EXERCISE 5: Assessing Your Self in Transition from the Perspective of *Menuchas Hanefesh* and *Pizur Hanefesh* Behavior**

At this stage I suggest that you take a few minutes to write down some of the thoughts and feelings that enable you to feel either love and closeness or isolation and conflict. I have included an initial example as a starter.

Thoughts and Feelings about Your Self in Transition

+ There are times when I am really grateful that we are seriously considering spending our lives together.

+ _____

_____

+ _____

_____

+ _____

_____

The Impact on our Relationship

When I am aware of feelings that bring us together, how does our relationship change?

_____

_____

_____

_____

_____

Thoughts and Feelings of Separation and Conflict

+ Sometimes I just feel that I cannot imagine us sharing our lives together.

+ _____

_____

+ _____

_____

+ _____

_____

The Impact on our Relationship

When I am tormented by thoughts and feelings that divide us, how does our relationship change?

_____

_____

_____

_____

_____

_____

_____

CHAPTER V

Transformations

◇ **The Miracle of Transformation and Change**

Transformations represent the ongoing miracles of human change and growth that Hashem has placed within the moment-to-moment experience of our lives. Within Torah life, each transformation is an opportunity utilized to redefine and deepen our relationship with Hashem and the world around us. Each *brachah, mitzvah* and *tefillah* throughout our day is an opportunity for growth and renewal. Shabbos, Yom Tov, Rosh Hashanah, Yom Kippur and other special days of our calendar year all epitomize spiritual environments for transformation. The transformations of this program are rooted in these same principles of growing and changing. The difference is that our focus is dedicated to learning to transcend states of *pizur hanefesh* to *menuchas hanefesh*, and from aloneness and isolation to union and fulfillment with your *bashert*.

Transformations mean that each of us carries the strength and capability to change in each of the five dimensions that comprise our experience of self. Even if we regularly find ourselves with troubled thoughts, feelings, physiology, behavior, or the overwhelming experience of our selves in transition — or with difficult challenges ahead of us in the search for our life partner — Hashem never deprives us of the power to transform these negative experiences of *pizur hanefesh* into a sense of balance and well-being that is integral to a *menuchas hanefesh* state of mind.

You may ask: If our lives are always engaged in an ongoing challenge of transformation — from states of anger to inner peace, frustration to acceptance, depression to joy, destructive behavior to *chessed* — how do these states of mind change? Where does one state come from and the other one go to? The answer is that *menuchas hanefesh* is a naturally inspired awareness of a deeper and truer self that is always within us. It is inherent in our spiritual design. And once it emerges, our states of *pizur hanefesh* recede, no longer creating insecurity and helplessness.

◇ The Fox and the Wolf: A Fable About Transformation

The *Gemara* in *Avodah Zarah* tells a parable, which I took the liberty to modify for the purpose of my work with couples. It gives us an insight into how Chazal understand our power to transform ourselves from one state to another.

> A tired and thirsty fox searched the forest for water and finally came across a well. When he looked down into the bottom of the well, his heart jumped with excitement. There, at the well's bottom, sat a pail of clear, cold water to slake his thirst. At the top of the well was an empty pail. He just needed to lower the empty pail, and it would bring the water-filled pail to the surface.
>
> When the fox attempted to lower the empty pail, he discovered he had no strength. So he circled the well for hours, looking for a solution that would save his life.
>
> Time passed and the sun set, giving way to darkness. The moon rose, shining its light right down into the well and

onto the surface of the full pail. The effect of the moon's reflection in the water was mesmerizing to the fox.

Just then, a hungry wolf passed by. The wolf saw the fox standing by the well and was relieved. He had not eaten all day. This fox was going to be his dinner.

"Hello, fox," said the wolf. "I'm going to eat you."

Weakened by thirst, the fox was clearly no match for the wolf. He seemed destined to die either of thirst or of being devoured by the wolf. But just at that moment, the fox had a sudden insight. He realized that the wolf's arrival was really a very positive event.

"I understand, wolf," said the fox. "You must be hungry and I'm in no shape to fight you. But I want to tell you that if you eat me, you will never be the world's richest wolf."

"The world's richest wolf? What are you talking about?"

"Look down into the well," said the fox. "What do you see?"

"That's the biggest diamond I ever saw!" said the wolf.

"That's right," said the fox. "But if you eat me, I can't help you get it."

"But how am I going to get down there to retrieve it?" asked the wolf.

Suddenly, the wolf had a great idea. "I know!" he exclaimed. "I'll jump into that empty pail, and you'll lower me down. Then I'll get the diamond and you'll pull me up."

"That's brilliant!" said the fox.

And so, that's what happened. The wolf jumped into the pail. The fox lowered the wolf down the well, and the wolf's weight was enough to send the full pail at the bottom up to the very top. All of a sudden, the fox's situation was very different. The cool, life-giving waters were in front of him, and the dangerous wolf was safely at the bottom of the well, never to bother him again.

Take a moment and consider the turning point in this fable. One minute, it seemed that the fox was finished. He was thirsty, weak and soon to be overpowered by a hungry wolf. But in the next instant, he had an insight that changed everything. Unexpectedly, he had an answer that freed him from his fate.

The fable is very clear in its message. Change can always occur, even when there seems to be no way out. And even more than this, the Alter of Kelm tells us, the answer is found in the very threat itself (a concept that we will also explore later, *b'ezras* Hashem). It is clear from this fable that the energy behind the solution is the wolf. And when it comes to learning to transform our negative states of personal experience, Hashem has created us with the capability to discover the right approach that elevates us from the emotional quagmire. Each time we discover an answer to the problem, we learn that we are never truly trapped by our thoughts and feelings.

◇ Transformation in Nature

Before we venture to understand what we can do to bring the gift of transformation into our lives on a moment-to-moment basis, it is crucial that we understand the meaning and significance of change and transformation in the world of nature. Within our natural surroundings, we observe how a caterpillar transforms itself inside its cocoon and emerges as a butterfly; a snake sheds its skin; the plant world is continuously reborn in the renewal of each spring. Nevertheless, transformation in nature is different than it is within us. Transformation in the world of nature is always meticulously guided by the irrevocable laws Hashem has designed for it. The same crawler always creates a cocoon around itself and emerges some time later as a moth or a multicolored butterfly. Whatever variations exist are coded into the genetic tapestry of a specific creature. There is no awareness, no choice, no growth of self.

In contrast, human transformation is based on the ever-present struggle for a true and authentic self to emerge, one that is in deep harmony with Hashem and the world around us. We call this growth *bechirah chafshis* (free choice). It is a gift that Hashem places in each of us; it is at the heart of all transformation and growth, and it is never denied us. At the heart of this approach is understanding the difference between the immutable rules that govern the world of nature, and our world as individuals created *b'tzelem Elokim* (in Hashem's likeness). This is the essence of appreciating our potential for growth and change.

◇ **The Snake and the Bird**

Rav Avigdor Miller, *zt"l*, in discussing how many of us may at times feel trapped in feelings of anger, shares a story about a bird and a snake. I later came across a similar story in the *sefer Cheshbon Hanefesh*, which was written by Rabbi Mendel of Satanov, *zt"l*, and published by Rav Yisrael Salanter, *zt"l*, in 1845. However, I prefer to present the story as I heard it from Rav Miller, while adding my own embellishments.

> A zoologist was in the Amazon rain forest studying the behavior of a rare snake and a particular species of bird. It was widely known that this snake fed off the bird, but no one had ever really understood how a reptile that slithers along the jungle floor could subsist by eating a bird that makes its nest high above in the canopy of trees.
>
> One day, the zoologist spotted the snake making its way through the jungle and followed it, hoping to solve the mystery. All of a sudden, the snake stopped dead in its path, raised its head and looked straight up. There, perhaps a hundred feet above, was one of these birds, sitting innocently and seemingly protected from its predator, joining in the riot of song and sounds of the rainforest. From

the perspective of the researcher, there was no way the snake could ever reach the bird. So he just waited patiently to observe the scene as it unfolded.

The snake opened its jaws and extended its fangs toward the bird. At first, the bird was oblivious. Then it caught sight of the menacing snake, and it began staring at its predator. Within a few moments, the mesmerized bird had become motionless. The singing had stopped, and soon the zoologist noticed the bird's first slight tremors. The trembling became more pronounced until the bird was shaking and shivering uncontrollably. Within a few moments, as if already dead, the helpless bird fell from its safe perch atop the jungle canopy and into the snake's waiting jaws.

After hearing Rav Miller describe this scene, I asked myself, "What if I cared about this bird? Perhaps I could speak the language of birds and, witnessing this macabre scene, attempt to rescue this helpless prey. What would I say or do?" I realized that I would want to tell the bird, "Hey, bird, wake up! Don't you realize that the snake has no control over you? Don't you remember that you have wings and you can fly? Don't you remember that Hashem gave you those wings, just as He gave the power to fly to every one of your ancestors since the very first days of Creation?"

Perhaps that bird would hear me and suddenly realize that he did have this wonderful power of flight. And even as he hurtled down toward the waiting jaws of his fearsome predator, he would shudder, snap out of his trance, spread his wings and pull out of his death dive just in time to save himself. Then he would triumphantly soar upward to life and freedom.

Of course, my image is all fantasy. The laws governing nature are very different and follow precise, immutable rules. Even though the wings were there, without the consciousness that they could be used, they were as useless to the bird as two lifeless wooden boards attached to its body. Just as the bird had lost its ability to fly during its fixation on the terrifying snake, we, too, become mesmerized by our own *pizur hanefesh* and lose our *bechirah*.

◇ Courage for a Princess

However, our own free will is different from the world of nature. We are created *b'tzelem Elokim* and therefore are never deprived of our power to discover the innate gifts that Hashem has implanted within our being. For us, the strength to overcome the mesmerizing effects of fear is very different. The capacity of the human will is limitless and never constricted by the same ironclad laws of nature. Hashem always gives us the skills to transcend our limits if we deeply believe in and are committed to the purpose of our lives to serve as *ovdei Hashem*.

To illustrate this, I want to share a tale, as told by the Baal Shem Tov, that can offer great insight into how our own human determination has the potential to transcend obstacles that are seemingly unconquerable.

> There was once a king with a very beautiful daughter. When it came time for her to marry, the king could find no husband courageous and intelligent enough for her. So he decided to permit every able-bodied man in his kingdom to compete for the right to win her hand. He placed her high up in a castle where she was in full view of the kingdom, and he built a fence around the castle. Then he informed his subjects that he would be placing fierce beasts and destructive forces within the fence to prevent anyone from reaching her. Finally, he proclaimed throughout the kingdom that even though it seemed impossible, there was a path to reach the princess, and anyone who could reach her would be rewarded with her hand in marriage.

From throughout the kingdom, able-bodied men seeking the prize of the princess's hand in marriage were drawn to the castle. However, as each arrived at the castle's perimeter, none dared to advance through the fence and into the field of horrors beyond. Each man simply melted in fear. For endless days, men arrived from every corner of the country and helplessly observed the princess from afar as she remained secluded, waiting for her suitor.

One day, a young man arrived. He observed the teeming crowd of men, saw the princess and understood their fear. As time passed, he became more enchanted with the maiden. Overcome by her beauty, he was determined to succeed in reaching her. *Such a beautiful princess must indeed be reachable,* he thought. Eventually, understanding that ahead of him there was a hidden path to the castle, he ventured through the fence. Nothing would stop him.

With great effort, he summoned all his might to race through the field of destruction − dodging, leaping and striking with all his might. Somehow, miraculously, he found himself triumphant and unharmed at the castle's entrance. He opened the door and made his way to the room of the waiting princess, who had observed his heroic advance.

When he entered her room, she greeted him as the bravest of all men − and the one she had been waiting for to take her hand in marriage. Then she said, "Now you can turn around to see the truth." He turned around and gazed through the window. He saw the throngs of frightened men assembled and standing helplessly at the periphery of the castle. To his shock, though, on the inside of the fence, between the men and the castle, there was only empty space. There were no ferocious beasts, no destructive forces.

"Where did they all go?" asked the young man.

"They were never there," answered the princess. "They

were all illusions of everyone's imagination. From where they stand, the beasts are still there. Now only you know the truth. Now that you are standing within the castle, only you can see those dangerous monsters for what they truly are. The monsters exist only in their fears."

In effect, the tale is a metaphor for what occurs throughout our lives. We feel ensnared by a painful feeling, anger, hurt, resentment or any other overwhelming feeling or thought. We believe there is no other way to experience life. Then we become aware of a higher understanding of life, a deeper vision — and suddenly, we find ourselves in the castle with the princess. We are free once again.

> I once told this Chassidic tale to a single young man who had been suffering from paralyzing anxiety that was keeping him from becoming engaged. I taught him a number of approaches to help him handle his anxiety; soon afterward he became a *chassan*. I was invited to his *vort*, and when I arrived, he asked me to walk outside with him for a moment. There he told me, "There is no way for anyone to understand how the monsters in that tale can seem to be so real and ferocious. That was how I viewed life before the engagement. But now that I am here at my own *vort*, I can look back and see that the monsters were all only in my imagination. They are just empty threats that never had any real power."

The difference between the stories of the bird and the princess lies in the contrast between the laws that guide change and growth in the world of nature and the power of free will in our own lives. In the first story, the bird cannot fly because the laws that Hashem has created to guide the world of nature are, in fact, immutable. The animal world possesses no ability to think. It is compelled to follow, without choice, the path that has been laid out for it. The second story, however, portrays our human gift of thought, hope, belief and strength that enables us to transcend the illusion of our helplessness and self-imposed limitations.

◇ ## Discovering My Own Free Will

The power of transformation is always in the air, and at times transformation can even occur in an instant.

> When I was growing up, cigarettes were just beginning to be considered a health hazard. At the age of about sixteen, I began to experiment with smoking. I had no father to guide me; he had died when I was ten. For me, that cowboy on the horse smoking Marlboros was a man to be admired and emulated. He was strong and free to roam, unfettered by life's limitations. So, like other foolish boys and men, I swallowed the message — tar and all — and believed that like the man on the horse, I would grow up to be strong and brave.
>
> The habit stayed with me for decades. Sometimes I would smoke a pipe and other times I would revert to cigarettes. I tried to stop on many occasions, but was always drawn back by the chemical and social tenacity of the habit. Then, one night when I was about forty and had been smoking for a quarter of a century, I had a dream. In it, I saw my children walking around a grave. I looked closely at it and saw ... guess who? I woke up in a cold sweat. The message had finally entered my brain. It frightened me as no warning on the cigarette package or Cancer Society commercial ever could. Nicotine had suddenly lost its power over me. I had a chance to be free. I saw it as a true gift from Hashem, and from that day on I never took another cigarette.
>
> Today I look around at young men — and even boys — smoking. I feel a sense of pity for how they have

relinquished their free will to the power of cigarettes and nicotine. And each time I see that cowboy on his horse, it is a powerful reminder of how we live in a society that takes our freedom away and replaces it with a childish fantasy and an addiction to black tar.

This potential for transformation is the inner strength that I consistently attempt to transmit to couples I am working with. Sometimes it takes laboriously hard work, and other times an insight similar to my own graveyard dream can make a critical difference in a realtionship.

◇ Transformation in Dating and Engagement

The challenge that many of us face is that we continually see all kinds of obstacles that distract us from cultivating close and caring relationships. The obstacles may be our fears, anxieties, moods, sensitivities or hurts. Whatever they may be, these are the illusions of the "fierce beasts" that prevent us from reaching the "castle" of a relationship that culminates in a successful marriage. The real power of these illusions is that we believe that we cannot overcome our negative feelings of anxiety, regret, numbness, obsessive thoughts, perfectionism, stomachaches — and all the other manifestations of *pizur hanefesh* that leave us feeling that we have no other choice but to end a relationship that once seemed to hold promise. As we will learn, no one is ever trapped. Hashem has provided us with many routes to freedom. And while many of these routes are skills we will be covering in depth throughout this book, I do want to share a few stories about the power of transformation.

◇ The List

Each of us always possesses the capability to make choices, to become aware of our true wings and our ability to fly. No one is ever destined to be entrapped in a pattern of failure or deprived of the chance to experience the gift of transformation.

My wife and I spent Shabbos with a couple, Ari and Rina, who seemed to be in their late thirties or early forties. Although they did not have children, they lived in a very spacious, newly decorated home. It soon became clear that this couple had been married for just a short while.

As I walked to shul with Ari on Shabbos night, we discussed his new life. He told me that he had been dating for almost twenty years and had met a staggering number of girls. He appeared to be a very serious person, certainly not one who wanted to exploit young women. So, while I told him that it was wonderful that he finally discovered his *bashert*, I asked him what he thought had caused him to date unsuccessfully for so long. He told me that when he finished his professional degree, he was deluged by *shadchanim* with offers. He was a very cautious person and wrote out a complete list of all the qualities he was looking for in a young woman. And with each date, he would actually visualize the list and would realize that the young woman he was dating did not fill his requirements.

After many years of failure, he went to someone he deeply respected to ask for advice. He was told that since he was financially comfortable, he should attempt to use his resources to do a significant *chessed*. Following this person's advice, he decided to help a single mother with a large family by purchasing a house for her, mortgage-free.

"Then a *neis* [miracle] happened."

"What was the miracle?" I asked him.

"With the next girl I dated, the list disappeared from before my eyes. And I married her."

Obviously, he did not marry her after the first meeting. However, it is clear that Ari had been entrapped in an obsessive concern with his list. He's not an obsessive individual, but in this area, his concern for details had imprisoned him for decades — in a pattern of thought and perception that had deprived him of life's greatest gift, his *bashert*.

◇ Three Fundamental Principles

There are three fundamental principles that govern our lives: The first is that we never lose our ability to transform ourselves. The second is that Hashem desires that we exercise our free will to be the loving individuals we have been created to be. And the third is to learn how to gain access to our true wings and never be deprived of the gift of flight, even when we are hurtling down from the tree and falling helplessly into the waiting jaws of the serpent.

Discovering this *bechirah chafshis* is at the heart of our history as a people. Isn't this what Yosef Hatzaddik was discovering as he saw the image of his father while struggling to break free from Potiphar's wife? And perhaps this is what Aharon Hakohen discovered as he silently accepted Hashem's will, upon learning of the death of his two sons on the day of his inauguration as *Kohen Gadol*.

◇ Transforming Tears to Laughter

While there is much to learn about acquiring the keys to transformation, many such events occur, even without our direct efforts, and almost instantly. And while our exploration of transformations will encompass more methodical and gradual approaches, I want to share three additional illustrations of how transformations can occur, as Chazal term it, *k'heref ayin* (within the blink of an eye).

There was a couple, Martin and Sarah, whom I had known before they were married. When we met again during their *shanah rishonah*, they told me the following story:

While they cared for each other very deeply, Sarah and Martin were both experiencing a very difficult adjustment, marked by continuous tension and even rage. The couple began to feel hopeless and the marriage seemed doomed.

During one particular fight, Martin's anger shot out of control. In his rage, he ran into the bathroom and slammed the door, all the while continuing the shouting with accompanying expletives. Feeling that all was certainly lost, Sarah sat on the couch and began to cry. She started to pray and beg Hashem for something to happen that would turn their marriage around.

Suddenly, she heard strange banging and scratching sounds emanating from the bathroom. *What's happening in there?* she wondered. Finally, she called out, "Martin, what are you doing?"

The voice on the other side of the door screamed back, "I'm locked in! The door is broken. I can't open it."

The image tickled her funny bone. "You're stuck in the bathroom?" she asked incredulously, and she began to giggle.

Martin heard her laughing. At first, it made him even angrier. Then, all of a sudden, the entire situation seemed absurd to him — even comical — and he began to chuckle, as well. Within an instant, both were laughing hysterically on opposite sides of the bathroom door. By the time Martin and Sarah finally figured out how to free him from the bathroom, their relationship had changed. Something funny had somehow transformed all their hurt and fighting. Their differences now all seemed ludicrous and certainly not worth losing their marriage over.

It's not that laughter turned their relationship around — although it may very well have helped. Rather, it's that now they had a new perspective on what had been perceived as a tragedy, and this new view may very well have saved their marriage from deteriorating to a point of no return.

Where did this strength to see the situation as comical come from? It came from that force within us that is always there to place life in the perspective from which Hashem wants us to view it. In our work, though, we will not resort to locked bathroom doors for this change in perspective. Rather, we will attempt to understand and utilize the keys that Chazal have provided us to live within that healthier state of self.

◇ At the Last Moment

Rav Eliyohu Goldschmidt, *zt"l*, the Mashgiach of Yeshiva Gedolah Zichron Moshe in South Fallsburg, wrote a book called *Dear Daughter*, a hypothetical account full of deep Torah insights, of a father's wise and loving guidance to his young daughter. He described another incident that shows how a marital transformation can occur in a flash.

Rav Goldschmidt shared the story of a couple from South America who were in the midst of divorce proceedings. (It is interesting to note that in the United States, seventy percent of divorces are initiated by wives. Following this pattern, here, too, the wife was determined to go ahead.)

> The husband had resisted greatly, but his wife insisted, and he was left with no choice but to proceed. He reluctantly agreed to meet with the lawyer to finalize the divorce arrangements. An appointment was arranged for 9:00 a.m.
>
> Early on the morning of the scheduled meeting, terrorists struck in the downtown area and caused many casualties. The wife, listening to the news bulletin on the radio, heard the name of her husband listed among the names of the injured and dead. She became very distraught,

knowing that she had pushed him to keep the meeting.

She realized, too, that the divorce process had taken on a life of its own. Her husband had been trying to persuade her to forgive and reconcile, but she had been swept away by her compelling need to end the marriage. Brokenhearted, she now understood that she had made a tragic error. She tearfully called the lawyer to inform him of the tragedy and tell him that her husband would not be attending the meeting.

The lawyer answered the phone, heard what she had to say and then told her, "You must be mistaken. Your husband arrived a few minutes early and he is sitting in front of me right now." The wife realized that another man with the same name as her spouse had been the unfortunate bomb victim. "Please put my husband on the phone," she requested.

When her husband got on the line, she said, "I have made a terrible mistake. Will you please come home?"

This story demonstrates the ever-present power of transformation, even as the powerful pulls of the divorce process are in motion. The potential for transformation can just as easily impact on a couple in the middle of a divorce as during any other stage of a relationship. Transformation is an integral aspect of how Hashem has created us. It only ceases when we cease to exist.

We have a mitzvah of *"V'ahavta l'rai'acha kamocha* — You shall love your fellow as yourself" (*Vayikra* 19:18). This mitzvah is most intensely felt within the husband and wife relationship. And while we may attempt to define our life experiences in many other ways, none approaches marriage.

Stephen Covey, the author of *Seven Habits of Effective People*, tells of a prominent executive who spent his life climbing the ladder of success in the corporate world. But when he reached the very top of the ladder and could see over the high wall, he came to a frightening realization. He suddenly understood that his single-minded focus on success had caused him to neglect his marriage. And when it was too late, he comprehended with great despair that he had spent his life climbing the wrong ladder!

These vignettes are a testimony to our ability to transform our lives and our relationships. In my work with both dating couples and married couples, I witness the power of transformation each time I sit with two people. It has become part of the spiritual logic with which I view life.

◇ The Power of Transformation

What is the source and purpose of this power? Each moment of our lives, Hashem places us between two diametrically opposing forces — *menuchas hanefesh* and *pizur hanefesh*. One will bring us closer to our purpose in life, and the other will send us far away from anything that can enhance our lives. In dating and engagement, these two forces constantly contend with each other, trying to influence the manner in which we view each other. Frequently it is the negative state of mind that locks us into a perception that seems inescapable.

Sandra and Lenny were both twenty-four. They had been dating for close to two months and had begun to discuss engagement. Sandra had been to see me after her last relationship with Moshe had suddenly ended, and she was deeply hurt because of the way she was treated. It took a while until she healed and was ready to begin dating again. When she and Lenny met, she maintained contact with me throughout their relationship and asked if I could meet with them both before they became engaged.

Two days before our meeting, Sandra called me and

asked that we postpone the session. At first, she was hesitant to tell me why. Then she revealed that someone had called her and offered the possibility of restarting with Moshe. Suddenly, all the hurt that had occurred with Moshe in the past, and the closeness and trust she had begun to feel for Lenny, were forgotten. Despite all she had suffered, she became obsessed with a need to see Moshe again. More importantly, she was ready to walk away from Lenny, who had given her so much of himself. She even insisted, "But Moshe was the only guy I ever really cared for. How can I ever get over him?"

I realized this was her *pizur hanefesh,* and that it could lead to another broken relationship. I was quite firm and direct with her and encouraged her to keep our meeting as planned. After a lengthy talk, she regained her perspective. I did meet with the couple and they were engaged shortly thereafter.

In every dating relationship and engagement, we are continuously dealing with our feelings, and sometimes it's very difficult to know whether they are justified or not. Yet, the source of the feelings is not the main issue. Once we have the troubled thought or feeling, we fall into a state of *pizur hanefesh.* At the same time, *menuchas hanefesh* always requires us to feel a deeper sense of balance and control over our troubled thoughts and feelings.

In each of the five dimensions we discussed earlier — thoughts, feelings/moods, physiology, behavior and trust/emotional closeness — we are never locked into a place where we are compelled to remain in our *pizur hanefesh* state. To the contrary, the Torah wants us to understand that each sign of our moving toward any state of mind that is associated with *pizur hanefesh* is actually a mandate for change and growth. And, therefore, each troubled thought or feeling offers an opening to respond in a manner that will actually bring us closer to *menuchas hanefesh.*

◇ **Dovid Hamelech and Transformation**

This concept of transforming our state of mind from *pizur hanefesh* to *menuchas hanefesh* is at the heart of how the Alter of Kelm describes the meaning of David Hamelech's declaration of loyalty to Hashem (*Tehillim* 94:19): "*B'rov sarapai bekirbi, tanchumecha yeshaash'u nafshi* — When my mind and heart are filled with many foreboding thoughts and feelings, Your comforts cheer my soul and bring me peace of mind."

The message that David Hamelech is conveying is that at no moment in our lives — such as a dating relationship or engagement that is going through a rocky period, or, *chas v'shalom*, when we are in the throes of a devastating illness — are we alone and helpless. Hashem always gives us the power to transform our *sarapim* — our foreboding thoughts and feelings. He enables us to discover the keys that unlock His ever-present comfort that warms and cheers our souls. This is the gift of transformation, and it resides in our potential to recognize each sign of *pizur hanefesh* as an opportunity to transform the moment into closeness to our own *neshamah* and to Hashem. This is why, at every moment of our personal and married lives, we are constantly monitoring our state of mind and learning how to transform adversity into opportunity. Our very fulfillment and joy in life result from learning to keep monitoring our state of mind — so we can experience life with all the potential that Hashem has placed within us.

Even when all seems lost, we are never the bird that is paralyzed; rather, we can more closely resemble the wily fox at the well. When it seemed that he was closed in on all sides, caught between his own thirst and the hunger of the wolf, he was given an insight that rescued him. In the same way, we are able to transform our own adversity into *menuchas hanefesh*.

◇ **Defining Our Experience of Life**

Our journey into understanding Hashem's gift of transformation begins with becoming more aware and appreciative of a phenomenon that has always been at the center of our life experience, but rarely is given much thought. This is our experience of our "self."

There is a question I pose to individuals and couples I work with: "Where does your experience of life come from?" The initial answer will usually be that we experience life through our thoughts, feelings and other senses. We automatically assume that whatever our thoughts and feelings are telling us is correct, and tend to accept this perception as the unquestionable reality. We tend to rely on these perceptions because our experience of self runs on autopilot.

I see a lot of this in my work with dating and engaged couples. A frequent statement I hear is, "But when I look at her, she really is too short. I never really minded it until we became engaged, and now I can't stop thinking about it." There are many variations on this "new perception" relating to height, weight, intelligence, *frumkeit* and *middos*. Still, I have rarely found that any of these new perceptions are based on anything but the increased anxiety that comes along with commitment and alters perceptions. From the perspective of the perceiver, the response is, "It must be true because that's how I see it." The message we give ourselves is clear. First is that "I am my perceptions," and second, "My perceptions are true and must be trusted, even if I decide to break my engagement."

The reality is that our experience of life is not solely our own and does not originate with us. Just like every other life function, our experience of self is a gift from Hashem. Whether we are experiencing *menuchas hanefesh* or *pizur hanefesh*, it all comes from Hashem. Without Hashem, there is no self. Yet we unthinkingly assume that our selves exist almost independently of Hashem.

◇ **Discovering an Awareness of Self in a Refrigerator**

> I know of a Rosh Yeshivah who wanted to help his children understand that we don't "just exist." Everything in life is a gift. He shared with me that when his children were young, they were taught not to go to the refrigerator and take any food without first asking permission. "We never refused them," he explained. "They just needed to remember to ask." His reason was that a child needs to learn that nothing is a given in life. Everything we have is a precious gift for which we need to feel a sense of *hakaras hatov*.

The lesson seems simple. Everything we have in life — even our sense of self — has been given to us by Hashem, and by those whom Hashem has entrusted with our well-being. Still, we rarely consider this novel thought, and it needs to be reinforced throughout our lives.

When a child is hungry, he says to himself, "I am hungry, and therefore I will eat." This translates into, "I am hungry and therefore I am entitled." In Yiddish, the saying is "*Es kumt mir* (It's coming to me)." The Rosh Yeshivah was teaching his children that the gift of food can never be taken for granted by instinctively saying, "I'm hungry, so I am just eating what's rightfully mine." The attitude of the child who believes that the sandwich he is holding is his because "I was hungry and I took it" is very different from that of the child who believes that the food was given as a gift from his or her parents because "I was hungry and my parents understood this, and this is the true sign that they love me and care for me." How much more true is this in relation to Hashem Who lovingly gives us the gift of our consciousness of self each moment of our lives.

The very first step toward *menuchas hanefesh* is to understand that our experience of ourselves, which means our consciousness and awareness, along with all of our other physical functions and senses, are all ongoing gifts from Hashem. And along with these gifts comes the responsibility of being aware of how our experience of self and our "right to harbor feelings and moods" must always be measured in relation to what Hashem expects from us.

◇ **Listening to your Deeper Self**

A *chassan* or *kallah* may feel in doubt about being engaged. She may say, "Did I agree to get engaged too soon? Did I do enough research? Did I overlook his behavior at the restaurant when he begrudgingly tipped the waiter?" Or he may say, "I realize she is one of the most wonderful people I have ever met, yet when I look at her I just don't feel the attraction."

With all these and countless other troubled thoughts and feelings assaulting and attacking from every side, the most commonly heard defense is, "These are my thoughts and feelings. How can I just make believe they're not there? It's not that I wanted to have them."

It's true that the thoughts, feelings and physiological reactions may appear in all their glory, but the only real change that can get us closer to the *chupah* must first begin with two questions that continuously determine our direction in life on a moment-to-moment basis. The first is, "Faced with these feelings, how can I discover my way to freedom from the oppressive nature of these thoughts and feelings?" And the second is, "If Hashem gives me my sense of self, what does He want me to experience that will enable me to understand the true essence and fulfillment of myself in this relationship?" Merely asking these questions is the first step to opening the door to real change and growth.

CHAPTER VI

The Principles of Transformation

The most important concept you will learn from this book is that we always have the freedom to access a state of mind that experiences *menuchas hanefesh*. Learning to access this dimension of ourselves is based on our awareness of principles that help us transform ourselves from *pizur hanefesh* to *menuchas hanefesh*. When integrated into the ebb and flow of our lives, these principles serve as the foundation for building, maintaining and strengthening relationships in dating and engagement.

These principles can be summarized as follows:

1. **Chiddush**: *Chiddush* is renewal. It is the awareness that at every moment of our lives Hashem recreates us as a physical, emotional and spiritual being that is capable of growing and changing, regardless of how limited we are in our own view.

2. **Tzomet**: *Tzomet* means crossroads. Through understanding this principle, we become increasingly aware that at every moment Hashem places us at the crossroads to experience two towering forces within us, *menuchas hanefesh* and *pizur hanefesh*.

3. **Mishkan**: *Mishkan* means sanctuary. Through an

appreciation of *Mishkan*, we gain greater clarity of how to cultivate a state of mind that brings us closer to a relationship rooted in a deeper appreciation of the meaning of caring, love, beauty and *kedushah*.

By understanding and following these principles, we open up the possibility of constantly transforming every aspect of our personal and shared lives.

Now we can take a closer look at these principles.

THE FIRST PRINCIPLE: *Chiddush* — We Are New Creations at Every Moment

◇ Receiving Life with Every Breath

The principle of *Chiddush* means we are aware that at every moment of our lives, Hashem is recreating us. Recognizing this phenomenon — that Hashem is constantly renewing our physical, experiential and spiritual selves — opens new vistas in our perception of the possibilities inherent in every moment. *Chiddush* is the knowledge that while we may feel entrapped in a state of *pizur hanefesh*, in reality we are in a continuous state of renewal, with endless choices to enhance our growth and well-being. The concept of *Chiddush* is based on the phrase we recite twice each morning: "*Hamechadesh b'tuvo bechol yom tamid*," which means that Hashem continuously renews the work of Creation with goodness. Our praise of Hashem for granting us life at each moment is also expressed by David Hamelech in *Tehillim* (150: 6), "*Kol haneshamah tehalail Kah* — Let all souls praise Hashem." Chazal interpret this to mean that with every *neshimah*, each breath we take, we are recreated by Hashem.

The Chassidic master, Rav Levi Yitzchak MiBerditchev, *zt"l*, deepens our understanding of this prayer as he explains that our soul is always yearning to leave us and rejoin its Master in Heaven. With each breath we take, Hashem returns our soul to us; as life is flowing away from us, Hashem is continuously breathing life back into us.

All this may sound very mystical and esoteric. Even so, when we appreciate the implications of *Chiddush*, we can begin to appreciate how being attentive to this continuous state of renewal holds the keys for discovering the possibilities for growth and fulfillment in every moment. Through this principle, we can become acutely aware that Hashem provides each of us with life in a very personal and loving way. We each receive precisely what we require to exist throughout every moment. And through this gift, life reaches every cell of our being. We experience the gift of life in our capacity to think, feel, breathe, move and perform every function that allows us to be ourselves. And all the while, we are also provided with another gift. It is the gift of self and soul that empowers us to be mindful of our moment-to-moment experience of life. This gift begins at birth and ends when we have finished our mission in life. Therefore, as we consider Hashem's love and caring for our existence at each moment, we can begin to appreciate the revolutionary impact this can have on how we view ourselves and our life partner.

◇ A Dialogue about "Self"

In a workshop that I frequently conduct on *menuchas hanefesh* and relationships, I attempt to teach participants how to appreciate that we each have a distinct and unique self, which is rooted in the eternal. I begin teaching this concept through a dialogue with a participant of the group.

The purpose of this dialogue is to create awareness that while our sense of self is always changing, reflecting the tapestry of our many thoughts and feelings, there is a deeper "self" that is constant and never changes. My goal is to help participants become more conscious of this eternal dimension of self that is anchored in the Oneness and eternal quality of Hashem. The practical implications of this awareness is that the "self" that yearns for a new car, or that feels anger and jealousy, is not the same dimension of "self" that experiences closeness to Hashem and to those we deeply care for. Our goal in life is to always strive to experience the deeper dimension of self.

I begin by saying that we all know that we possess a unique self that enables us to face our moment-to-moment sensations of life. Yet how do we know that what we experience is really our unique self?

This is how the dialogue is conducted:

S.O.: What is your name?

Chanah: Chanah.

S.O.: Do you remember the first time you knew your name?

Chanah: No. But it was probably at about the age of two or three.

S.O.: Do you associate your name with your "self"?

Chanah: Yes.

S.O.: So you have known that you are Chanah for about twenty-five years?

Chanah: That makes sense.

S.O.: Was there ever a time when you did not know you were Chanah, or you didn't know you were yourself?

Chanah: I always knew I was myself, perhaps except when I was sleeping.

S.O.:   Where do you think you received your ability to know that you are really you, and that your experiences represent who you are?

Chanah: I imagine that my brain cells, synapses and many other functions of my intelligence and nervous system enable me to know that I am Chanah.

S.O.:   Did you know that at your age, most of the cells you had in your childhood have since died, and new ones have taken their place? And while your physical cells may have changed, you are still Chanah?

Chanah: I know that my cells die and are regenerated. But I never really thought about how my self continues, despite the death of the cells. That's very interesting. So tell me, where does my consciousness of self come from?

S.O.:   You know that you are yourself because self has a dimension of Hashem's eternal Being. It is beyond the physicality of cells and it gives us the power of awareness and consciousness.

When you daven Shemoneh Esrei, you say, "*Ata chonain l'adam daas* — You (Hashem) bestow on man wisdom." This includes your ability to know that you exist and experience your own life and the world around you. No other creature in the world has the power to think and be aware.

Do you know why I am placing such an emphasis on being aware of your consciousness of self?

Chanah: No. Please tell me.

S.O.:   The foundation of everything I am teaching you is based on being aware that Hashem gives us life at each moment, and Hashem gives us a deeper self at each moment. This deeper self, which is a part of our *neshamah*, always has the ability to discover the road to freedom and *menuchas hanefesh*, regardless of where we are and what we are experiencing.

Therefore, the "self" that feels trapped and insecure and hurt is not the "self" that Hashem wants you to experience as the true and unique reflection of your *neshamah*. And we recognize this deeper self through *Chiddush*.

You see, Chanah, our *Chiddush* and our deeper self always hold the keys to our transformation.

Chanah: I always believed that Hashem gives me life, but I never really thought about being recreated at each moment. I also need to be more mindful of how my deeper experience of my self is a gift from Hashem.

◇ We Are Always in a State of Receiving Life

This first discovery is that living is not a passive or reactive process. We have choices between experiencing our lives from either deeper or more internal dimensions of our "self" or from a superficial dimension of our being. True living is understanding that our self is the result of our constant state of receiving through Hashem's flow of love. Just like the children who were taught the meaning of receiving by asking before they took food from the refrigerator, we, too, learn to be appreciative of our state of receiving life from Hashem on a moment-to-moment basis. This awareness is the first step toward transforming our *pizur hanefesh* to *menuchas hanefesh*, and it transforms our relationship with those who share our lives.

A Power Beyond Self

Even when I feel angry and hurt, the "I" who experiences this anger and hurt is still receiving its ability to experience these emotions from Hashem. Even so, the same Hashem Who gives me the ability to come into contact with these emotions does not wish me to be stuck in them. The implication, especially in relationships, is that even as I may harbor these feelings, Hashem allows me to feel them, only because He wishes me to change them. Understanding this choice and learning to transform our negative perceptions is the essence of *avodas* Hashem.

The Freedom of Creation

The knowledge that I am being recreated at each moment informs me that I am always given the opportunity to rediscover my freedom from the strong pull of *pizur hanefesh*. We are never created to be imprisoned by our present negative perceptions. We may not yet understand how to find the key to freedom from our anxieties, anger, sadness or any other negative state of mind. At the same time, the realization that we are being continuously created comes with the belief that along with our renewal, Hashem will also make it possible for us to discover the gateway to our freedom.

Experiencing Time as a Loss of Control

Another aspect of this awareness is that of time, because when I live in an awareness of *Chiddush*, I am experiencing life in Hashem's dimension of time, rather than being pushed by my own internal compulsive drives.

In reality, we have no concept of Hashem's dimension of time, for He is beyond time and not bound by its finite limitations. We, on the other hand, will always have to answer to insistent demands of time. It's the nature of our mortality. Nevertheless, some are more bound and imprisoned in time than others.

For example, some people always feel impatient and in a rush. They have no awareness of their choice in life to slow down. It's like their engines are running at full speed, yet the gears are in neutral. They're not really going anywhere. The reality is that their lives are driven by tension, insecurity and the inability to feel quiet within. They are always in a rush because *pizur hanefesh* always distorts time. It causes them to feel impatient and jumpy.

Imagine waiting at a traffic signal for a red light to turn green, and there is a car next to you with its driver revving his engine impatiently. Suddenly, the light changes — and he's off, leaving burning rubber and a trail of exhaust smoke in his wake. What was his rush and what will he do with the three seconds he saved before he needs to stop at the next light? The answer is that his behavior is being driven by *pizur hanefesh*. His concept of time is distorted because he possesses poor internal controls. His impatience is a reflection of inadequate self-control masquerading as success behind the wheel of a high performance car. Internally, he is just a little boy who has never learned to gain control of the forces that are relentlessly driving him. He cannot appreciate *Chiddush* because the engine of his drives is louder than the sound of his deeper self. This deeper self can only emerge when we attempt to aspire toward *menuchas hanefesh*.

◇ **How a *Gadol* Experiences Time**

The minute we recognize Hashem's renewal of our lives at each moment, we are able to feel greater internal control and become less driven by tension, impatience and internal anxiety. Rav Dovid Feinstein, *shlit"a*, spoke of how his father, Rav Moshe, *zt"l*, always had patience for anyone. One moment he would appear to be in a rush, but the next — if someone needed his attention — he was able to speak calmly and carefully and never give the impression that he was rushed or tense.

This ability to experience Hashem's time empowers each of us to be a *savlan* — a tolerant and patient person. With this strength, we can each be more caring and understanding to that individual with whom we are learning to build the delicate bonds of a relationship.

◇ *Hakaras Hatov*

The final awareness related to *mechadesh b'tuvo* is that since I am receiving life at each moment, Hashem expects me to be cognizant of and grateful for this gift of life. Chazal call this *hakaras hatov*.

We demonstrate our *hakaras hatov* to Hashem by caring for those Hashem wishes us to care for. And this relationship is personified between life partners.

◇ **Exercises to Cultivate Our Awareness of** *Chiddush*

To help you internalize this first principle — our awareness of receiving the moment-to-moment gift of life — I would like to suggest a few activities or exercises that you can integrate into your daily schedule.

1. The Awareness Walk

+ Take a walk on a quiet street while staying focused straight ahead.

+ Be aware of the trees, birds, clouds, sky and everything around you that is receiving the gift of life from Hashem.

+ Now, focus on your own self receiving these gifts of life that make you think, feel, walk, hear, see, breathe and perform every other function that enables you to be a living being.

+ Remind yourself that every moment, Hashem is a loving Creator, continuously breathing life into you and every molecule in this universe.

2. Awareness of Receiving Life

+ Throughout your day, whether alone or with others, be aware that regardless of what you are experiencing in your relationship with yourself or others, you are receiving life from Hashem at this very moment.

+ Take this moment to express to Hashem that you are grateful for the life He is breathing into you.

3. Your Awareness of Time

+ Learn to quiet the feeling of impatience or being rushed by taking a minute to remember that Hashem is renewing your life at every moment.

+ Follow this awareness by a deep breath.

+ Observe how this quiets the inner drive that creates tension, intolerance and impatience.

THE SECOND PRINCIPLE: *Tzomet* — We Live at the Crossroads

The second principle is recognizing that we are always standing at the crossroads (Hebrew: *tzomet*) where we are given the freedom to choose between two states of being. In one direction, we face a state of mind that reflects *menuchas hanefesh*, and in the other direction, we face toward *pizur hanefesh*. We need to learn how to exercise this freedom.

◇ **There Are No Accidents in Our Lives**

In the classic *sefer Chovos Halevavos*, the Gate of *Bitachon* defines the meaning of *bitachon* as our belief that no event can occur in our lives that is not the direct result of Hashem's intervention. Chazal tell us that no one can even lift a finger here below without the consent of Heaven. As the *Gemara* in *Brachos* (33b) teaches: "All that occurs is from the hands of Heaven, except for the fear of Heaven." Nothing is ever "accidental" or "by chance." At every moment of our lives, Hashem is placing us at the crossroads. Our responsibility is to first define which route leading from the crossroads brings us closer to Hashem and to those with whom we are cultivating our closeness, and which course distances us.

Being aware of our lives at the crossroads means that we can become aware of shifts in our choices of how we perceive life at any given moment. At one moment, we can undergo a sense of well-being and security, and the next moment, insecurity and emotional despair. We may look at our partner and feel a sense of trust and closeness, and just hours later feel disinterested and distant.

Where do these shifting thoughts, feelings and sensations come from? They may be coming from many possible external or internal sources. Perhaps we can say they come from our daily pressures of work, our memories of past events from earlier life experiences or challenges that we are facing in our relationships, or any other significant area of our lives.

◇ **A Story of Entrapment and Freedom**

> I met a young woman, Andrea, who had been dating unsuccessfully for many years. During one of our meetings, she confided that the home she grew up in was very dysfunctional; she felt she would carry the scars of these relationships wherever she'd go in life.

One incident she shared occurred when she was five or six as she was jumping rope. She missed a jump and fell on her face. As she lay on the ground in tears, she put her hand to her face to discover she was bleeding from her mouth and cheek. She noticed that her mother had been watching the entire incident. In her panic, she began running toward her mother, who stopped her short with a stern warning of, "Don't come near me. Just get into the house and wash up." She cried as she told me the story and then admitted, "How can I ever trust anyone after being exposed to this throughout my childhood?" My position was that we are never locked into our past. Hashem always gives us opportunities to discover our wings and soar.

A few months after our session, Andrea was introduced to Mark. He was a gentle and very kind young man who had grown up without a father. Mark had also suffered in his dating, as many of the girls viewed him as "nerdy." In truth, because of the challenges of his younger years without a father, he had developed acute sensitivities for the feelings of others. Because of his unsuccessful dating of other young women, he began to feel hopeless.

When he and Andrea began to know each other, they connected in a deep and very meaningful way. Neither had ever believed it was possible to discover another individual who could soothe the hurt feelings and insecurities of the past. Today, the couple is raising a family, and learning to appreciate Hashem's gifts of life that were missing in their younger years.

Bitachon is the awareness for Andrea — and certainly for Mark — that their challenges are not strange and unknown to Hashem. The events in their lives have unfolded to bring them to this crossroads. Each has a different challenge. For Mark, it's the challenge of using his sensitivities to care for another. And for Andrea, it is learning to trust that someone could deeply care for her.

Each of us stands at these crossroads between our two states of mind of *menuchas hanefesh* and *pizur hanefesh* at every moment. We are brought to this place by our upbringing, our life experiences, our biology and our hard-wiring. And we are always challenged to emerge from the crossroads with a greater understanding of Hashem's will and our own latent strength to fulfill this will.

Eating the Bread of Embarrassment

"Why do we have to be challenged throughout our lives?" This is a question many have asked me. The answer, as I have come to understand it, is that each of us is given a *neshamah* that accompanies us throughout our lives. Each morning, we thank Hashem for this gift. And while our physical selves are mortal and finite, our souls are immortal and infinite. Eventually, after 120 years, our *neshamah* will leave our bodies and will stand face-to-face with Hashem. At that time, Hashem will want to give us many rewards because of His love for each of us. But we need to feel that we deserve this love.

> Imagine that a friend asked you to accept an award for an organization that he was running, and you agreed. Now imagine further how, at the award ceremony, he spoke of your dedication to his organization — but you knew that his accolades were not based on fact. You had done very little for this organization, and felt truly embarrassed. Had you done something to deserve the award, you would have felt much more comfortable with the praise.

Chazal tell us that it's the same way with our life challenges. Hashem has a deep love for each of us and wants to bestow this love on us. However, we need to feel that we deserve it;

otherwise, it is what Chazal call "the bread of embarrassment." We need to know that we worked hard to deserve this love. And this is why we are always at the crossroads. We are accumulating the experiences to be able to say to Hashem, "I acknowledge my own struggles to deserve Your love."

Therefore, each moment when we realize that we are at the crossroads, we come to understand that Hashem has actually placed us in this position. We are placed in this challenging moment so we can transform *pizur hanefesh* to *menuchas hanefesh* and gain an additional gem in our crown of pride and accomplishment that made our journey in this world worthwhile. These are events that occur in the here-and-now, but their impact resonates for all eternity.

THE THIRD PRINCIPLE: Mind as *Mishkan*

Let's do a brief review. There are three steps in the process I have been describing. The first is realizing that we are in a troubled state of mind that is threatening our most precious relationship. This opens up our vistas and informs us that we are not imprisoned in our *pizur hanefesh*. The second step is our awareness that we are standing at the crossroads between the two states and that there are other, more productive ways to experience our relationship. And the third step is to navigate our state of mind in a direction that can heal the wounds and bridge the gaps in our relationship.

To move toward this choice, we need to sensitize the internal compass that points us in the right direction. And the direction we will be following is the *Shechinah* — the Presence of Hashem in our lives. By defining the states of mind with which the *Shechinah* can be compatible, we are also defining the states of mind that are compatible with *menuchas hanefesh* and relationship building. And since the *Shechinah* rests within the *Mishkan*, we can appreciate how the third step in this process is cultivating the value of Mind as *Mishkan*.

Before I describe the process of how we learn to cultivate this concept of Mind as *Mishkan*, I would like to describe a young man who came to see me.

> Yisrael was a young doctor who had been brought up in a home without his father, who died when he was ten. He vividly remembered his feelings of hurt and loss when his father died. The feelings returned to him when he observed other boys in shul or school together with their fathers.
>
> As he dated, he realized that each time he felt close to someone, he was overwhelmed by a feeling of "I'm afraid that a terrible event will deprive me of marrying this person." And over the years, this fear was responsible for sabotaging many promising relationships. He realized that he continued to harbor the same troubled state of mind, but his hurt and fear were always directed toward the person he was dating. He viewed himself as trapped in an emotional darkness, and believed he would never experience the light of healthy feelings toward anyone.

Yisrael had become aware that he was stuck in the same fear of loss that had pervaded his childhood. Yet, to take the next step toward relationship building, he needed to believe he possessed an internal compass that could guide him toward a healthier state of mind and relationship with a woman who could become his wife.

His sense of deprivation had caused Yisrael to feel that life had offered him no real opportunity to grow. Yet through learning to focus on the concept of *Mishkan* through a guided walking meditation, he learned that he possessed the internal strengths to overcome this fear and was able to cultivate a relationship with the woman he married.

◇ **My Reflections at the Kosel**

As an introduction to how the concepts of *Mishkan* and *Shechinah* play such a crucial role in our internal compass, I would like to share some personal reflections and observations about the Kosel, from a recent trip.

> As I approached the plaza and saw the mosque standing where the *Bais Hamikdash* once stood, I tore my shirt, thereby fulfilling this special mitzvah of mourning, just as we have done at this site for over 2,000 years.
>
> The July sun intensified the whiteness of the Kosel's immense stones. Approaching the Wall, I observed throngs of visitors drawn, as if by a magnet, to feel a spiritual presence that exists nowhere else in the world. It's difficult to articulate exactly what this presence is. Nonetheless, most people who have been there will testify that "something extraordinary happens" at the Kosel.
>
> As I davened Minchah, I sensed I was standing closer to the living Presence of Hashem — the *Shechinah* — than was possible in perhaps any place else on earth. I experienced Hashem's nearness in the profound clarity of each word of prayer I uttered. The act of praying here in this place, coupled with my prayers themselves, evoked within me a sense of the possibility of being a deeply spiritual — *ruchani* — individual. This is a feeling experienced by so many in this spot.

I have many memories of the Kosel, but the one that stands out actually took place away from the site.

> A number of years ago, when I was traveling from Eretz Yisrael to America, I sat next to a software developer who was busily writing programs on the plane. For the first few hours, no words were exchanged between us. After a while, he finally closed his computer and we spoke.

Jim hailed from California, where he lived in a beach house on the Pacific coast, and was now returning from his first visit to Eretz Yisrael. I asked him how he had enjoyed himself. "Well, I really enjoyed the nightlife in Tel Aviv!" he replied enthusiastically, obviously referring to everything that Hashem does not wish Eretz Yisrael to be. Still, I understood that his superficial view of Eretz Yisrael was tied to his beach house/bachelor lifestyle. Yet I also believed that somewhere within his memory of Eretz Yisrael was a deeper, more spiritual and meaningful impression.

I asked him if he had been to Yerushalayim. He courteously told me he had visited the Wall and the Old City. However, while his parents are Jewish, he explained, he had never had any religious education, so these sites meant little to him.

It struck me as strange that someone could visit Yerushalayim and the Kosel without a memorable moment to share. But as we continued our conversation, Jim's attitude began to change. The more I asked him about his first impressions of the Wall and the Old City, the more his memories brought him back to the experience. He now seemed more willing – even eager – to share what had happened. It was almost as if he had a deeply moving experience at the Kosel that had been forgotten and was now being remembered. It's somewhat similar to a dream that we can't seem to remember, until an association is made – and suddenly it reappears in our memory. In the same way, he was now remembering with great excitement what had occurred within him.

It only took a few minutes before he began to describe a deeply moving memory of seeing the Kosel for the first time and approaching it with great reverence. He could remember getting close to the Wall and uttering prayers to a G-d that he had never felt existed before that moment. Then he shared with me what he had prayed for – that he would be able to find a Jewish woman with whom to share his life.

I gazed at him in amazement. One minute, all he could remember was the Tel Aviv nightlife, and he had no recollection of Yerushalayim at all. The next moment, he divulged a personal experience that transcended his present life of living in a beach house, pursuing women and enjoying the nightlife of a foreign country. Somehow, just being at the Kosel evoked his deeper thoughts and aspirations about belonging to Am Yisrael and bringing a Jewish woman into his life.

Before that moment, Jim told me, he had never understood why he should marry a Jewish woman. Suddenly, and without any rational explanation, it made clear and profound sense to him. Obviously, "something" had called out to him and had touched his uneducated, yet receptive, Jewish soul unlike anything before in his life.

I'm sorry to say that I did not pursue a relationship with Jim. Yet, this and countless other personal experiences that we have all had cause us to ask, "From where does the Kosel receive its immense spiritual power?"

We all understand the answer. The Kosel stands on the *Har Habayis* (the Temple Mount) — the center of the universe. It is on that specific place that Hashem has chosen to rest His *Shechinah*. When we are in its proximity, we can sense its Divine and holy beauty.

This is where Avraham Avinu brought his son Yitzchak to the *Akeidah* (the Binding); where Yaakov Avinu laid his head and in his dream envisioned the Presence of Hashem atop the ladder; and it is the place that Dovid Hamelech purchased as the site of the *Bais Hamikdash*. The vessels of the *Mishkan* found their ultimate home in the *Bais Hamikdash*, which was eventually built by his son Shlomo Hamelech, and then rebuilt under Herod. Today's Kosel represents the sparse remains of the Second Temple.

Moshe was commanded to make a holy place for Hashem, and He would dwell among His People. The vessels that were contained in the *Bais Hamikdash* were fashioned in the desert and were contained in the *Mishkan*, which Moshe Rabbeinu had constructed before B'nei Yisrael entered Eretz Yisrael. We read about this in the weekly Torah portion of *Parashas Terumah* (*Shemos* 25:8), "V'asu Li Mikdash v'shachanti b'socham — they shall make a Sanctuary for Me, and I will dwell among them."

The *Mishkan* was a fitting place for the *Shechinah* to rest, as its sacred beauty was unique. It was filled with wondrously beautiful vessels crafted from precious metals. Its fabrics were colored using rare dyes. Intoxicating aromas of incense wafted through its space and beyond. And the enchantment of the song of *Leviim* (Levites) filled the air. This was the daily ebb and flow of spiritual life that was the *Mishkan*. And all this was accompanied by the offering of sacrifices and the ever-burning light of the Menorah. There was no other place in the world fitting enough for us to experience the Presence of Hashem as the *Mishkan*.

◇ The Whisper of the *Shechinah*

Clearly, our state of inspiration at the Kosel today is distant from even a faint whisper of what it was when the *Bais Hamikdash* was standing. But even today, close to 3,500 years after the building of the *Mishkan* in the desert, just the sight of the stones and the throngs who come to soak in the Kosel's *ruchnius* (spirituality) is so deeply inspiring. The mere spectacle opens our hearts to realize that Hashem has placed this power of beauty and *kedushah* in our world that elevates our lives. Merely standing at the Kosel gives our lives clarity, focus and an awareness that is unavailable anywhere else on earth. Through the spiritual presence of the Kosel, we can feel a sense of connection to the precious and infinite gift of life that Hashem gives us all.

I have come to understand when I am near the Kosel that even this faint whisper of the *Shechinah* is transforming. And each experience of transformation brings us a small step closer to being the individual Hashem has wanted us to become, ever since we opened our eyes to the world around us. At the Kosel we are all equal. Standing near these holy stones, we no longer carry the illusion that we are defined by our possessions, the size of our house, the make of our car, the label on our clothing or our place on the dais. Here we realize life's true value when we permit the power of the *Shechinah* to permeate our consciousness. At this holy site, even a beach dweller without a moment of Jewish education can sense a yearning deep within himself for a life partner who will permit him to attach himself to this place forever.

Along with this understanding about life, we also become aware of our human vulnerability. We can appreciate the meaning of our relationships with the people who share our lives. We realize how deeply we need human love and caring. We understand that life's true treasures reside in our capability to receive and give love. This is why the crevices of the Kosel are filled with tiny notes with prayers for *shalom bayis*, health and finding *shidduchim*.

Taking leave of the Kosel is never without a deep sense of loss. I notice how many visitors walk backward in respect, maintaining visual contact, perhaps as an expression of their wish to maintain their feeling of connection. It is as if prolonging the sight will allow them to fully incorporate its treasure into their everyday lives. It is here, at this Wall, that each of us is able to experience some sense of the *Shechinah*. And because of it, we are able to experience our deeper and truer selves.

◇ **The *Mishkan* of Our Lives**

I have shared these thoughts because they introduce us to the third principle, that of Mind as *Mishkan*. When are we truly our "selves"? We are only our real selves when we are aware of Hashem's Presence in our lives. This is how we were intended to live. The entirety of our lives is intended to be a *Mishkan* — a resting place for Hashem's Presence — whether we are in Yerushalayim, New York, Toronto or Los Angeles. Anywhere we are, and at each stage in our moment-to-moment experience of life, Hashem has given us a mind and a *neshamah* to emulate the *middos* that approximate the beauty of *Mishkan*. And our awareness of this potential within us is transforming, just as praying at the Kosel is transforming.

Hashem has placed countless opportunities for the *Mishkan* and *Shechinah* to reside in our lives. And each of these opportunities helps us experience the true depth of who we are.

First, there is the dimension of prayer. We recite the Shemoneh Esrei at least three times daily. Each time we daven Shemoneh Esrei, we enter the domain of the *Shechinah*. When we begin, we take three steps to prepare ourselves to enter Its domain; when we end, we take leave of Hashem's Presence by stepping backward. Perhaps this is why Rav Kook, *zt"l*, the late chief rabbi of Eretz Yisrael, said that whenever he davened Shemoneh Esrei, he always saw the Kosel in front of him.

Another area of our lives where the *Shechinah* is present is in Shabbos. In shul on Friday night, we greet the *Shechinah* when we sing *Lechah Dodi* ("Come, my friend, let us greet the bride"). Throughout the twenty-five hours of Shabbos, we cultivate this relationship to the *Shechinah* through our dress, eating, pace of life, family experiences, Torah learning, davening and achieving a state of *menuchah*. Through the Shabbos, we become a suitable place for Hashem to rest His Presence.

The *Shechinah* yearns to reside within our relationships, through the ongoing experience of trust and caring. Where does Hashem find it suitable to permit His *Shechinah* to dwell? In this relationship that is growing between a man and woman.

> There is a wonderful and well-known story about Rav Shlomo Zalman Auerbach, *zt"l*, who, while walking home, paused to straighten out his clothing and smooth his beard. When asked the purpose of his behavior, his response was that he was going home to his wife. Since there was *shalom* (peace) between him and his wife, the *Shechinah* rested there. Thus, he was going to greet the *Shechinah*. This same *gadol* stated publicly, at his wife's funeral, that it is customary to ask for *mechilah* (forgiveness) from the deceased for anything hurtful he may have done to her over the many years of their marriage. But he was not aware of a single moment when he did not treat her with respect and kindness. This is the essence of a relationship where the *Shechinah* dwells.

All these experiences of our lives permit the *Shechinah* to reside near or within us. However, perhaps there is one dimension that encompasses all of these, and without it, the others are not possible. It is in our state of mind. Without a suitable state of mind, our connection to Hashem's Presence would not be possible.

◇ Where the *Shechinah* Rests

The *Gemara* in Shabbos says that the *Shechinah* never rests in a place of sadness. It only rests in a place suffused with the joy of the ongoing *mitzvos* of our lives. This means that we need to be in a positive and secure state of mind for the *Shechinah* to reside within us. Using the familiar example of the glass of water, when the glass seems half full and we are grateful to Hashem for all of life's gifts, our mind is a resting place for the *Shechinah*.

But when the glass seems half empty, even when the quantity is unchanged, we have lost our opportunity to be a resting place for the *Shechinah*.

It is not as if I really have a choice in the perception. When one state of mind brings me closer to who Hashem wants me to be and how He wants me to perceive the world, then I am actually being myself. And when I enter a negative state of mind that distances me from Hashem and myself, I no longer serve as a vessel for His Presence.

This is why I call the third principle Mind as *Mishkan*. It is based on our awareness that we are all created to experience thoughts, feelings and an experience of life that enable us to achieve our own human potential as individuals and to share a close and caring relationship.

◇ The Rambam and the *Shechinah*

This concept of Mind as *Mishkan* took on even greater clarity as I read the thoughts of the Mashgiach of Mir, Rav Yeruchem Levovitz, *zt"l*, in his *sefer*, *Daas Torah*, which deepens our appreciation of the meaning of the *Mishkan* in our lives. He cites the Rambam's view that all the vessels of the *Mishkan* were designed to serve as metaphors for each of us. For example, the spreading of wings of the angelic figures, the *Keruvim*, above the *Aron Hakodesh*, served to bring life-giving *kedushah* from the Heavens into our world. The Rambam sees this spreading of the wings as a metaphor for the manner in which we breathe, where the opening and closing of the chest cavity brings life-giving air into our bodies. Just as the *Keruvim* used their wings to bring life into the world through their wings, so, too, do our lungs bring life-giving air into our bodies.

Another sacred vessel was the *Aron Hakodesh* — the Ark containing the Tablets of the Ten Commandments, as well as the Torah itself. The Rambam explains that the Tablets and the Torah represent the heart of the Jewish people, and are concealed within the Ark, like the heart of man, which is concealed within the chest cavity.

The Menorah, which illuminated the *Mishkan*, represents wisdom and all human enlightenment, and contained seven branches. Here, too, the Rambam cites these seven branches as a symbol for our five senses, plus our powers of imagination and speech.

In each of these and other comparisons, Rav Yeruchem shares his understanding of Rambam's vision of how Hashem commands us to create a *Mishkan* that He will dwell in. By creating the vessels that are a metaphor for each of us, Hashem is telling us that just as He desires to dwell in the *Mishkan*, He desires that we recognize that we are all the embodiment of the *Mishkan* and it is an embodiment of us. As we learn that we can think, feel, see and live as the *Mishkan*, then we are being ourselves and fulfilling our purpose in life.

What is there about the *Mishkan* that causes it to be a suitable place for Hashem to reside? The *Mishkan* is where Hashem's love for us and all mankind is most evident. It is a place of peace and harmony. In the *Mishkan* and in the *Bais Hamikdash*, no metal tools were used to fashion the vessels contained within. In the *Mishkan*, the two golden *Keruvim*, which signified Heavenly beings, were placed on top of the *Aron*, the Ark, which contained the Ten Commandments. The position of the *Keruvim* signified Hashem's love for us. When Am Yisrael is united as one, they face each other lovingly. And when there is conflict among Hashem's People, they turn away from each other. The floor of the *Mishkan* is called *Ritzpas Ahavah* — the Floor of Love. The inner chambers of the *Mishkan* were filled with the beauty of song; the illumination of the Menorah; the aesthetic harmony of colors, textures and materials; and the sublime feelings and thoughts that permeated it.

◇ **The *Mishkan* in Our Lives**

The *Mishkan* is the paradigm of beauty, *kedushah*, closeness, pleasantness and clarity in human life. It represents the environment that brings us closer to our own natural beauty with which Hashem endowed us all, and our potential to share lives of love and closeness together. Our awareness of the *Mishkan* is our internal compass that directs and guides our deepest yearnings to be ourselves and share our lives in love and peace.

The Rambam and the Mashgiach are telling us that throughout our lives, we are all accountable to remember that each moment Hashem wants our state of mind to be an experience of exquisite and sublime beauty. Hashem desires that our thoughts and feelings and every aspect of our beings emulate the beauty of the *Mishkan*. And it is only when we experience this state of mind that we are truly ourselves. Remembering *Mishkan* as the paradigm for our state of mind means that we have a "gold standard" for defining how Hashem wishes us to experience life. In summary, being aware that Hashem created us to serve as a *Mishkan* empowers us to fulfill the purpose of our existence.

This doesn't mean that our lives are free of stress and distress. It means that we are created with a mandate to discover how to go through life from within the *Mishkan* even when our lives are challenged. For example, our sense of gratitude and *menuchas hanefesh* can pervade our lives even under the most difficult trials. When Rav Shimon Schwab, *zt"l*, lost the power of his legs in his later years and was confined to a wheelchair, he was asked what gave him the strength to maintain his sense of hopefulness and belief. His answer was that he had so much to be grateful to Hashem for, how could he even consider feeling upset over what was missing in his life? In marriage, as well, when we fall into a trap of feeling upset with our spouse, we have forgotten all the countless ways that our lives are intertwined that bring our lives a sense of stability and continuity.

There is an exercise I give dating couples called the Sharing Tree. It is composed of considering all the myriad of ways that our lives are connected at the roots. It has the power of reminding us to be aware of a sense of gratitude for all that we do and are for each other. This awareness of *hakaras hatov* is redolent with the aroma of the *Mishkan,* as are all other positive perceptions.

This third principle teaches us that regardless of what we are experiencing in life, Hashem desires that we cultivate a state of mind of mutual caring and trust that enables us to be a resting place for His *Shechinah.* Not only has He fashioned this yearning within us as native to our minds and hearts, He has also filled our lives with countless impressions and experiences that point us in this direction. The mere mention of *Mishkan* evokes our internal longing for beauty, delicate refinement, *kedushah* and the most gentle of human emotions that bring our lives together in love and closeness.

The practical implication for this principle is that when we remember that Hashem created our minds to be a *Mishkan,* we can now evaluate how our state of mind compares with the concept of Mind as *Mishkan.* We are contrasting our present thoughts, feelings and forms of behavior with the beauty and *kedushah* of *Mishkan,* because this is the only experience of life that is a fitting place for the *Shechinah* to reside.

◇ **The Interior Decorator**

Our striving to discover that state of mind that is compatible with the *middos,* thoughts and feelings of *Mishkan* is analogous to an interior designer in search of the ideal colors and textures that will blend well with a design pattern. The designer will bring swatches of fabrics and samples of materials into a showroom to determine the overall visual and aesthetic harmony of all the objects when they are brought together. In the same way, we are constantly "matching up" our present state of mind with *Mishkan,* which is the state of mind in which Hashem wishes us to be. This means that the *middos* of being patient, loving, empathic, gentle, understanding, giving and humble all enable us to be appropriate environments for Hashem's Presence. And this is what we are searching for.

Therefore, as we learn to monitor the shifting patterns of our state of mind, we learn to remind ourselves: "My responsibility in life is to remember that I can transform this thought, feeling or behavior from *pizur hanefesh* to *menuchas hanefesh* through remembering that Hashem has created my mind to be a *Mishkan.*" And this is the essence of the third principle. It uncovers a vast area of sublime human experience that we all have within us that points us in the direction of *Mishkan* and enables us to be who we truly are. When we can remember this third principle, we are empowered to recognize and distance ourselves from negative and even toxic states of hurt, anger, resentment and all the other states of mind that lock us in the quicksand of *pizur hanefesh.*

◇ Defining the Desired Achievements of *Mishkan*

Once we have defined *Mishkan* as the direction of *menuchas hanefesh,* we can define what we can achieve as a result of our freedom. This could include aspirations such as, "Hashem wants my mind to be a *Mishkan* ... so I can be a better dating partner, *chassan, kallah,* etc." Articulating these desired achievements signifies a broad and promising vision of the future, as opposed to the myopia and paralysis of *pizur hanefesh,* which we were caught up in before employing these principles.

REVIEWING THE THREE PRINCIPLES AND THEIR MEANING FOR TRANSFORMATION

At the heart of all transformation is an unshakable sense of *emunah* that along with the personal challenges that Hashem has placed in our lives, He has also given us the resources to keep on rediscovering the pathways that lead us toward *menuchas hanefesh* and shared trust and closeness. And among the many resources he has given us to achieve this, the three principles of *Chiddush*, *Tzomet* and *Mishkan* serve as our lighthouse, constantly guiding us back home to our deeper and truer selves. And when we understand this, the experience of *pizur hanefesh* is similar to driving on rumble strips that warn us when we begin veering off the highway. It's a signal to find the correct pathway to be re-inspired and reconnected.

The implication of these three principles in our lives is that we have mastery over our own destiny through learning to constantly transform ourselves. As we learn to return to these principles and use them as our compass in life, we discover inner strength and wisdom that we never realized exist within us.

With this in mind, I'd like to review the principles and embellish their meaning for each of us in our personal lives and relationships.

◇ **1. The First Principle is our awareness that Hashem creates us as new beings at every moment of our lives.**

When we are experiencing a state of *pizur hanefesh* through our thoughts, feelings, physiology, behavior or relationship, there is always a sense that not only is the negative perception true, but that it will never change. This first principle immediately rescues us from the entrapment of the negative perception. Once we are aware that we are receiving life at this very moment, we open our vistas of life and realize that we can free ourselves from the myopic, narrow and self-centered perception. We realize that there is a Hashem in the world, and that even our very consciousness, which is presently ensnared in the iron grip of *pizur hanefesh*, is actually being given life by Hashem.

It's a remarkable thought to realize that while we may feel resentful or are angry at the very person with whom we are attempting to build a relationship, Hashem is giving us the power of consciousness to be in this negative state of mind. And in the same way He gives us the power to be aware of our negative states, He also gives us the power to transform ourselves to a positive state. In essence, with this principle, we acknowledge that there is a power even greater than our anger, hurt, impatience, addiction or resentment. This is the power and domain of Hashem. And we express our awareness that all change comes only through Hashem, by expressing our desire to grow through articulating a *tefillah* in which we ask Hashem for His assistance in transforming our state of mind.

The *Chiddush Tefillah*:

This *tefillah* corresponds to the three principles we have learned and are recited together. However, we will learn each *tefillah* individually. You can express the *Chiddush* principle by saying:

> *"Hashem, You create me every moment and You don't want me to be in this state of pizur hanefesh."*

◇ ## 2. The Second Principle is our awareness that at every moment we are standing at the crossroads.

This principle informs us that regardless of the intensity of our state of mind, our troubled experience is only one path of a crossroad, and a second route exists at this very moment. We may not know what it is, but we accept that it was Hashem Who placed us here. And it is Hashem Who desires that we discover a portal into the other state of mind, which is *menuchas hanefesh* and shared trust.

The *Crossroads Tefillah*:

You can express the Crossroads principle by saying:

> *"Hashem, You have placed me at the crossroads between my expression of pizur hanefesh and menuchas hanefesh, and You want me to learn to transform myself."*

◇ ## 3. The Third Principle is that our mind was designed to be a *Mishkan*.

This third principle now provides us with a direction in life that we have internalized many times. Now we can match our present state with internalized thoughts, memories and feelings of the beauty and *kedushah* that is *Mishkan*. We don't even need to select a specific aspect of *Mishkan*. It can be very general and impressionistic. Even so, once we are able to artic- ulate this all-encompassing definition of how Hashem would like us to experience our lives, we can define the many expres- sions of this positive state of mind. In essence, we have pre- pared ourselves to receive a transforming gift of wisdom and insight from Hashem.

We can now wait securely and patiently for that transforming state of mind that is compatible with how Hashem has created us. It may be experienced through a clearer and more positive thought, a better feeling, a quieting of symptoms and urges or a feeling of closeness in our dating relationship. The possibilities for experiencing our capacity to experience *menuchas hanefesh* are endless, and they are available throughout our lives.

The *Mishkan Tefillah:*

You can express your *Mishkan* principle by saying:

> *"Hashem, You want my mind to be a Mishkan because it will help me be a better dating partner, chassan, kallah, etc."*

Finally: *Yegiah* — Transformations are the Discovery of a Gift

There is a final dynamic that enables transformation to occur. I do not include *Yegiah* in the principles as it does not need to be articulated. It is our realization that, like all else in life, transformation is a gift from Hashem. It is the reward for our belief that all our efforts are *l'sheim Shamayim* (for the sake of Heaven) — what Hashem views as our own inner preparation to be deserving of the gift of transformation. Throughout our lives, whether we are looking for a *shidduch*, earning a living wage or finding the beautiful *esrog*, we are required to make the effort. Yet, we must always realize that the results come only from Hashem. Success for our efforts is the gift. All else is an illusion.

This concept is even true when we are attempting to free ourselves from powerful and negative thoughts, overwhelming and disabling feelings, physiological states of anxiety or physical distress, a behavioral addiction or a relationship conflict. It is up to us to make the responsible effort, but it is only through Hashem's loving guidance that we can become familiar with new insights that are the key to our well-being and our maturing relationships.

The Sfas Emes Defines *Yegiah*

This experience of discovering new insights or our emerging sense of empowerment is explained so eloquently by the Sfas Emes, Rav Yehudah Aryeh Leib Alter of Ger, *zt"l*. The Rebbe uses the term *"yagata u'matzasa"* (you toiled and found; *Megillah* 6b) to define this process of discovery. In the Torah reading of *Terumah*, the Sfas Emes describes how Moshe Rabbeinu found that visualizing how the Menorah should look was beyond his human capabilities. But as a result of the depth of his desire to fulfill the commandments of Hashem, he was not only provided with a visual image of it, but Hashem Himself actually created the Menorah as a gift for Moshe and the *Mishkan*.

For us, this means that when we have invested our deepest possible human effort to achieve a lofty goal that exceeds our human limitations, Hashem rewards us with this *metziah* (discovery) as a gift for our efforts.

This is the concept of *yagata u'matzasa*. It is unlike anything we have otherwise come to understand in our acquired concept of how we achieve results in our lives. Whether our strivings are to build the Menorah for the *Mishkan*, to achieve freedom from a troubled state of mind or to transform a relationship conflict into caring and trust, the reality is that, on our own, we are helpless to transcend our limited dimension of self. However, through deep and noble yearning and striving, we are able to receive this gift directly from Hashem. This is why Chazal use the word *"matzasa*, you found."

A *metziah* is something that was found. We are surprised to find the money that suddenly appears in front of us lying in the street. A moment ago it was not there. We had no previous relationship to it. Now it's there and it's ours. In the same way, Hashem suddenly sends us the *metziah* of transformed thoughts, feelings, inner strengths and perceptions that continuously bring two lives closer together. These "discoveries" are loving gifts from Hashem.

CHAPTER VII
Acquiring the Tools of Transformation

◇ *"Mayim Amukim Eitzah B'lev Ish"* —
The Treasure Beneath the Surface

Countless discoveries in human history have led to a new paradigm for understanding the world we live in — from the journeys of Columbus to the calculations of Einstein. However, one of life's great discoveries is available to us at all times. It is the ongoing gift of *Chiddush* that occurs each time we discover that we are never the bird who loses its ability to fly. In each moment, Hashem gives us the gift of wings. In *shidduchim*, dating and engagement, we become aware of this power of discovery as we learn to transcend the seeming limitations of the moment, escape the quicksand of *pizur hanefesh* and feel the clarity of *menuchas hanefesh*. Transforming our state of mind to *menuchas hanefesh* is the single most important dynamic that makes it possible for every dating couple to continue cultivating their relationship, and each *chassan* and *kallah* to walk together toward their *chupah* and toward building a *bayis ne'eman b'Yisrael*.

The potential to experience insight and inspiration is always present within us, even at those moments when we feel a sense of abject hopelessness and powerlessness. Our power to receive these gifts from Hashem is always there. We need to know how to access them. We may not always be aware of our choices, because the wisdom and clarity that comes with *menuchas hanefesh* reside deep within us. This treasure never sits on the surface. Like the water at the bottom of the well waiting for the wily fox to bring it to the surface, the insight is always there, waiting to be grasped and understood. Our task is to know how to retrieve it.

Water is an apt metaphor for this wisdom. Shlomo Hamelech teaches in *Mishlei* (20:5): *"Mayim amukim eitzah b'lev ish, v'ish t'vunah yidlenah — Counsel in a man's heart is like deep water, but a man of understanding will draw it out."* The Malbim, a noted nineteenth-century *talmid chacham* who wrote a commentary on the entire *Tanach*, explained the meaning of this verse. He wrote that there are deep waters within us containing great wisdom and insight, but to gain access to our own potential, we need to draw this wisdom from the depths of our mind, as if by a pail tied to a long rope. The wisdom that helps us emerge from our entrapment is always waiting within us to emerge to the surface. We need to know how to free up these treasures that Hashem always wants to give us.

When an insight suddenly illuminates our thoughts, it has the effect of a lightbulb being switched on in a dark room. Such an "aha!" moment can occur while dealing with a personal problem, pondering a decision, seeking to understand a difficult Torah concept or facing any of life's countless other daily challenges. The answer that had been so elusive earlier is suddenly right there, shimmering with crystal clarity.

> Yisrael had been dating Sarah. He had been in shidduchim for about three years. This was the first girl he truly felt he could marry. Yet every time he was close to proposing, he took a close look at Sarah and asked himself, "Am I really attracted to her? What will happen after the wedding and I no longer find her attractive?" Just asking the

question always seemed to create a sense of uncertainty, and with it, anxiety.

As he learned to focus on a quieter and calmer state of mind, closer to *menuchas hanefesh*, he then said, "I get it. When I'm in doubt, she actually loses her attractiveness because I'm seeing her from a troubled state of mind. And when I'm in *menuchas hanefesh*, she actually looks prettier." For Yisrael, this was a great discovery, for now he understood that Sarah's attractiveness was more a function of his state of mind than an objective reality. He finally grasped that his negative perception of her appearance would pass, and he would be able to see her as the same sweet and lovely person he knew her to be. Once this clarity was in place, he was able to propose to her.

Once his "light" went on, his path was crystal clear. Until then, he had been gripped by uncertainty and anxiety that had distorted his perception. Now he had a clearer understanding that had been unavailable to him in the past. The wisdom was always there; he just needed the time to regain that sense of clarity and gain access to his "deeper counsel."

◇ Learning the Skills to Go Deeper

Entering the state of *menuchas hanefesh* occurs through gaining access to our *"mayim amukim,"* the deep waters of counsel and wisdom. This is how Hashem has created us. This deeper wisdom is a guiding voice from within that constantly attempts to direct our lives toward the fulfillment of who we truly are. Just as the *neshamah* regulates our immune system, which maintains the delicate balance of our physiological well-being, it also grasps the deeper truth inherent in each moment of our lives and attempts to have its thoughtful and wise counsel heard and understood.

Our capacity to make wise decisions and gain insights is

never available to us on a superficial level and without efforts. The guiding principles of many of the tools we will be learning are based on understanding how to permit this deeper, wiser voice of our *neshamah* to once again be heard. Once we can recognize the guidance emanating from our *mayim amukim*, we can then become suitable vessels to receive the gift of *menuchas hanefesh*.

Thus, the approaches and exercises in this section help us gain access to our *mayim amukim* in order to achieve the following goals:

1. Let go of troubled thoughts and feelings that entrap us in *pizur hanefesh*.

2. Ease stress and anxiety that lead to relationship conflict and personal insecurity.

3. Learn to tap into a deeper wisdom and insight that Hashem has placed within each of us.

4. Modify *pizur hanefesh* forms of behavior that destroy dating relationships and engagements, and replace them with behaviors that bring two lives together.

5. Reawaken deeper emotional connections that have already been developed within a relationship.

With these goals in mind, we can now proceed to learn the skills of transformation.

◇ Transforming Thoughts and Feelings

In dating and engagement, it's so easy to slip into negative thoughts and feelings.

> Chani is engaged to Yehoshua and their wedding is just two weeks away. To Chani, Yehoshua is the most special boy she ever met. No one ever spoke to her before with such sincerity and caring. Her parents love him, as well

as her siblings. Yet as the wedding approaches, she finds herself looking at other couples and comparing herself to them.

"First, I look at other couples and they seem so much happier together. I know he is so special, but I always wanted an outgoing husband, and there are times when he is so quiet. Then I look at the clothing he wears. He tries to look neat, but his pants always seem to look baggy. I look at other *chassanim* and my brother's friends and they look so put-together and sharp."

Chani is conflicted. On the one hand, her *menuchas hanefesh* permits her to appreciate the exceptional qualities that she has observed in Yehoshua. At these moments, she appreciates that he possesses all the qualities that will make her feel like a cared for and deeply loved wife. However, when she finds herself sliding into her *pizur hanefesh*, she sees Yehoshua from a very superficial perspective. His baggy pants, ten-year-old car and nerdy shoes make her feel that she is being cheated out of life's most special rewards. If I were to speak to her *pizur hanefesh* side and say to her, "But look at all his *middos*," her response would be, "Don't I deserve to have a sharp, with-it and outgoing *chassan*?"

There are times when Chani, or others like her, will actually tell Yehoshua, "Can I be honest about the way I feel?" She would then go on to share her *pizur hanefesh* feelings — only to discover that Yehoshua is deeply hurt and the damage can't be repaired so easily.

One couple came to see me three years after their wedding. Just a week before their wedding, Manny had told Cheryl that he wanted to be honest and share with her something that was bothering him. He then told her that he did not feel attracted to her. Cheryl was mortified. "It was like a dagger in my heart," she told me, three years later. And that feeling never left her.

✦ ✦ ✦

> Simcha and Karen were almost engaged. However, Simcha was having obsessive thoughts about old dating partners, so he shared his thoughts with Karen. She broke out in tears and left the car. Simcha called me. "What did I say? I was only trying to be honest!"

In truth, in all our *pizur hanefesh* moments, we are convinced we are doing the right thing. "I'm only trying to be honest. Shouldn't I share what's on my mind?" The answer is: You can share what's on your *menuchas hanefesh* mind. You should never share what's on your *pizur hanefesh* mind.

◇ The Ski Slope

When we are in this *pizur hanefesh* mindset, we are on a very slippery slope, where something can be said or done that will change the course of a relationship forever. One moment the air is quiet and calm, and then someone says or does something that triggers an unexpected sequence of events that causes the relationship to spiral downward in the blink of an eye.

This lightning-speed process of the downward spiral reminds me of a story shared by a close friend describing a scene he had witnessed on the Swiss Alps many years ago.

> A father was enjoying the adventure of watching his young son run down the snowy foothills of the Alps. The proud father placed his child on a gentle and seemingly safe slope and encouraged him to run down. The boy would start running, fall and roll in the snow. The father and the son would then laugh and start all over again. The father repeated this playful game a number of times until the boy felt more confident as he ran down the snowy slope.
>
> The next time the boy started running, he was able to keep his balance. The snow and the hills were now his

friends. He made his way down the slope again, this time with greater speed and glee. The boy was mastering the art of running down a snowy hill, and he and his father laughed triumphantly. But the father's laugh was suddenly cut short and replaced with shock, fear and panic; his son had become so proficient that he was running downhill at a speed far greater than either had anticipated. At this rate, the child would pass the father in a few seconds and continue to build up speed as he headed toward a precipice perhaps two or three hundred feet below them! The man had failed to judge what would happen if his son learned to keep his balance while running at full speed. The father's laughter turned into an ear-piercing scream as he realized that with every passing nanosecond, his son's life was closer to slipping away.

The desperate father lunged headfirst toward his son, tripping the child as he was about to pass by. His fingers barely touched the boy's legs, but it was just enough to upset the child's delicate balance and send him tumbling harmlessly off to the side. Father and son were both crying — each for very different reasons.

Here, a father and son were enjoying the moment, surrounded by the breathtaking peaks of the Alps. An idyllic scene was suddenly transformed into a nightmare when the boy was helplessly pulled by a downward spiral toward a precipice. How long did it take for the father's laughter to turn into a scream of pain and torture? Did it take a second, or just a nanosecond?

I ask the question not because there is an answer, but because I want to create an awareness of how long it takes for a statement to be made between dating partners or a *chassan* or *kallah*. It occurs in an instant, even faster than a child running helplessly down a slope. It's faster because the child is running, pulled by the physical gravity, while with a couple, all we need is a gesture of the hand, a word, a reference to an event — and then suddenly not one, but two, individuals are racing downhill toward the precipice. They push and pull and provoke each other to build up breakneck speed, faster than the ear or eye can detect. And it's all because when negative thoughts and feelings emerge from *pizur hanefesh*, they take on a destructive power that accepts no limitations.

What We Learn from Monkeys

Why did Simcha have to blurt out his thoughts about previous dating partners? He would say, "I couldn't help it. I was just trying to be honest." It is so difficult for couples to let go and break away from these thoughts and feelings. Just as there are forces of nature propelling the child toward the precipice, there are also natural forces within each of us that drive us toward conflict, even if it is in no one's best interest.

> In his classic book on therapeutic communication, *The Language of Change*, Paul Watzlawick describes how members of a tribe in Africa capture a live monkey. They place a banana into a wicker basket that is attached to a tree. The top of the basket is large enough to accommodate the open hand of a monkey, so it can place its hand in the basket to grab the banana. However, the opening is not large enough to permit the closed fist of the monkey to be pulled out of the basket while holding the banana. When the monkey grabs the banana, the hunter knows that no force on earth will make that monkey willingly let go of its prize. The helpless animal will now be trapped by its own determinedly closed fist, unable to let go for even a moment. Losing its freedom and probably its life is a steep price for a monkey to pay for holding on to a banana.

There are many individuals who simply can't let go. I have lost track of the number of times I've heard a dating partner or *chassan* or *kallah* admit, "I knew I shouldn't have said that," or "I know it's killing our relationship, but I can't help myself." And along with these negative thoughts and feelings comes the inevitable perception, "It feels almost impossible to let go." In reality, the question I hope couples will ask is, "How can I let go of the banana?" In my own work with dating and engaged couples, I have met individuals who have held tight to their bananas for decades and just can't let go.

We see this in particular with men who have been dating for years; as they grow older, they still insist that the girl of their dreams is just as young, pretty and fertile as when they first started dating. To many of us, there seems to be an element of absurdity to their expectations. But when you are holding on to that banana with a clenched fist, it seems quite natural.

◇ E.A.T.

How do we begin to let go of the banana? How do we learn that we have the strength and power to change? I use the acronym "E.A.T." to describe three steps in the transformation process.

E is for Experience: We experience the negative thought, feeling, physiological sensation or the quality of our connection toward our dating partner, *chassan* or *kallah*.

A is for Awareness: We become aware that our thoughts, feelings, physiology, behavior and relationship experience are in conflict with the state of mind that Hashem has intended to bring us closer to each other.

T is for Transformation: We become aware that we are not entrapped and can employ specific thoughts, perspectives and behaviors to transform our present state.

We can now take a close look at the tools that can be helpful toward transforming a person's state of mind and lifestyle in a way that is aligned and in synchronization with the *retzon Hashem* (the will of Hashem).

TOOLS FOR TRANSFORMATION

TRANSFORMATION TOOL #1:
Using the Three Principles

The first and most important of all the tools you will learn in this program is to integrate the three principles of *Chiddush, Tzomet* and *Mishkan* into your moment-to-moment experience of life.

◇ **Internalizing the Three Principles**

First, be aware of the negative thoughts or feelings that are constantly flowing through your consciousness and realize that you have the ability to transform your state of mind. It's so crucial to understand that nothing justifies these feelings. Even if something was said or done that causes you to feel you cannot continue with the relationship, the first step is to realize that you do have the ability to quiet your state of mind by utilizing the three principles.

If you are a young woman and you look at the person you have been dating for a month and view him as a "failure," be aware that these thoughts and feelings are expressions of *pizur hanefesh* and will only keep you isolated and apart. Just because you think or feel this way does not make it the undisputed "reality." We need to assess whether these thoughts are bringing us closer to the state of mind that Hashem has created us to experience — or further away. Only then, after we have quieted our minds, can we assess the validity of these perceptions.

Let's look at some of these possible thoughts and feelings:

+ You look at your dating partner or *chassan/kallah* and

notice there is something a bit off with a mannerism, the use of a word (non-offensive), a gesture, etc. You say to yourself, "This really gets me nervous. I'm ending this relationship."

+ You are in a public gathering and see someone else's date or *chassan/kallah*. You think, "This is the kind of partner I deserve."

+ You are waiting to meet and your partner is late. You say, "If I have to put up with this for the rest of my life, this is not for me."

+ You feel your partner is a failure.

+ You find your partner unattractive.

+ You feel your partner is insensitive.

+ You think your partner is unintelligent.

+ You are concerned that your partner is not *frum* enough, or too *frum*.

I could write a list that would fill volumes ....

Even if a panel of blue-ribbon judges agrees with you, there is no objective reality that can determine your state of mind. This is your domain and responsibility; your state of mind only exacerbates and feeds the problem. While it may very well be that your partner is challenged in a particular area, your state of mind locks you into *pizur hanefesh* and it will drive you away from the relationship. In *pizur hanefesh*, all the moments you may have shared together when you felt comfortable seemed to have never occurred. All you have are the troubled thoughts in this troubled moment. It seems as if the perception has become an indisputable reality. Here the role of the *pizur hanefesh* state is to cause you to remain alone and to believe that your troubling thoughts are your only option.

The first step is to realize that regardless of the validity of your feelings, your thoughts and feelings are steeped in the quicksand of *pizur hanefesh*. Your first goal is to rebalance yourself and rediscover your *menuchas hanefesh*. Deciding that this is your direction is the most important decision you can make. Once you make it, you will discover solutions to the perceived problem. Once you understand that your primary problem is with your state of mind, you can begin to use the principles of *Chiddush*, *Tzomet* and *Mishkan* to be open to meaningful solutions. This does not mean that you can marry anyone you date. That was a reality in earlier generations. It does mean that you will be able to make decisions that will determine your future from a more reliable, stable and insightful perspective.

To prepare you for using this tool, I suggest you spend a few moments learning to internalize these three principles by focusing on the four concepts and also repeating the appropriate *tefillah* for each principle:

1. Chiddush

To start with, be aware and accepting of the reality that your very existence is the result of being given life every moment by a loving and nurturing power that emanates from Hashem. This life-giving energy imbues every cell of your body with the power to think, feel, behave and perform every physical function required to exist, thrive and be free to fulfill your potential.

2. Tzomet

The next step is to realize that Hashem has placed you at these crossroads. While you are presently experiencing *pizur hanefesh*, where your thoughts and feelings are troubled, there is also another dimension to your self, which can be felt as *menuchas hanefesh*. Regardless of the reasons, Hashem wants you to transform yourself.

3. Mishkan

The third step is to be aware that the only way you can select which direction Hashem wishes you to take in the crossroads is by learning to access a state of mind that is similar to the beauty and clarity of the *Mishkan*. Hashem desires that your state of mind be a resting place for His Presence — the *Shechinah*.

Yegiah

Finally, realize that once you have invested your best efforts, your *yegiah*, Hashem will provide you with the insight that you deserve and require — the *metziah*. For with each new insight, we are discovering Hashem's ongoing love for us, which is the *metziah*. All we needed to do was to make the effort, the *yegiah*.

After following these steps, you can begin to be aware that Hashem always leaves you with a key to discover new possibilities and pathways to transformation. They emerge as deciding to take a needed time-out; reframing a perception in a more positive light; engaging in a meditation to reduce stress and become more tolerant and patient; taking a walk; opening a *sefer*; and many other options and insights that are always available to you.

Once we learn to use these three principles, they will help us become more attuned to living in that state that Hashem desires for us. As we create appropriate states of mind that invite the *Shechinah* into our lives and homes, we also come in contact with the revitalization of our healthy thoughts and feelings for each other. So, whenever your thoughts and feelings bring you to a negative place, using these principles will enable you to discover your *mayim amukim*, those deeper insights and feelings that enable you to quiet your mind and bring about new possibilities in your dating relationship or engagement.

◇ The *Tefillos* for Transformation

Now that we have covered the principles of transformation, we can put the three *tefillos* together in the proper sequence. First, let's take a scenario that I see often in dating and engagement:

> Mark is sitting in his car with Shira. In his pocket is the engagement ring he plans to give to her tonight. Suddenly, he remembers Sarit, a girl he was almost engaged to last year. He tells himself, "If I'm still thinking about her, maybe it means Shira and I are not meant to be." There is a moment where he feels frozen, as if the apparition of Sarit is some kind of *Bas Kol,* redirecting him at the last moment. Truth be told, at this moment he has no relationship with Sarit, while he has come to feel understood by Shira better than anyone he has ever known. Yet, his confusion, which is a result of his *pizur hanefesh* state of mind, will accept the thought about Sarit as believable, and he will spiral into a state of anxiety that will jeopardize the engagement.

Mark has a choice. He can accept his distraction over Sarit, or he can take a few seconds to change his state of mind. The process would sound something like this:

The *Chiddush* Tefillah:
"Hashem, You create me every moment, and You don't want me to be in this state of pizur hanefesh over my thoughts about Sarit.

The *Tzomet* Tefillah:
"Hashem, You have placed me at the crossroads between my expression of pizur hanefesh and menuchas hanefesh, and You want me to learn to transform myself."

The *Mishkan* Tefillah:
"Hashem, You want my mind to be a Mishkan, so I can

remember those moments that brought Shira and me together."

During her dating with Baruch, Shalva could not let go of a thought that had crept into her mind. Baruch had been engaged before, and she never really understood why he broke the engagement. He was always unclear and evasive. Now her mind was occupied with worry that perhaps he was abusive, or maybe there was something else that should be of concern to her.

Baruch heard the concern in her voice and attempted to reassure her. Still, she was not calmed and comforted. Within a few days, her obsession with his previous engagement reached dangerous levels. Whatever he told her was unsatisfactory. She remained troubled in her thoughts and feelings and was considering ending the relationship.

Learning to use the principles in their interaction enabled Shalva to shift away from her runaway thoughts and feelings and quiet herself down. "It felt like I had a choice," she explained. "I didn't have to react in fear and destructive thoughts. It freed me up to be who I really am."

Many therapists would see Shalva's thoughts as "sabotaging" the relationship. They may, in fact, have had that effect. Nonetheless, her will and desire to undermine the relationship should not be confused with her *pizur hanefesh*. Thus, when she began to learn and use these principles, it was an empowering awareness. Suddenly, she was no longer pulled into the vortex of fear or driven by her runaway thoughts. A small light seemed to go on which made it possible for her to say, "There's a way out of this trap. I can keep myself free of the dangerous reasoning or entanglement." It was a reassuring awareness to feel that she was off the ski slope.

◇ **A Suggestion for Integrating the Principles Into Your Life:**

For one week, repeat the three principles and their corresponding *tefillos* three times a day. You can select a specific time or place. By repeating the principles, you will enhance your awareness of them so they can be effectively used when you go through a troubled state of mind caused by *pizur hanefesh*.

TRANSFORMATION TOOL #2:
Living in the Flow of Life

◇ **Reynolds Channel**

Near my home in the Rockaways, along the Atlantic coast, there is an inlet from the bay called Reynolds Channel, where a number of small boats are docked. There are times when I walk by and the water level is so low that the boats are actually sunken in the mud near the shore. Then, when I return in the evening, or whenever the tide is in, the boats are bobbing in many feet of water. One day, I realized that had I only been there in the morning, and never seen them bobbing during high tide, my perspective would be that these boats are always stuck in the mud. I would naturally think that they were abandoned, or I would wonder why anyone would want to dock his boat in the mud.

However, once I realize that the boats rise and sink with the natural rhythms of the tide, my perspective is very different. I call this Hashem's flow of life, and there are countless expressions of this flow of life in the world around us and within us. It exists in the small channel outside my home; in the revolution of night and day; in the changing of the seasons; within our own bodies; and even within the flow of our own thoughts and feelings.

◇ *Ba'erev Yalin Bechi …*

When we appreciate how Hashem's flow of life fills our world, it gives us a perspective that quiets our moments of insecurity and helplessness. Each morning, we recite the phrase of David Hamelech's hope for the future (*Tehillim* 30:6): "*Ba'erev yalin bechi, v'laboker rinah* — In the evening I lie in tears, but in the morning I will hear the song of joy." It is a belief that life is an expression of Hashem's flow of life. And just as the tide changes, even when we go to sleep at night feeling helpless, Hashem will enable us to wake up with a renewed sense of hope and strength.

This song of hope is not just for the hours of darkness. At any moment, we may feel the gloom of night descend. Yet we have the ability to realize that Hashem is preparing the song of morning for us. When we acknowledge this, even when the boats are in the mud and we are subjected to the pain and gloom of the moment, we can wait for the tide to turn and the morning to come. When we maintain this perspective, darkness never seems permanent. Perhaps this is what the *Tanna*, Nachum Ish Gamzu, meant when he said of all events in his life, "*Gam zu l'tovah* — This, too, is for the good."

This recognition of Hashem's flow of life enables us to perceive life from a more elevated perspective. It's as if we are seeing life from 30,000 feet up rather than at eye level. We look at the bigger picture. We understand that our hurt feelings at the moment will pass, given the opportunity. Our thoughts of criticism will yield to healthier thoughts that bring us closer together.

◇ *Kiddush Levanah*

I was reminded of this one *motza'ei Shabbos* as I stood outside of shul and waited for the clouds to clear so we could bless the new moon by reciting *Kiddush Levanah.* Although some people wanted to leave, I decided to wait. Then the moon, as if on cue, peeked out from behind the night cloud cover. This, too, is part of Hashem's flow of life. Sometimes we need to be patient, to wait and permit Hashem's flow of life to allow the moon to emerge.

Becoming aware that we are living within Hashem's flow of life brings on a deeper sense of security and inner stability. It is a perception that we can learn to cultivate and internalize into our lives. Here are a few personal thoughts regarding how I have come to bring this understanding into my own life.

◇ Life Flowing through Our Beings

There are times when I take a moment, listen to myself breathe and imagine the air entering my lungs and flowing through my bloodstream to find its way to every cell of my being. I realize that regardless of what is occurring in my life, there is a continuous inner river of life bringing nourishment and sustenance to every cell of my being. This is part of Hashem's flow of life.

I can walk on a tree-lined street and see clouds in gentle motion, birds in elegant flight, flowers and trees in bloom. I can smell delicate aromas and hear the sounds of nature, even the voices of people in my environment. This, too, is Hashem's flow of life.

What do all these phenomena of life mean to us? Hashem has placed the flow and rhythms of life within us and all around us. It's in the animated world of nature that envelops us — in the air, trees, clouds, rain, sun and living creatures that populate our world. This flow of life brings us the energy to have healthy, loving and life-giving thoughts and feelings, and an experience of our selves.

Our appreciation of this flow of life that Hashem continuously causes to pulse through the universe has crucial implications for our thoughts and feelings. We learn to appreciate that a thought and a feeling never exist independent of countless other functions that are occurring simultaneously. For example, it's very fascinating to realize that Man is the only being in the universe that can think and talk. As I mentioned earlier, each day we recite "*Atah chonain l'adam daas*" in the Shemoneh Esrei It means that Hashem lovingly bestows the power of thought within us.

Yet, these thoughts are not an isolated phenomenon. They exist in a larger system, as well. They emerge into our consciousness through the cells of our mind that Hashem nurtures at each moment. These cells are fed through the circulatory system that is an inner river of life constantly maintaining them. The system is driven by a beating heart and balanced by the delicate biochemical environment of our physical beings.

In the totality of this delicately balanced universe of self, we are aware of our thoughts and feelings. Even when we believe we have "nothing on our minds," our minds are never at rest. Throughout each moment of our lives, our minds are filled with a veritable stream of both positive and negative thoughts and feelings. Some have the potential to bring us closer to *menuchas hanefesh*, and some will drive us further away.

◇ Don't Feed the Bully

Frequently, when we have a negative thought, our tendency is to view it as the enemy and fight it off. Many find that this approach merely "feeds the bully," and intensifies the thought or feeling. At the same time, when we realize that even our thoughts and feelings are part of Hashem's flow of life, we no longer feel the need to do battle with them; we have the real choice of learning to quietly "let them pass." Chazal (*Brachos* 9b) say that when we are worried about a future event that we can't influence, our best approach is to quiet the worry by realizing, "*Dayah l'tzarah b'shaatah.*" It's enough to worry about it when it happens.

By saying this, we realize that there is an ebb and flow to our consciousness, which is part of the rhythm of Hashem's flow of life. And many of these thoughts and feelings will frequently "self-correct" when we realize that we have the ability to drop them. This awareness is the same as knowing that as I pass by Reynolds Channel and see the boats stuck in the mud, with a bit of patience I'll see the boats bobbing freely when the water returns. When I am feeling down and hopeless, or have a negative thought about my dating partner, *chassan* or *kallah*, then the awareness of David Hamelech's song of hope — at night there may be tears, but there is hope that the morning will bring song — empowers me to let go of the iron grip of the mood or thought. We need to get beyond the impulse that stays rigidly focused on the negative; otherwise, we compound the problem.

◇ *Sur Meira, Va'aseih Tov*

Rav Nachman Bulman, *zt"l*, from whom I learned many precious lessons of Torah and life, shared with me the need to move beyond negative thoughts to discover the positive. David Hamelech expresses in *Tehillim* (34:15), "*Sur meira, va'aseih tov* — Move away from evil and commit yourself to do good.*" Rabbi Bulman explained to me that there are many who are obsessed with the *sur meira* (leaving evil) side of the phrase. The problem is that they repeat it over and over until they become like a broken record and make a lifestyle out of it. They never really get to the marrow of life's precious experiences that exist in the second phrase of the verse: *aseih tov* (do good). According to Rav Bulman, the task at hand is to realize that the negative side requires us to leave it quickly — *sur meira* — and then, just as quickly, jump to the positive — *aseih tov*.

On a practical level, this means that we frequently become entrapped in how we feel about negative thoughts and feelings, and this makes us feel even worse.

> Karen was twenty-three and she had been dating Sammy for two months. She met with me to discuss whether to continue in the relationship. First, she described how she was uncertain about whether she really liked and respected him. Then she described how guilty she felt about her uncertainties. "I feel like such a bad person when I say these things." My response was, "Which is worse? Is it the initial doubt you had, or your feelings of being guilty over the doubt?" She thought for a moment and answered, "I guess I can live with the doubt and see how things progress. It's the guilt for feeling the doubt that makes me feel even worse."

For this young woman, the guilt itself became a source of even greater hurt, when she said to herself, "I feel so terrible about feeling guilty." Once again, we are compounding the problem by "feeding the bully."

◇ **Digging Deeper into the Ditch**

This is what I refer to as "digging deeper into the ditch." For me, it creates the potential for a dialogue that goes like this:

> "Hey, what are you doing with that shovel?"
> "I'm in a ditch, so I'm shoveling myself out."
> "Well, how deep was the ditch when you first got in?"
> "It was up to my knees."
> "But now you've shoveled yourself in up to your hips. Looks like you're just getting in deeper."
> "So what do I do?"
> "Well, first, I suggest you stop digging."

◇ Milton Erickson's Morning Light

There is a good deal I would like to share about Milton Erickson, M.D., who died in 1982. Erickson was a larger-than-life figure, who reshaped our conception of how people can change. I want to share a story that Erickson told about himself that is very germane to our discussion of Hashem's flow of life.

Erickson was brought up as part of a large family in the Minnesota plains. As a teenager, he was stricken by polio. At the initial stages of the disease, his condition was extremely critical. The attending physician told his mother, "Mrs. Erickson, it seems that Milton will not live through the night." His mother began crying uncontrollably. The young Erickson was very upset to see his mother crying. He sensed the overwhelming gloom that pervaded the cabin. Although the use of his limbs was very limited, his mind was still very crisp and clear. Before he closed his eyes and slept for what was believed to be his "last night of life," he motioned insistently to his mother to move the dresser away from the window.

Contrary to the doctor's prediction, he awoke the next morning. Erickson went on to achieve a lifetime of unparalleled accomplishments in his field of psychiatry and clinical hypnosis. Some time later, when he was able to communicate, he was asked about his insistence about moving the dresser. His response was, "They thought I was going to die and they were very depressed. However, I wasn't about to buy into that gloom. I knew I would live to see the sun rise in the morning. But the dresser was blocking the window, and I wanted to make sure I was able to see that sun the moment it started to rise."

◇ A *Brachah* from Rav Aharon, *zt"l*

An event that occurred in my own family is seared indelibly into my mind. In 1960, my younger sister was taken to the emergency room with spinal meningitis. The physicians told my mother not to expect her to live through the night. We were four children and my mother; my father, *a"h*, had died six years earlier. We heard the doctor's report and were all in a state of shock. My brother-in-law, Rabbi Shmuel Kaufman, contacted the *gadol hador*, Rav Aharon Kotler, *zt"l*, and informed him of the impending tragedy. Rav Aharon slammed his fist on the table and stated with unswerving certainty, *"Zi vet nisht shtarben* (She will not die)."* And in the morning, after a night of *Tehillim* and *tefillah*, I entered her room and she was indeed still alive. Here, too, we see David Hamelech's prophetic words: *"Ba'erev yalin bechi v'laboker rinah."*

We understand that on a *ruchnius* level there is a vast difference between the *emunah* of a *gadol* such as Rav Aharon, *zt"l*, and the hope and determination of a young boy stricken by polio on the plains of Minnesota. Still, the power to believe and trust in the goodness of Hashem's flow of life is inbred and instinctive, even when the moment seems dire and even hopeless. So when you are feeling critical of your dating partner, the first instinct may be to believe the criticism as the unquestionable truth. That is the nature of *pizur hanefesh*. A wiser approach would be to take a step back and say, "I may be experiencing negative thoughts or feelings, but I have many different thoughts and feelings within me that are all a part of Hashem's flow of life. Therefore, I can drop this negative state of mind and be open to more positive states that I am not yet aware of."

Our awareness that even the troubled thoughts or feelings are connected to Hashem's flow of life creates an immediate respite from the compulsion to fight or flee. Perspective is a far better tool than combat or retreat. And even more important, the respite and freedom create an opening for us to receive the wisdom of our own *neshamos*, as we are now capable of focusing on our *mayim amukim*. The ability to quiet our negative thoughts and feelings now makes it possible to receive new and healthy perceptions from the inspiration that Hashem has placed deep within each of us, just below the surface. And by being conscious of the countless manifestations of this flow of life, we are opening ourselves up to other thoughts and possibilities.

TRANSFORMING PHYSIOLOGY

◇ Our Body's Pathways

The primary tools we have learned are more helpful for transforming the thoughts and feelings that impede *shalom bayis*. Yet when it comes to transforming physiological patterns of *pizur hanefesh* and distress, I have frequently found that we require more sensory and behavioral approaches. This is because once the body has developed its own neural pathways of experiencing insecurity and discomfort, these patterns are triggered by anticipation, association and habit.

> Shimmy is a twenty-six-year-old lawyer. He has dated many young women, and felt that a large number were suitable as a life partner. Still, as he gets to know someone a bit better, he feels himself becoming physically tense. "Just knowing that we're going to be in each other's presence in the next few moments causes me to feel a sense of physical tightness and anxiety. I feel it in my joints and my head; my hands become sweaty. Even if I wanted to, how can I continue?"

Whether the cause of anxiety is real or anticipatory, the effects are frequently measurable.

> I worked with a young woman who had severe stomach cramps after each date with a certain young man. At night, she would awaken in severe pain. She was convinced

that this was a sign that they could never get married. *Baruch Hashem*, she was able to develop skills in quieting and managing her physiological reactions.

In dating and engagement, as I described in the last chapter, the physiological manifestations of *pizur hanefesh* are staggering. They include headaches, backaches, tightening of the jaws, panic attacks, high blood pressure, hyperventilation, stomach problems and many other similar physiological expressions of our negative state of mind and body that we call *pizur hanefesh*. Frequently, I am asked whether any of these are purely physical. The answer is that they certainly can be, and it's always prudent to consult with a physician before any other diagnosis can be applied. On the other hand, when a physician feels the source of the symptom may have an emotional element, then it's wise to apply some of the approaches that have the potential to quiet down the symptoms that may very well be rooted in a *pizur hanefesh* state of mind.

> Yussie was engaged, and he had always experienced some degree of anxiety in the past. When he was confronted with the unexpected pressures of engagement, his symptoms grew in their intensity. Even beyond the physical tension, he began experiencing fatigue and headaches. He had been to both traditional and homeopathic medical practitioners with poor results. But as he learned to apply approaches that enabled him to transform his *pizur hanefesh* to *menuchas hanefesh*, Yussie came to appreciate that his symptoms were not a "message" that he had made an error. More important, he learned that he had far more control over his symptoms than he had ever imagined.

In *Devarim* (4:15), the Torah commands us to watch over our health: "*V'nishmartem me'od l'nafshoseichem* — And you shall be very careful with your souls." This *mitzvah* comprises more than just being aware of our vital life signs. It extends to developing a lifestyle that connects our positive emotional and cognitive well-being to a healthy physical experience of life. It means being attentive to how these factors contribute to our physical functioning, and learning to apply effective approaches that have a positive influence on how our body behaves.

◇ Overcoming Paralysis

As we look at this interface between mind and body, I am invariably drawn once again to the groundbreaking achievements of Dr. Milton Erickson.

Like many others who suffered from polio, Erickson was unable to move a muscle. His mother would place her motionless adolescent son on a chair in the middle of the cabin, where he would sit all day. While there, he used his sharp mind to observe life moving all around him.

During this period, his mother gave birth to a girl. From his chair, young Milton observed how his infant sister learned to use every muscle in her body. She used her hands and feet to roll over and eventually crawl, her fingers to grasp and her knees to balance herself as she prepared to walk. From his observations, he came to understand that it was the mind's ability to focus on muscle groups that caused each of these skills to be learned. Sitting motionless in his chair, he wondered whether he, like his infant sister, could connect his thoughts to his muscles and regain the use of his body.

One day, the family was shocked to see that Milton had fallen off his chair. Everyone knew that since he was paralyzed, he must have been pushed. However, for him it meant that somehow his thoughts had caused his muscles to move his body. It was the beginning of a new life. Within a year and a half after that event, he had mastered the ability to regain control over almost all of his muscles. At the age of nineteen, he went on a solo canoe trip of 1,500 miles.

Erickson then went on to use his unique understanding of how the mind controls the body to become a psychiatrist and one of the world's foremost clinical hypnotherapists. His achievements were monumental. His accomplishments have always provided me with a sense of inspiration for our innate capacity to overcome the limitations of our physiological responses.

◇ Leibel's Speech Impairment

A Chassidic young man, Leibel, came to see me about a severe stuttering problem that had prevented him from dating. He was the only one left in his *shiur* who was neither married nor a *chassan*, and was very depressed about his situation. Since his stuttering was so evident, he never had the opportunity to even meet a young woman. Leibel's family had spent many thousands of dollars on treatment over the years, without any appreciable effect.

As part of understanding *menuchas hanefesh* and change, Leibel learned a meditative and focusing exercise: the Pulse of Life. After practicing the meditation for a week, he felt capable of having his first meeting, or "*besho*," as it is called in Yiddish. He met with the young lady for the required time and was able to maintain sufficient mastery over his stuttering for the girl and her family to feel confident that this was no longer an issue of concern.

All this occurred without my knowledge. As I was driving home from a meeting, I received a call from him.

"This is Leibel."

"Hello, Leibel. I'm glad to hear from you. I was expecting to hear from you two days ago. Have you been doing the exercise?"

> "Yes, I did the exercise many times, and I had a *besho.*"
> I was surprised. "That's great. And what happened?"
> "*Mazel tov,*" was his answer. "I had the *besho,* and now I'm a *chassan.*"

This story may seem somewhat unbelievable. However, consider that Leibel and others suffering from this impairment can usually sing, *daven* and even read out loud without stuttering — provided it's not in a one-to-one situation. The ability to speak fluently and unimpeded is learned. Leibel had learned that he could gain mastery over his vocal organs to control his speech in the social context, as well.

My intention is to demonstrate that Hashem gives us the ability to gain mastery over our physiological functioning and transform it when necessary. This is not a new concept. There are many well-respected approaches that use the mind/body connection to improve health and well-being. Dr. John Sarno's methodologies have gained worldwide recognition for reducing back pain by overcoming stress.

◇ **Rav Gustman's Root Canal**

For our work, I prefer to consider our own *gedolim* to appreciate the possibilities of how the mind can overcome the limitations of the body.

> I know a dentist in Eretz Yisrael, Dr. Josh Daniels, who performed a root canal on Rav Yisrael Ze'ev Gustman, *zt"l,* one of the *gedolim* of the previous generation. The root canal procedure is particularly painful and always requires an anesthetic. Rav Gustman, however, told Dr. Daniels that there was no need for any anesthetic. He would simply review his Torah learning during the procedure.
> I recently met Dr. Daniels at a wedding in Eretz Yisrael, and he shared that while the Rosh Yeshivah had insisted

that he not use any anesthetic, Dr. Daniels continuously apologized and asked for his *mechilah* for the pain he was causing him. The Rosh Yeshivah reassured him that he was in no distress, and thanked him for taking care of him. During the procedure, Rav Gustman sat peacefully as he reviewed his Torah learning.

The Rebbe's *Niggun* and the Rav's *Tefillin*

There are many similar stories, such as the one in which the Modzhitzter Rebbe, *zt"l*, composed a beautiful and well-known *niggun* (tune) during a surgical procedure.

There is also the episode about the Tchebiner Rav, *zt"l*, who was required to stay awake during neurosurgery. The dilemma was that without anesthesia, no one can withstand the pain. But with anesthesia, he would succumb to sleep. His response to the problem was to wear his *tefillin* during the surgery. Since there is a halachah that one may not sleep while wearing *tefillin*, he was certain that he would not fall asleep as long as he wore his *tefillin*. To the astonishment of the surgeon, the anesthesia was administered and he remained alert throughout the surgery.

The Art of Transforming Physiology

My intention is not to focus on dealing with any specific physical discomfort or how to undergo a root canal or neurosurgery without anesthesia. It is to guide individuals and dating couples toward overcoming the influence that adverse physiological symptoms can have on their efforts to discover their life partners, because the presence of these symptoms exacerbates and deepens all the other issues.

This is because whenever we feel we are losing control of our physical functioning because of our partner, it depletes us of our strength and desire to continue in this delicate building process.

This is why I usually attempt to help the individual learn to transform the symptom. Even if nothing else is accomplished, if we are successful in quieting the symptom by learning to bring it under control, this in itself makes for a profound difference in our sense of personal empowerment. Beyond the correction of the physiological problem, I also attempt to enhance a dating couple's quality of life through exercise and strategic activities that contribute to a greater sense of *menuchas hanefesh* in the physical dimension.

◇ The Garden Hose

Physiological symptoms that are related to personal and dating stress are analogous to a garden hose. If the "hose" is unblocked, then the physical and emotional energies within us flow naturally. Conversely, if the "hose" is knotted or constricted, the flow of "water" will be inhibited until something gives. All of a sudden, there may be a surge of emotions, or the pressure will continue to build up and create small fissures that enlarge, until the walls of the "hose" are like a sieve, with "water" squirting out from everywhere. In other situations, the blockage may be hermetically sealed, leading to the effects of profound emotional repression.

We can see the effects of these phenomena through high blood pressure, hyperventilation, rapid heartbeat, teeth grinding, stomach disorders and many other similar symptoms. One man told me that while he was on his way to a job he dreaded, his nose suddenly started bleeding. Clearly, the pressure in his blood vessels built up as a result of his emotions, until the delicate capillaries of his nose gave way and became an exit for the pressure.

◇ *Kotzer Ruach* in Mitzrayim

It is worth repeating that in our own history we can see this phenomenon. When Am Yisrael was enslaved in Egypt, we are told that they suffered from *"kotzer ruach"* (*Shemos* 6:9), which means shortness of breath. It is only when Hashem relieved the pressures of servitude that they were once again able to take a full and deep breath, and then pray to Hashem.

◇ Exercises in Transformation

In order to transform physiological symptoms that I have found to be widespread in relationship building, I teach couples three approaches, which comprise the next three transformation tools. These are:

1. The Power of Focused Walking
2. Centering
3. The Pulse of Life

TRANSFORMATION TOOL #3:
The Power of Focused Walking

◇ Rachel's Walk

Rachel is one day away from her wedding. She calls me to say that she does not know whether she can go through with it. She has been feeling very tired, and her mind is filled with contradictory and confusing feelings about Moshe. I suggest that she take a Focused Walk. At first, she responds with frustration, "I don't know if anything is going to help." Then she agrees.

Rachel begins her walk. On this autumn day, she has chosen a quiet street near her home in a New York suburb. The street is lined with trees and has relatively little traffic. And just as important, it is unlikely that she will meet anyone she knows who may interrupt her exercise in Focused Walking.

Rachel walks at a comfortable pace and appears to

be looking straight ahead. The walk lasts for about thirty minutes. We assume that she has used the opportunity to get some fresh air and exercise. While this is certainly true, something far more important is occurring. During this Focused Walk, Rachel is exploring the causes of her fatigue, as well as her confusion about Moshe and her upcoming wedding. During this time, her enhanced focus enables her to sort out many thoughts and feelings. She finishes her walk with a sense of clarity. She decides that her marriage will have its challenges. In spite of this, she decides that she does want to marry Moshe. She is ready for her wedding, which is less than twenty-four hours away.

This section will explore the importance of Focused Walking as an essential tool to help you regain the delicate balance between your mind and your body, which is so crucial in overcoming the physiological symptoms of *pizur hanefesh.*

◇ The Benefits of Walking

There is no need for me to advocate the health benefits of walking. That would be similar to promoting breathing. I am an avid walker and I recommend it for others.

When Rav Avigdor Miller, *zt"l*, was given a ride home from a wedding, he insisted that he be left off about two miles from his house. The *bachurim* in the car would not hear of it and insisted that he be driven home. He patiently explained that if he would be taken all the way home, he would simply walk a mile back in the direction they just came from and then return another mile. He had not yet had the opportunity to walk that day, and this was his opportunity.

Simply stated, there is probably no better and healthier exercise than walking. Yet I am advocating walking both as a physical and daily transformational activity, which enables the body and mind to achieve a synchronization of awareness, insight and physical well-being.

Physiological symptoms of *pizur hanefesh* are a sign of an imbalance between our thoughts and feelings as they impact on our physiology. The headache, fatigue, palpitations, anxiety and panic attacks may certainly have their roots in our hard-wiring. I know of one young man who has suffered from countless somatic disorders. "That's just the way I'm wired," he informs me. Another man, Moshe, feels he developed colitis through pressures at home and at work. And a young wife, Malkie, is sure that her migraines got worse as a result of family pressures. As mentioned, in all these situations, there is a need to examine the physical aspect of the symptoms. But once this has been responsibly explored, we can take a closer look at how we can recalibrate the delicate mind/body balance.

Focused Walking is an approach I have taught many dating couples and individuals in order to help them discover how their troubled thoughts and feelings may be contributing to their physical symptoms that undermine their relationships.

There are countless benefits for integrating Focused Walking into your life. A brief list of benefits includes:

+ Overcoming physiological symptoms of stress
+ Problem solving and resolution
+ Exploring and clarifying thoughts and feelings
+ Regaining access to our more human and caring emotions
+ Experiencing emotional catharsis
+ Calming hurt, anger and frustration

The Dynamics of Focused Walking

At the beginning of this chapter on transformation, I discussed the principle of *mayim amukim*, the deep wisdom that is within each of us, waiting to ascend to the surface of our consciousness. This wisdom is at the heart of our intellectual, emotional and physical rebalancing. It is a powerful insight that frees us from the compelling and repetitive patterns of *pizur hanefesh*, which are the causes of our physiological symptoms. These symptoms are the body's blind and chaotic way of trying to regain balance, and they never work. Hashem places this deeper wisdom within each of us to delicately assist in the regulation of our functioning, whether it's our body temperature, blood pressure, blood sugar, immune system or the myriad of interrelated systems that enable us to fulfill our life tasks.

Pizur hanefesh keeps us distracted and emotionally "unintelligent," causing us to be imbalanced in a way that leads to physiological symptoms. Focused Walking, on the other hand, enables us to reach deep into the well of our own selves and gain access to our "*mayim amukim*," our deep waters of wisdom and insight. It's as if we are sending a pail deep down within the well of our selves to draw up waters of clarity. This clarity has a way of correcting the imbalance and helping us overcome our symptoms.

Why do we use walking? Through the synergy of forward movement, while focusing on a specific goal and using a visual focus, we gain access to insights that have eluded our consciousness. Focused Walking is effective because through the experience, our minds are able to receive insights and clarity that emerge from our *mayim amukim*. Armed with this wisdom, we gain new options for spiritually and emotionally healthy living that make it possible for us to find better solutions to our challenges, rather than repeating dysfunctional physical symptoms.

The concept of Focused Walking is based on how the Alter of Kelm, *zt"l*, encouraged Focused Thinking to reveal hidden treasures in our thoughts. In Focused Thinking, he would suggest that a student close his eyes for a three-to-five-minute period and focus on one specific issue without opening his eyes. Many *talmidim* of Kelm practiced this every day as a way of strengthening their power of focus. The difference is that in the Focused Walking exercise, you are literally "on the go."

◇ How to Create Your Own Focused Walking Exercise

The principle behind Focused Walking is that we use our visual focus on an external object, usually a tree, to learn how to resist distractions, which are the essence of *pizur hanefesh*. When we overcome the tendency to be distracted, we gain access to our deeper sense of wisdom. And through learning to maintain our visual focus, we create a deeper inner clarity on an issue we are thinking about.

As you begin the walk, you will notice how easy and compelling the need to be distracted is. This is the pattern of *pizur hanefesh*. Once you become aware that the distractions are caused by *pizur hanefesh*, you will see that you are capable of resisting them. The moment you learn that you have this strength, your thoughts and insights from the *mayim amukim* begin bubbling to the surface of your consciousness. Therefore, the challenge is to use the walk to continuously maintain a visual focus while concentrating on a specific question or thought.

The procedure for the Focused Walk is the following:

1. Decide on a Focus

Select a question or issue that will be the focus of your walk. The goal could be one of the following:

a. Talking to My Physiological Symptom

+ What does my physiological symptom (fatigue, headache, etc.) say to me about my lifestyle, my relationship, etc.?

b. Clarifying My Relationship

+ Can I remember a moment when I felt connected to my dating partner or *chassan/kallah?*
+ Can I remember a moment when I felt a sense of gratitude toward my dating partner or *chassan/kallah?*

c. Problem Solving

+ How can I learn to discuss the issues that I am defining as problematic?

2. Select the Place to Walk

Choose a tree-lined street, a park or anywhere you can walk with a minimum of traffic, people and distractions.

3. Get Focused

Start walking, and as you walk, look straight ahead or preferably at a tree. Maintain your focus straight ahead or on the tree, and silently repeat your focus for the walk. For example, "What are the factors that may be contributing to my headache?"

4. Get Ready for Distractions

Permit your mind to be aware of any thoughts or images that it may perceive. Yet you should also be aware of how you will be distracted from your visual focus. When you are pulled away, return your visual focus straight ahead or to the tree, and repeat your focus: "What are the factors that may be contributing to my headache?" After about five or more distractions, you will realize that being distracted is the result of *pizur hanefesh*. At that moment, you will resist the pull.

5. Monitor Your *"Mayim Amukim"* Thoughts

Once you have resisted distraction and can maintain your visual focus, you will discover that your thoughts become clearer.

Unexpected flashes of impressions, insights and memories will bubble to the surface. As you resist your *pizur hanefesh* tendency to be distracted, you are able to reach *mayim amukim* insights that emerge from the bottom of the well. You will discover that once you have a single memory or insight, the next insight will be almost instantaneous. Once you are in this focused zone that we call *menuchas hanefesh*, you can walk for as long as you wish to continue to deepen your understanding of the many intricate and delicate connections that create your physiological symptom. And with each insight, you are coming closer to a sense of mastery that reestablishes the balance between *neshamah* and body, which enables you to once again be in control of your physical functioning.

In my work with dating couples, I frequently suggest that they each take a daily Focused Walk. They repeatedly share that they use these walks to gain valuable insights into their own behavior, transform their moods and develop approaches to resolve their relationship issues.

TRANSFORMATION TOOL #4: Centering

Cindy is sitting in a restaurant with Charles. She has a tendency to feel agitated on dates. This causes her to blurt out things that she wishes she can take back.

Simcha is a thirty-year-old lawyer who has been in a number of relationships that end when he shows signs of stress and tension. He needs a way to quiet his anxiety.

When Asher picks up his date, he always feels uncomfortable and edgy. While he feels confident and calm in just about all other areas of his life, for some reason, this is where all his self-doubt is felt and communicated.

These examples are very common to dating, since the experience of attempting to develop a relationship with someone who

may have been a stranger a short while ago engenders a heightened sense of emotional and physiological tension. I believe this
is because dating couples are processing an enormous amount
of impressions and information about each other. This creates
an unusually high stress factor.

When you are attempting to learn about a relative stranger's
life and are assessing *middos*, physical attributes, mannerisms,
financial security, level of Yiddishkeit and so many other factors,
the result is frequently a heightened state of discomfort, uncertainty and even physical anxiety. I learned to view this overload
as the quintessential expression of *pizur hanefesh*. There seems
to be a "loss of self" when dating partners are flooded by the
sheer quantity and quality of stimuli they are experiencing as
they consider each other's differences and uniqueness.

In my attempt to help singles maintain their own sense of
self, I came to appreciate the deeper meaning and implications of
a concept I had earlier alluded to. The Mashgiach, Rav Yeruchem
Levovitz, *zt"l*, taught that within us there is a *neshamah*, as soft
and gentle as silk. It is an entity that Hashem places inside us
each day. We thank Hashem for our *neshamah* each morning as
we recite, "*Modeh ani lefanecha* — I gratefully thank You." This
neshamah is the guiding force to our inner sense of well-being,
balance and *menuchas hanefesh*. When we are in an overload
mode, and feel tension and anxiety, we not only lose our sense of
our self, we also become cut off from this silken *neshamah* that
resides quietly and peacefully within us. The *neshamah* is the
reason we are so sensitive to the nuances of words and feelings.
When we are cut off from our *neshamah*, we tend to define ourselves by the tense and jarring quality we experience in our state
of hyper-stimulation and overload.

The challenge that I faced in workshops I presented to singles was how to enable each individual to maintain a clearer
and calmer sense of self during the demanding relationship-

building process, meaning, how could we make it possible for each individual to remember that regardless of the emotional overload of dating, he could still maintain his sense of intactness and inner balance? Even more important, how could each one learn to remember that within them there was a soft and silken *neshamah*? What would be an appropriate reminder or "anchor" that would enable them to remember who they really were within?

This led me to consider an observation I have repeatedly made over the years in my work with couples. When individuals are tense and anxious, many exhibit a tendency to express these feelings in their hands through emphatic movements and gesticulations. It is as if the movement of the hands creates a more decisive exclamation than the words themselves. And when they are calmer, they tend to keep their hands closer together, with far less emphatic and tense movement. I came to view these movements as a barometer of internal agitation or calm. In essence, I discovered that the greater the agitation, the busier the hand movements.

Chazal have always recognized the concept of busy hands, which they refer to as "*yadayim askanios.*" And because Chazal recognize that our hands are always busy and continuously touching things, they incorporated the ritual of washing our hands when we awaken in the morning, when we daven or upon entering a shul. I was told that Reb Yeruchem Levovitz, *zt"l,* said that there was really no reason for him to wash his hands in the morning, as he was always aware of what his hands were touching, even in his sleep. Nevertheless, he washed them.

In Jewish life, the concept of *yadayim askanios,* or busy hands, is viewed in a negative manner. When we are davening to Hashem, Chazal recommend that we gently hold our hands together, quietly and calmly, over our hearts, to emphasize our deep and calm sense of devotion.

As the workshop participants and I explored this phenomenon of tense hand movements, I came to suggest that the participants learn to gently hold their hands together or even have their fingers delicately touch when they go through this sense of emotional overload in dating. In this way, they would be reminding themselves that just as their hands are soft and gentle, there is a soft and gentle *neshamah* in each person, in themselves and in the person they are dating. Thus, I felt it would be possible to enable singles to be in greater touch with their "selves" and be aware of their own *neshamah* during these important moments. I called it Centering, as it enabled them to return to the center of self.

The results were immediate and extremely positive. One young woman sent me an email that read, "We were at the restaurant together and I was very disappointed and impatient, and wanted to leave. Then I decided that this was the time to get centered. Once I did, I was able to feel calmer, more relaxed and focused." I also began to hear that workshop participants were using Centering in their professional work, with friends and family and even in their own *tefillos*. This was when I began to teach the method of Centering to married couples, particularly to those who experienced high degrees of physiological stress. The results have been very effective in getting these couples to feel calmer and more in control of themselves, particularly as they interact around challenging issues.

Yet, as I learned more about Centering, I came to understand a more important dimension of its benefit. Initially, I had understood its value in calming the anxiety related to emotional overload. Later, I came to appreciate its deeper value as a way of cultivating an inner dialogue with our deeper selves and our *neshamos*.

Gently touching our hands, palms and fingers becomes a method of deepening our sensitivity to who we are within. It's not just helpful to remind ourselves of our silken *neshamos* in times of stress; it is even more important to cultivate this gentle touch — as a violinist learns to touch the delicate strings of his instrument. In this way, Centering becomes an effective skill in helping individuals continuously feel in touch with a quieter, gentler self on a tactile and sensory level. It becomes a tactile and sensory portal to our inner world of gentle *ruchnius*.

Once we have cultivated this gentler tactile experience of who we are, we can reassure ourselves that we are never our unsafe impulses, nor our anxiety. We are never really the "third rail." And once we can feel safe with our inner self, we can help others around us feel just as safe as we do. Once we trust ourselves, we can enable those we care for to feel trust and security, as well. This is what I have taught many dating and married couples — a stratagem that has enabled them to maintain this deeper relationship with their inner selves as a way of quieting the physiological effects of tension and anxiety.

◇ Learning the Art of Centering

You can easily learn to center yourself in a few moments by following these steps:

a. Bring the tips of your ten fingers together. Permit them to touch gently. Then close your eyes and feel the delicate nature of your fingertips.

b. Now gently rub your palms and permit your fingertips to run over your palms and the back of your hands. Feel the soft and gentle touch of your skin.

c. Place your fingers within each other, so they are interlaced, while keeping the touch as soft as ten feathers.

d. Place your hands on your abdomen, so you can feel the steady rhythm of your breathing.

e. Finally, close your eyes and spend a few moments exploring the gentleness of touch.

When you have completed this initial exercise, you can use Centering in a dialogue.

Approach someone you know and center your hands in any way that feels comfortable. You may wish to have your fingertips touch, or your fingers touch the back of your hands or your palms. You may create a slow motion or just keep your hands still. And, as I suggested before, you may also find that placing your hands on your abdomen helps you to feel even more centered.

As you speak, be aware of how the experience of Centering enables you to feel calmer, more relaxed and focused. You are able to listen better, respond more thoughtfully — and even be aware of emotions that were not previously available. Most importantly, it makes you feel more secure and centered within yourself, and this is conveyed to whomever you are communicating with.

You will discover that using Centering in this manner allows you to feel a circuit of comfort that is created as your hands and fingers make contact. This sends a very tactile and sensory message to your whole body that you are safe and secure, and reminds you that within, there is a very gentle *neshamah* that brings life to your every moment.

I suggest you begin to explore the many benefits of Centering as you speak to your dating partner, *chassan/kallah*, colleagues and family members. It will facilitate a more secure dimension of your physiological self to emerge.

TRANSFORMATION TOOL #5:
The Pulse of Life

The two previous transformation tools we have learned, Focused Walking and Centering, are used to handle nonspecific physiological symptoms and to gain greater clarity of your deeper thoughts and feelings. This next tool, the Pulse of Life, is used to transform a specific symptom. The Pulse of Life is experienced as a personal encounter between one's own body and *neshamah*.

I have explained how our thoughts and emotions impact on our physiological functioning. We can experience its effect on our circulatory, digestive, nervous and glandular systems as our emotional imbalance and insecurity is expressed through our bodies. In effect, in our sense of distress, our body acts on its own to attempt to correct what it views as a problem. The difficulty is that it acts in its own limited, unguided manner, and the results are always problematic.

Perhaps we can use the metaphor of someone receiving a kidney transplant. After the transplant, the body's immune system starts to recognize the life-giving organ as an "intruder," and sets off an elaborate system to defend itself. If I was having such a procedure and my immune system was to act negatively, I would want to say, "Listen, immune system, I need this new organ to survive. Back off. You are working for me, and right now you are not acting on my behalf." Without proper medication, my body's immune system would reject the organ, causing disastrous results. This, in effect, is what happens when our body compensates for signals of distress. It acts blindly and instinctively to attend to the emergency and creates a whole new set of difficulties.

The Pulse of Life is a guided imagery experience that uses our awareness of our pulse beat to regain control over our body's misguided functioning. It uses the synergy of relaxation, a higher vision of life and the beat of our pulse to create a mind/body dialogue. The effect of this dialogue helps the compelling drives of our physical functioning surrender to the higher wisdom of our mind and soul. By learning to focus on your pulse beat and understand how it affects your physical functioning, you learn to create a new language of inner peace, in your thoughts, feelings and physiology.

◇ The Pulse of Life Meditative Exercise

It is always best to be personally guided through this exercise. A CD of this exercise is available from my website: gatewaystomarriage.com.

In this section, I will provide the basic elements that I teach couples. These contain thirteen steps and should take from seven to ten minutes. Of course, you can take as much time as you wish.

a. Select a relaxed and quiet place to sit or lie down, where you will not be disturbed for about ten minutes.

b. Locate your pulse on your wrist, neck or temple. Then, close your eyes and count five beats of your pulse, followed by a full breath.

c. Repeat the count of five pulse beats followed by a full breath, four more times.

d. Imagine a white light on top of your forehead (approximately where a man wears his *tefillin*).

e. Imagine this white light is your *neshamah* and it represents the essence of all the spiritual and meaningful aspirations you strive for in life. This can include *shalom bayis*, Torah, *nachas* from your children, personal happiness or any other meaningful life goal.

f. Realize that the white light is a sign that Hashem is always giving you life — always protecting and loving you, and that you are never alone or forgotten.

g. Feel your pulse once again and be aware that the beat of

your pulse is the sound of an inner river of life flowing throughout your body.

h. Be aware that your pulse also carries feelings of tension and anxiety that you would like to quiet down.

i. Imagine that your pulse can speak to the white light, and says, "You, white light, have so much *chachmah* (wisdom). Please teach me to quiet my fears and anxieties."

j. Imagine that your pulse says, "I surrender myself to your wisdom."

k. Imagine a mountain in the distance covered with ice and snow. As the sun rises, the snow and ice melt and trickle down the mountainside.

l. Imagine your own pulse and your anxieties becoming softer and gentler and melting, just as the ice and snow are melting.

m. Last, imagine the white light descending into your mind and slowly bringing its warmth to every part of your body. Start by feeling the warmth of the white light in your head, moving down your neck, arms and hands, continuing down your chest and stomach and finally down your thighs, legs, knees and ankles.

TRANSFORMATION TOOL #6:
The Meditative Walking Exercise

Another very effective tool I have developed for individuals and couples is Meditative Walking. There are two programs, one for walking alone, called "Walking toward *Menuchas Hanefesh*," and another for couples, called "Walking Together." Both programs are available on the gatewaystomarriage.com website.

CHAPTER VIII

The EMBERS Program:
Cultivating Commitment and Closeness

◇ **The Biosphere — Where Orchids Bloom in the Bronx**

I always marvel when I visit the New York Botanical Garden in the Bronx. It's where I can see and smell flowers from the world over in all their beauty and lushness. Even in the dead of a dreary and freezing New York winter, I can enter a glass-enclosed world where tropical flowers are blooming in all their glory, just over the waters of the Bronx River. The secret is that within this glass-enclosed world, the conditions for growing orchids and other exotic plants are ideal. The humidity, temperature, light and soil are all perfectly balanced to encourage a tropical plant to bloom in New York City in February.

In many ways, the biosphere of the garden is similar to the environment required for trust to evolve between a child and mother during the early years of life. When a mother is caring for the needs of her helpless and dependent child, especially in the first year of life, the mother must provide her child with a protective embrace of love and gentle attentiveness. Only through this protective environment can the self of the child gradually grow in trust, self esteem, identity, responsibility

251

and the ability to give and receive love.

The concept of the biosphere is true of the emerging selves that bring the lives of a dating or engaged couple together. Relationships that lead to marriage require a protective envelope of meaningful experience to facilitate trust; then our deepest sense of self can emerge, and a relationship that leads to marriage can follow.

In Chassidic communities, this process takes on a different pattern, where the trust is not between the couple, but between the parents who have selected the *shidduch* and with the *kehillah* (community) in which the couple will remain an integral part. Within this context of the community, the couple will gradually learn to trust, understand and care for each other. In contrast, in other communities — whether Agudah, Young Israel, Y.U., R.C.A., etc. — there is an expectation and a need for the couple to know each other and develop a closer relationship before they agree to become engaged. This occurs through the emergence of this inner self that determines a sense of readiness between a couple, whether they have dated for a month or half a year. And it is our behavior that determines the emergence of this inner self. There are behaviors that encourage this deeper aspect of self to emerge and behaviors that scare the self into hiding.

EMBERS AS A GUIDELINE TOWARD TWO EMERGING SELVES

A couple's true feeling of creating a relationship occurs when they share memorable and meaningful experiences that allow the deeper self to feel secure enough to be expressed. Moments of stress, distraction and anxiety, on the other hand, cause the opposite effect and their relationship is undermined. This chapter focuses on those behaviors that create memorable moments and those behaviors that destroy relationships. EMBERS is the acronym for the behaviors that create connections — which represent six dimensions of our shared experiences that enable the self to safely emerge.

Our behavior and the ability for a dating or engaged couple to develop and sustain growing feelings of commitment and closeness are always the result of how we gain mastery over our *pizur hanefesh* impulses, which plant seeds of doubt and discomfort and prevent a relationship from growing. A relationship grows through an emotional environment that is continuously created through our conscious use of language and behavior and sharing moments of mutually rewarding pleasure, as well as our ability to express our inner aspirations — our *ruchnius* (spiritual yearnings). A couple's ongoing sense of trust, happiness and fulfillment is never accidental. In essence, at each moment we are either creating embers that unite us as a couple — or we are creating hurt, alienation and disappointment, which fragment and weaken the fragile bonds that are developing. In developing this most important and sacred of all human bonds, there are never moments of neutrality.

This section will identify six areas of your growing relationship that impact on the behavioral, spiritual and emotional climates that help couples create an emerging sense of commitment and closeness between them. I call these areas EMBERS because as an acronym, "EMBERS" encompasses issues that I have found to be crucial elements of each relationship. In addition, the word embers evokes images of quiet sparks inside each of us that are longing to be rekindled within a relationship to each other and in our relationship to Hashem.

This final section, therefore, deals with the integration of six areas of your relationship that promote the behavioral and emotional climate leading to commitment and closeness. Together they create EMBERS, which include:

1. Expressions
2. Moods
3. Behavior
4. Enjoyment
5. *Ruchnius* (Spirituality)
6. Sensitivity

EMBERS represents a rich and full palette of colors and experiences in a relationship that empowers a couple to continuously bind their lives together. When these six elements are in synchronization, they create tones as rich and delicate as the strings of a Stradivarius violin. Each element of these EMBERS brings a couple closer and more conscious of their potential for deeper and more meaningful human emotions that Hashem has implanted in all of us. These are the shared emotions that marriage has always been destined to fulfill.

With this in mind, we can now take a closer look at the EMBERS that enable couples who are dating or engaged to enhance their experience of mutual understanding and trust — through the ways they behave toward each other, and through their learning to keep each other safe and balanced through the relationship-building process.

1. EXPRESSIONS

The EMBERS Principle: *Expressions that emerge from menuchas hanefesh bring a couple together in a shared bond of commitment and closeness. Expressions that emanate from pizur hanefesh destroy this potential.*

When was the last time someone said something that made you smile deep within? Look back into your life and try to remember individuals who said special things in special ways. Perhaps it was something that affirmed you or that enabled you to be positive about yourself. It could have been something personal that was shared and deeply valued as an expression of openness and honesty. Or it may have been an expression from the heart that touched you very deeply.

> Almost forty years ago when our first child was born, I returned from the hospital to daven Minchah in the *bais medrash* of Mesivta Tifereth Jerusalem on the Lower East Side, and I was walking on air. As I entered, I was eager to share this wonderful event in my life. The first person I noticed was the Rosh Yeshivah, the *gadol hador*, Rav Moshe Feinstein, *zt"l*. Rav Moshe had been our *mesader kiddushin*, and it had taken a few years for us to have our first child. I literally ran over to him to share the news with him. To this day, I can still feel and experience his warm and loving response. I was overwhelmed by the sincerity of his joy conveyed through his piercing eyes, the warmth of his smile and the warm gentle hands that folded over mine in a loving gesture of shared happiness. At that moment, I learned how to wish someone *mazel tov*, or even, *chas v'shalom*, how to give condolences over a loss. Decades later, Rav Moshe's expression from the heart is still with me, and when I wish someone a *mazel tov*, I still attempt to convey this same warmth and sincerity to others.

For everyone else in the *bais medrash*, the moment was unnoticed. Yet for me it has lasted through all these years. This is because each of us yearns to feel a deep sense of connection with another. This is how Hashem has created us. And when these connections are created, a relationship is formed.

During dating and engagement, there are many opportunities to create these memorable connections, which I refer to as "threading the needle" because these shared moments require precise and delicate expressions that come from deep within our selves. There are countless ways to miss these opportunities, just as there are a million ways to miss the eye of the needle. Here is one of many examples that come to mind.

Every year, I receive a call from a young woman in Yerushalayim wishing me a *shanah tovah* (good year) and expressing her *hakaras hatov*. It was about seven years ago when Shani was dating Moshe. Shani felt that Moshe had the qualities she had always looked for in a *chassan* and was ready to proceed if Moshe would ask her. However, Moshe gave no indication of his readiness and this stage in the relationship seemed to be dragging on.

Moshe then told her that he was confused and uncertain and wanted to "take a break, and think things through." Shani felt distraught and saw the chances of this going anywhere as remote. After about a week of not hearing from him, she was informed by a friend that he had not been at work. She learned that he was at home with the flu.

Shani called me to discuss the relationship. At the end of the conversation, I suggested that she Fed Ex him a get well card with a small assortment of chocolates, which she told me he liked. At first, she was hesitant about appearing too aggressive and not "giving him his space."

A few days later, though, she called to say that she and Moshe were engaged. The flu had hit Moshe pretty hard, and he was home feeling quite ill and alone. When the Fed Ex envelope arrived, he thought it was business related and had no desire to open it. But he gave in to his curiosity and saw the letter and candy. He returned her gift with a phone call of gratitude. He had been touched very deeply. Suddenly, the relationship made more sense than ever before; he was moved by her expressions of sincerity and caring. "It was the most wonderful surprise I ever received," he later told her. They were engaged just a few days after.

◇ ## A Thought About "Honest" (Negative) Expressions

One of the most memorable phrases from my initial training in marital therapy back in the 1970s is, "You cannot *not* communicate." In relationships, we are always communicating, whether we are verbal or silent. The embers that lead to trust and commitment never result from being "brutally honest." I can't remember any time that the expression of negative feelings and thoughts played a productive role in bringing couples closer. Deep and real connections only grow from positive expressions that bring two lives together.

I have found with many dating and engaged couples that someone will feel the need to share negative "but honest" thoughts in a phone conversation. The phone is a relatively easy place to express these issues as there is no one in front of you. It's like dropping a bomb from 30,000 feet up. The pilot does not have to face the consequences of his action. In these conversations when something negative is expressed, there is a powerful and destructive effect that cannot be corrected, especially on the phone. I always tell couples that feelings need to be expressed in a way that can be heard and understood, so it allows the relationship to grow, rather than damage it. When negative thoughts are expressed on the phone, they are never helpful. The result of expressing these feelings on the phone is frequently, "I told Chaim my feelings about the way he acted the other night and we spoke for three hours. In the end, we were even further apart." Another common statement is, "When we began to vent our negative feelings in an attempt to be honest with each other, we found ourselves digging deeper and deeper into the negative stuff. All of a sudden, we were left feeling it's all over, but neither of us knew how we got there so fast."

Everything you have read in this book has pointed in one direction — Hashem has created us in a manner that enables us to grow from positive expressions. Sharing negative feelings is almost always destructive, unless done in a manner that permits the message to be heard in a caring, thoughtful and safe manner. Therefore, a crucial principle of expressions is that sharing negative emotions simply because you have "a gut feeling" that needs to be expressed is guaranteed to weaken or destroy a relationship.

You may start with a "gut feeling"; then invest the time to understand and evaluate its veracity; and then spend a lot more time and effort to decide the next step that can help the relationship grow from it.

Many insist that this approach is an unhealthy stifling of our emotions. Yet in Torah life, we are always guided to avoid negative expressions and emotions, even where it seems almost impossible to restrain them. I want to give a very personal example of how a person can hold back from expressing painful emotions that are welling up inside with volcanic force.

> The halachos of Shabbos require us to refrain from any outward expressions of grief or sorrow. This is because Shabbos is a time when the *Shechinah* is present in our home.
>
> How well I remember when my father, *a"h*, tragically died on a Shabbos morning when I was ten years old. My grandmother, a woman of great courage and personal strength, had just lost her precious son, a true *talmid chacham*, who suddenly passed away at the young age of forty-six. Yet throughout that entire Shabbos, she did not utter a single note of grief or pain. But as soon as Shabbos was over, she let out a cry of agony that still reverberates in my mind more than a half century later.

Not expressing negative emotions is much more than sealing our lips. We need to appreciate the reasons that we are not sharing our thoughts and feelings. In essence, we are attempting to maintain our *menuchas hanefesh* state to determine what it will take to preserve the relationship and move beyond the challenge. Still, withholding these negative expressions while holding on to the feelings is futile, because we are always communicating.

> Meir shared his futile attempt to hold his emotions in check. "I'm not happy with Chaya's decisions about our plans after the wedding, but I keep my mouth shut and say nothing." To which Chaya responded, "I appreciate that you work hard at not criticizing me. But do you know what it's like to have someone — the person I am engaged to — glaring at me? I know you're seething inside; I can feel it. It makes me feel terrible. You might as well be screaming at me."

Perhaps this is why Chazal tell us that a sour face is like a *"bor birshus harabim,"* which means that a bad mood is like a ditch in a public place. Everyone nearby is affected, and people invariably fall into it.

In our relationships, our expressions — whether verbal or silent — have the power to build bridges of love and closeness toward *shalom bayis,* and they have the ability to destroy our homes and lives. Perhaps this is close to the meaning of Shlomo Hamelech's words in *Mishlei* (12:18), *"Yaish boteh k'madkeros charev, u'leshon chachamim marpai* — There is one who speaks like the stabbings of a sword, while the language of the wise heals."

In relationship building, we are exquisitely attuned to the countless ways that we and our partners express ourselves — through our words, the tone of our voice and our facial expressions, and in all the ways we communicate in our lives. Because of the profound need for closeness and caring that Hashem has placed within our very beings, we can sense the slightest nuance of interest, sincerity and caring, and, of course, any feelings of rejection, indifference and alienation. Therefore, in order to maintain and cultivate a relationship, we must learn to express ourselves in ways that turn each moment into a shared experience of trust and security. The only acceptable expressions between a dating or engaged couple are those that make each of them feel emotionally safe, respected, cared for and secure.

◇ ## The Art of Listening

Take Responsibility for Your Communications

Your expressions are a function of your state of mind. If you're in a state of *pizur hanefesh*, you will express yourself accordingly, and if you are in a state of *menuchas hanefesh*, it will be expressed and felt. We know this concept from *Mishlei* (27:19) where Shlomo Hamelech says, "*Kamayim hapanim lapanim, kain laiv ha'adam la'adam* — As in water face answers face, so the heart of man to man."

Therefore, your communication has the potential to either evoke a positive response that will strengthen bonds, or provoke a negative reaction that will cause conflict and hurt.

I came across the following concept in Dr. Pransky's excellent book on marital relationships, *The Relationship Handbook*:

If you are critical, you will cause hurt.

If you are angry, you will damage others.

If you are hostile, others will fight you.

If you are indifferent, others will be hurt by you.

If you are annoyed, others will drag their feet.

However ...

If you are patient, others will join you.

If you are appreciative, others will put themselves out for you.

If you are caring, others will pull out all the stops to help.

It's time to realize that it all depends on you.

Pizur Hanefesh Expressions

Being in a state of *pizur hanefesh* causes you to focus on yourself, particularly when you are feeling insecure, needy, upset and disconnected. Falling into a state of *pizur hanefesh* will cause you to use expressions that divide and hurt.

Pizur hanefesh expressions are frequently heard in the following way:

Criticism
"I can't stand when you wear that ugly tie. I'm just telling you the truth."

Loudness
"I realize that I'm raising my voice. I'm just trying to make my point."

Anger
"You're darn right I'm angry — and I have every reason to be!"

Vulgarity and Inappropriate Language
"There's nothing wrong with a few choice words. That's the way people speak today. If it makes you feel embarrassed, you're just too squeamish about these things."

Impatience
"I realize I'm impatient. It's my nature."

Coldness, Silence and Not Caring
"You may feel hurt, but I don't have to buy into your hurt."

Tension
"If my tension is getting you nervous, that's your problem."

Abuse (Physical or Verbal)
"It's not my fault. There's nothing I did to you that was harmful. You're just too sensitive."

Expressions that Flow from *Menuchas Hanefesh*

Menuchas hanefesh expressions reflect a quieter, healthier state of mind that allows you to express yourself in a way that rekindles the embers of trust and closeness. Elevating yourself to a state of *menuchas hanefesh* activates the inner wisdom of your *neshamah* to discover creative and positive expressions of self, which include:

Affirmations: Sharing thoughts and feelings that recognize each other's striving for greatness:
"I really admire the way you devote so much effort to being such a sensitive person."

Gratitude: Learning to say "thank you" is a giving act:
"I deeply appreciate how you helped me out this morning when I was in a rush. I realize it was an imposition. It showed how much you care for me."

Sharing Expressions of Caring: Learning to share your human need for warmth:
"It really makes me feel special when you say and do things that show you care about me."

Empathy: Demonstrating your interest and sincerity:
"I know what you've been going through, and I want you to know that I care about what's been happening."

Vulnerability: Learning to share your humanity:

"I guess there are times like this when I realize how fragile I can be. Thanks for being there for me."

Interest: Demonstrating you care enough to be genuinely interested:
"I was thinking about you and called to see how you are doing."

Acceptance: Learning to accept and value differences:
"I've come to understand that we don't have to be the same. I've come to appreciate you for your differences and uniqueness."

Judging Favorably (being *dan l'chaf z'chus*): Being able to see the positive side:
"I've learned to trust that whatever you are doing, your intentions are correct; and if I'm patient, I'll find you've made the right decision."

Compassion and Warmth: Understanding that your dating partner or *chassan/kallah* needs you to be caring through challenging times:
"I really feel what you are going through. I just want you to know that I'll be there for you."

Expressing Commitment: Learning to share that you are in this forever:
"I understand that things are difficult right now. I want you to know that I am dedicated to seeing you through this rocky patch."

Some Additional Guidance on Expressions

Be Aware of Your Tone: When you are communicating something important, speak softly and gently:
"I've learned that when I speak softly and gently to you, you feel

that I understand you and it helps you listen, as well."

Maintain a Positive Way of Communicating: Speak in positive and gentle terms. Raising your voice or using profanities always horrifies and destroys everything you have created together.

Always Give Feedback: Learn to provide clear and coherent feedback so your partner feels heard and understood: *"I believe I understand what you are saying. I think you are saying that ..."*

Communicate Clearly and Directly: If you have something complex and difficult to say, perhaps you should write it down first to clarify it in your mind. You can then share it verbally or in a letter.

Listen Thoughtfully: You don't always have to speak. Then again, you do have to listen carefully and avoid all distractions, such as cell phones, other people, newspapers, looking at a TV and anything else that will distract you from giving your dating or engaged partner your full attention.

Maintain Frequency of Contact

Dating and engaged couples often forget that their relationship needs to be watered and tended to like a sapling. Many professionals permit their career to get in the way of their relationship-building. Whether it's tax season, a shift in the emergency room schedule, grading finals or a difficult closing, we need to remember that maintaining contact is crucial to this delicate nurturing process. If someone says, "I won't call and I'll see if I miss him," it is like gluing two pieces together that require an hour to set and testing the bond after a few seconds. Relationships take quite a bit of time to develop.

Therefore, remember that you demonstrate your desire to build this relationship by carefully learning to express yourself in every way that helps the EMBERS emerge between yourselves. This is your most important tool.

2. MOODS

The EMBERS Principle: *In a state of menuchas hanefesh, we experience moods that are secure, trusting and loving, and each of these positive moods and feelings contributes to building this most precious of all relationships. When we are in a state of pizur hanefesh, we experience moods that are emotionally insecure, isolating and hurtful. Our goal is to learn that we can always transform our moods and regain our ability to fortify the bond that is being created.*

Dating is an emotionally exhausting experience. It tests every fiber of your being because so much is at stake. This is particularly so for couples who have dated others before and have been hurt and disappointed. Who would not have his guard up and ready in order to be protected against hurt? Then, when we factor in other issues such as professional pressures, family and our emotional ups and downs that have so many possible sources, it's easy to get caught in negative moods. When these moods hit us, they immediately distort everything we know and feel about the person we are dating. Suddenly, nothing is right. Everything seems dark, without a future. A typical comment that emerges from such a mood is, "I don't know what I ever saw in him."

As a relationship evolves, moods change. Consider this very common scenario:

> Sandy is dating Kalman and feels that he has all the qualities she has been looking for. Kalman, as well, initially feels that Sandy is one of the finest people he has ever

met. Both return from the first date with a palpable feeling of hope. Each is able to picture the other as the ideal life partner, who fits well with their ideals and even fantasies.

Yet, as Sandy and Kalman get to know more about each other, they both begin to cue into subtleties and differences that are not quite in synchrony with the idealized fantasies each harbored. They are confronted with a constant need to adjust the fantasy to accommodate the reality, and with each accommodation there is a growing feeling of compromise and disappointment. Before long, their dating is "not going anywhere." In reality, the negative feelings and moods are now obscuring what was and could be right about the relationship — with a cloud about what feels wrong about it.

In truth, every relationship requires continuous readjustment in our emotions and perceptions. The more time we spend with someone, the more we need to readjust to our new realizations of who this person truly is. Still, at no time do we ever really grasp the essence of the individual. I have been married for forty-five years, *Baruch* Hashem, and I still feel that as our lives are unfolding, there is so much more to learn about each other. The art of building a relationship is based on being able to continually adjust our mutual understanding, while learning to maintain the stability and positive quality of our moods.

I referred to this earlier when I discussed the self in transition, where as two people get closer together, they must give up the old perceptions of each other. They are losing the old and incomplete perceptions in order to grasp a newer and more realistic sense of each other — while holding onto a positive state of mind. This is a very great challenge, with a very great reward. It's called discovering your soul partner.

It's important to remember that for younger couples who meet, date and get engaged in a rather short period of time, this challenge in dating is not as great. Their knowledge of each other doesn't require this deepening understanding of each other. Nevertheless, it can be more problematic during the engagement period.

For more mature couples or those who require a longer period of time to get to know each other, moods that set in over time can be a daunting challenge.

> Marion and Steven began dating about a month ago. Both were in their late twenties and had had many disappointing dating experiences in the past. When they began dating, they were mutually elated over their ability to communicate, their shared interest in a Torah home and many other common interests. Both felt they had discovered the right person.
>
> But after about a month, they began to discover differences that caused each of them to fell "less positive" about the relationship. After another month, both were feeling it was going nowhere. Marion actually felt "down" and Steven was "frustrated" at the lack of progress. Now both were back where they'd started from and were ready to end the relationship and move on, as painful as this seemed. What both needed to learn was that moods and feelings have a way of overtaking our positive memories and perceptions. Suddenly, everything they initially saw and felt about each other that created a sense of optimism and promise had disappeared under the foggy bottom of negative moods, or *pizur hanefesh*. Once they learned that we always have the ability to gain mastery over these moods, they were able to continue building their relationship

As I mentioned before, for younger couples, this challenge of shifting moods can be especially problematic during engagement when there is more time to ruminate, to compare your *chassan* or *kallah* to others or harbor misgivings and fears.

Brenda and Michoel were young and engaged after a couple of months of dating. All had gone smoothly and everyone was joyous over the *shidduch*. Yet just a few weeks into the engagement, Michoel began to feel down about the engagement. Nothing had occurred to trigger his moods; then again, his mother did tell me that throughout his growing up, Michoel had experienced episodes of moodiness, and tended to place the blame on others.

Now it seemed that he was having one of his mood episodes once again, but this time he was blaming it on Brenda. His statements sounded like this, "The more I observe her, the more I think I acted too hastily. I should have given it more time."

Michoel trusted his moods. He had been living with them for many years and watched them come and go. Now he saw Brenda as the reason and was ready to jettison his *kallah* for it. As he learned that he was not a prisoner of his moods, he was able to regain a sense of security about Brenda and the engagement.

I have already cited the well-known concept that a face is similar to a *reshus harabim* — a public domain. Our moods and state of mind affect us and those around us. A negative mood, or, as George Pransky calls it, a low mood, is actually contagious. No one can escape its influence. We pass it around like a flu virus. The result is that our young and growing relationships are either enhanced or endangered by our moods. While we can usually ascribe a reason for them, I have found them to be a dimension of our emotional functioning over which we have little control.

When a dating partner or the person you are engaged to has a long face and you don't know why, suddenly the fragile relationship is in jeopardy. Or when you have this glum mood and feel, "I'm stuck in this feeling and helpless to escape from it.

I have no choice but to accept it as real and true," you can come to see your negative moods as reality. I have learned to tell dating couples, "Don't ever trust a negative mood. It is never your friend."

Some people will be aware of their frustrations throughout the day. Others may feel hopeless and depressed, while others will harbor anger. Most will defend their state of mind. Yet, in all my years of working with both married and engaged couples, and even in my own marriage of over four decades, I have never witnessed a negative mood that I came to appreciate as ultimately legitimate. It's the same as someone telling me that they have a body temperature of 103°, and that's where it should be — while I know that our bodies were not created to accommodate such a high temperature. It's all part of our *pizur hanefesh* state. The fundamental principle is that regardless of the trials and challenges that Hashem gives us, we are always expected to cultivate the inner strength to overcome our negative moods. If there are issues that need to be addressed, or changed, they can only be corrected from a state of mind that is experiencing *menuchas hanefesh*.

This is why moods are so essential to our ability to kindle EMBERS. I consistently tell couples that regardless of the past, even if you have become accustomed to expect disappointment, resentment or frustration, the ability to build your relationship depends on not permitting your negative moods to be a significant driving force in your life. Love, trust and closeness can only emerge when you learn to take the first step and begin creating an environment free of these moods.

This is why we build relationships through these EMBERS. We learn to take responsibility for our *pizur hanefesh* moods by being aware of their presence, and then take measures to transform them.

◇ **Some Rules to Remember About Moods**

1. There is no negative mood or feeling that can define your experience of self.

2. Never trust your negative or low moods. They are never your friend. These moods will follow three characteristic patterns:

   + They will always distort your perception about yourself and those closest to you.
   + They will always cause you to make the wrong decision.
   + They will never apologize for having misled you when you realize how tragically you have acted as a result of your negative mood.

3. You can change your moods. Appreciation and trust are just a thought away.

4. You are never your *pizur hanefesh* thoughts or moods. There are always "healthier ones" waiting inside you to be discovered.

5. You are not the bird who is paralyzed by the sight of the snake. Hashem always gives you the keys to discover your wings to freedom.

6. Your negative moods have consequences:

   + A chip on the shoulder creates animosity.
   + Frustration and anger create fear.
   + Depression creates distance.

7. Your turning point for discovering your freedom from your negative moods is to remember the three principles of *Chiddush*, *Tzomet* and *Mishkan*.

8. Focused walking is an excellent way of transforming your moods.

◇ **A Story about Being a Master Over Your Moods**

There are many moods that can undermine relationships. This one was presented in my first book on marriage as it speaks so deeply to me. I believe you'll appreciate why I chose to repeat it here.

> Yaakov and Naomi were married in 1970 and had raised a family of seven children. In 1990, Naomi was diagnosed with cancer and began radiation treatment. Her prognosis was poor.
>
> The couple and their children managed to see themselves through the initial stages of Naomi's treatment, and the illness was brought under control. Even so, Naomi's condition was never quite stable. Hospital stays and an ongoing fear for her life had become part of their marriage and family experience.
>
> About seven years after the initial diagnosis, Yaakov, a computer analyst, filled in one day to teach a *daf yomi* class. It took him many hours to prepare, but the experience was very meaningful. He decided to continue. Meanwhile, Naomi's condition slowly deteriorated. But somehow, she, Yaakov and the children always found the strength to continue on to the next round of radiation, the next hospitalization and the next crisis. In 2009, Naomi passed away. By that time, they had seen all their children married, and Yaakov had completed teaching the *daf yomi* cycle, uninterrupted from the day he began.
>
> Just before her passing, when all the treatments that had succeeded in keeping her alive for almost twenty years could no longer extend her life, it was time to finally say good-bye. Yaakov gathered all the children and their families together around their mother's bed. And as a family, they sang the *Shir Hamaalos*, Psalm 128, that we say

each night before we go to sleep and on Shabbos before it draws to a close (at the end of Maariv).

A Song of Ascents

Fulfilled is each person who fears Hashem, who walks in His ways.

In the labor of your hands when you eat, you are worthy of praise and all is good with you.

Your wife will be like a vine, fruitful in the inner chambers of your home; your children will be like shoots of the olive tree around your table.

So is the blessing of the man who fears Hashem

May Hashem bless you from Tzion and may you gaze at the beauty of Yerushalayim all the days of your life.

And may you see children born to your children. May peace be on Yisrael.

At the funeral, Yaakov eulogized his wife. His message was moving and inspiring. But one thought rang out beyond every other, when he cried, "Naomi, we won!"

The victory was over every moment of torturous pain, despair and hopelessness. They emerged the winners over every battle of the body and mind and defeated every conceivable mood and thought to keep the family growing and loving. And at the end, with their children around her bedside, and the *tehillah* (praise) of David Hamelech on the lips of each child and grandchild, they understood the meaning of their victory.

For most of our lives, our challenges are, *Baruch* Hashem, far less painful. But like Naomi and Yaakov, we are all tested to win the moment-to-moment victory of our *pizur hanefesh* moods and emerge with relationships solidly embedded in the delicate emotions of trust and closeness.

3. BEHAVIOR

The EMBERS Principle: *In a state of menuchas hanefesh, we appreciate the value of behaving toward each other in ways that engender closeness, inclusion, caring and sensitivity. In a state of pizur hanefesh, we behave in ways that are self-serving, exclusionary and uncaring.*

The essential difference between behavior that emerges from *menuchas hanefesh* and that which springs from *pizur hanefesh* is that in our *menuchah* state we are acting in the fullness of our beings. We are relating to our deepest yearnings, fully cognizant of the feelings of those we care for and very much connected to our own deeper *ruchnius* that is our connection to Hashem. *Pizur hanefesh* behavior always gravitates toward our own narrow needs and self interests; it is never sensitive to the deeper needs of others and has no inherent value.

◇ **Having a Good Time**

himon, who was dating Suri, discovered that he "enjoyed going to Atlantic City once in a while." Suri was upset enough to want to stop dating him. When I discussed it with him, his response was, "What's the problem? I spend a lot of time learning; so what if I have a little enjoyment once in while?"

Shimon's statement of innocence triggered a scene I witnessed many years ago, which I continue to see as a paradigm of "socially acceptable" *pizur hanefesh* behavior. Shimon's innocent plea for a good time spoke volumes about him.

273

A number of years ago, my wife and I attended a professional conference on the Jersey Shore. In the evening, we took a short ride to Atlantic City. I had never been in a gambling casino and was curious to view one firsthand.

We entered a massive hall filled with countless slot machines. There were perhaps fifty people in the room. All were hunched over the slots, their hands automatically inserting the coins and pulling the lever as they watched the wheel spin. It was a mindless — almost lifeless — repetition, without thought or soul.

I was reminded of a story I had once read by the author Jack London, about a man in the Klondike, freezing to death. He kept himself alive by running around a frozen lake. And even when he was losing consciousness and close to death, the thrust of his forward movement kept him running. He was essentially a dead body given movement by the sheer instinct of repeating the motion of his legs.

I walked out of the casino shaken to the core. I had witnessed the phenomenon of how living and breathing human beings can become emotionally and spiritually dead, while automatically shelling out money.

I later learned how the industry had designed slot machines so that gamblers feel compelled to continue playing in this thoughtless way. I hoped that professional psychologists were not part of the nefarious design team.

What Shimon did not understand was that his sense of entitlement to have a good time was exposing a deeper trait of enjoying behavior that entraps him in self-perpetuating patterns of mind-numbing repetition. In this socially accepted state of *pizur hanefesh*, Shimon is oblivious to Suri or anyone else. All that matters is the need to continue to try and win, even if it costs him the relationship.

◇ ## The Frog Kickers

Addictions — whether to work, gambling or any other activity — are expressions of *pizur hanefesh*. What these forms of behavior all have in common is a lack of any redeeming emotional, spiritual or relationship value. They are always the result of our not having learned to master our impulses, coupled with the need to mindlessly repeat learned patterns of behavior. I have a name for this population that claims to be unable or unwilling to overcome these impulses. I call them the "frog kickers."

To understand what I mean, let's go back to our history as slaves in Egypt. The second of the ten plagues was the plague of frogs. Yet, a careful reading of the description of the frog invasion reveals that only one frog was initially sent. It was only when an Egyptian hit or kicked that single frog that it multiplied. Then, with each subsequent striking of a frog, the frog population grew geometrically, until there were millions of them. The Brisker Rav, *zt"l*, asked, "What if the Egyptians had not hit that first single frog? Then there would only have been a single, lone frog in all of Egypt. This is certainly not a plague!" He explained that Hashem knew the personality of the Egyptians. He knew they couldn't control their rage, even if they understood that the frogs would only multiply when they were struck.

My principle of repetitive behavior is simple. A frog kicker feels he can't control himself. He or she can be an outraged Egyptian, a gambler, a smoker, a workaholic or a shop-aholic. All these people are driven by forces that create the illusion that their behavior is beyond their control.

Yet, we now understand that Hashem always gives us free will. Shimon really can find a better way to relax and enjoy himself. Nonetheless, in his present distorted concept of relaxation, he sees giving up gambling as a sacrifice he is unable and unwilling to make. As I have said repeatedly, we are never the bird falling helplessly into the mouth of the predator.

> An excellent example I can give of the power of trans-formation that lies within us is based on my own experience as a former smoker. While I now understand that I acquired my addiction through my gullibility and confusion, there was one aspect of my smoking that always fascinated me. On Shabbos, my urge to smoke disappeared. This was very strange, as I know cigarettes create a nicotine addiction. Still, somehow the power of Shabbos quieted that gnawing and perpetual need for the next cigarette.

This power of Shabbos to subdue a strong addictive urge has always demonstrated to me how the spiritual dimension of our being will inevitably prove to be stronger than our physical urges. Unquestionably, this is the strength behind the twelve-step programs that have proven to be the only effective approach to treating severe addictions of almost every kind.

◇ Expressions of *Pizur Hanefesh* Behavior

Most *pizur hanefesh* behavior is not addictive, just repetitive, self-centered and thoughtless. Here are a few examples of those I have come across:

> Chaya had an irrepressible need to text her *chassan*, Dovi. She had a need to keep him filled in on every small and large event in her life. This was her concept of "being close." At first, he found her texting cute. Then he began to feel it was intrusive. "I always feel like if I don't answer, I'm avoiding or even rejecting her. I don't think I can toler-ate being in this kind of marriage."

Clearly, Chaya's texting was driven by a sense of insecurity and the need to feel that Dovi was always there, just waiting to hear the minute-to-minute news of her life. Her inability to feel secure within herself and in their relationship was expressed through the *pizur hanefesh* behavior of incessant texting. Learning to bring her behavior under control and cultivate her sense of security probably saved her engagement.

> Shaul is a lawyer who works long hours in his firm. He had been dating unsuccessfully for a number of years until he finally met Chanah, who he saw as having great potential as a life partner. Yet he was always preoccupied with his work, continuously taking calls, being delayed for almost every date and cutting off calls with Chanah to take office calls. The relationship was in jeopardy. Yet, despite this, Shaul insisted, "I have no choice. This is my profession and these are the demands of my job."

I am not the one to say whether or not he needs to take a call or arrive an hour late. At the same time, I can say that being with Shaul caused me to feel like he was attached to that third rail, which is electrified. He was always plugged in and couldn't stop himself from living every moment in the fast lane. He claimed he had no choice, as he was under nonstop pressure from his firm. From my perspective, Shaul was using the job as much as the job was using him. He did not know how to slow himself down and take control over his need to be living with his foot on the accelerator. Although this works at the office, in relationships it's pure *pizur hanefesh* behavior. Learning to slow down was essential in enabling him to cultivate a trusting relationship with Chanah.

Here are some more examples:

+ Debbie and Shalom were dating seriously. Both had spent a number of frustrating years attempting to discover their *bashert*. They had been dating for about six weeks when Shalom found himself looking on dating

websites to see which of his old dates were actively looking for dates.

+ Alex had indicated to Marcia that he was interested
in getting engaged, yet he was seen by one of Marcia's
friends at a local singles gathering.

+ Moshe loved his new Acura. He especially enjoyed driving at speeds that made Sheila nervous. She asked him
to slow down many times, yet he insisted that she "sit
back and relax."

+ Pearl is a physical therapist who believes it's essential
that she always have a series of questions she will go
through with every new person she is dating. She justifies this behavior by saying, "I went through a very difficult life. I know what it is like for people to hurt people.
I need to make sure I don't fall into the same hole in my
marriage."

We can give countless illustrations of *pizur hanefesh* behavior
and never run out of examples. They will include offensive language, smoking and other addictions, excessive use of the internet, maintaining contact with a large number of social network
"friends," the inability to curb cell phone use and a myriad of
other behaviors that are the direct result of distractedness.

Yet perhaps the most prevalent area of *pizur hanefesh* behavior is when a couple is engaged and they are planning their wedding. This is when all the *pizur hanefesh* floodgates are opened
and the *chassan*, *kallah* and their parents go rushing headlong
into a veritable sea of excessiveness, debt and absurd positions of
inflexibility that destroy the delicate bonds between two people
waiting to start the enterprise of life together. Permit me to
share with you just a few of these absurd, sometimes laughable
and all too frequently tragic forms of *pizur hanefesh* behavior.

Sharon and Meier were sitting with her parents just a few days before the wedding, planning the seating arrangements. Each table provided a daunting challenge. Suddenly, Meier stood up and declared. "I've had enough of this. If this is what my life is going to be like, I don't want it." And with this declaration, he stormed out. The next morning, Meier's parents called to notify Sharon and her parents that he was not continuing with the engagement.

✦ ✦ ✦

Just one week before their wedding, Tziril's father, Mr. Slotney, asked Yechiel, his future son-in-law, to meet him at a New York City steakhouse. He wanted to discuss the children's plans of moving to Eretz Yisrael after the wedding. Yechiel had believed this was agreed upon. In fact, it had been. But Tziril's mother was not yet ready to part with her daughter, so she told her husband to speak to their future son-in-law and ask him to reconsider.

As they sat in the busy steakhouse with aged meat platters flying out of the kitchen at $75.00 a plate, Yechiel was astonished to hear of his future father-in-law's about-face on his support of their move to Eretz Yisrael. As Yechiel turned red and almost choked over the marbleized steak he was trying to digest, Mr. Slotney saw that Yechiel was not very happy with what he was saying. The two men stayed with each other for another half hour or so, and then both went on their way. The next day, Yechiel received a text from his best friend, Chaim, "Y, how come you didn't tell me the wedding was off?"

That's right. After Mr. Slotney left the steakhouse, he called Yechiel's *rebbi* and let him know it was over. The word of the broken engagement reached Chaim before the *chassan*, Yechiel, who learned of his own broken engagement through a text from a third party.

✦ ✦ ✦

Mrs. Lederer was a successful businesswoman, with her own well-known designer store in the heart of the *frum* community. The marriage of her only daughter, Rivka, was an event she had been waiting for since her daughter's birth. Now that Rivka was engaged to Simon, she was determined not to disappoint all her friends, customers and community members. The wedding was planned in the area's most expensive hall. The band size grew to fifteen pieces. The smorg would feature duck, rack of lamb and a sushi extravaganza that would be etched in everyone's memory. The flowers, table arrangements and gowns would set a precedent that would be difficult to repeat.

The only problem was that with each demand, Simon's family grew increasingly outraged. The couple never made it to the *chupah*. Three years later, Rivka is still unmarried.

I realize these are all difficult to absorb. Yet, can we permit these unnecessary tragedies to go unchallenged? Permit me to share a few more, and then I will release you from the horrors of reading about *pizur hanefesh* behavior during engagement.

- The *chassan's* parents broke the *shidduch* because of the struggle over who would be the *mesader kiddushin*.

- The mother of the *kallah* told the caterer before the *badecken* (veiling the *kallah's* face right before the wedding ceremony), "Tell your people to start clearing everything away. We're leaving."

- Sonya was a *kallah* who had been brought up in a home with all of life's gifts placed at her feet. After becoming engaged, she decided that her *chassan* was not the kind of person she was looking for. So one day, she shared the following emotional statement with him, "I feel like I'm ready to jump off a bridge unless we stop this wedding."

What all these stories attempt to illustrate is that our newly acquired pursuit of meaningless superficialities has become the death knell to countless engagements and relationships. It leaves everyone feeling empty, vacuous and isolated from each other. It deprives us of our *tzelem Elokim* and creates fantasies that are impossible to achieve.

I am aware of the reasons. We live in a country that has enabled us to grow financially, numerically and in our Torah learning. However the price of our revival is that so many have bought into its excesses and superficialities. The result is an emptiness that hurts deeply while it ensnares and destroys lives. When Rav Yecheskel Abramsky, *zt"l*, arrived on these shores after the war, he remarked that he could not remain in America, as it was a country founded on *sheker* (lies and deceit). Many have been able to transcend the illusions of America and build wonderful Torah lives here. On the other hand, far too many have succumbed to the influence that drove Rav Yecheskel to seek his *ruchnius* elsewhere, which eventually brought him to Eretz Yisrael.

When we are in a *menuchas hanefesh* experience of self, our behavior is the result of our *bechirah chafshis*. It is focused, meaningful, productive, inclusive and relationship-building. When we are in a *pizur hanefesh* experience of self, our behavior tends to be self-centered, need-gratifying, unaware and uncaring of consequences, insensitive to others and compelled by destructive forces within us.

◇ **You are expressing *pizur hanefesh* behavior when:**

+ You have a need to date as many people as possible.
+ You feel you can determine whether someone is for you after one date or even a few minutes.

- You spend excessive time on the internet.

- You need to continuously text.

- You watch inappropriate movies or television shows.

- You are addicted to any of the following:
  - Cigarettes
  - Alcohol
  - Gambling
  - Working unnecessarily long hours

- You use aggressive and inappropriate language.

- You find yourself shouting and threatening.

- You find yourself compulsively complaining that "there is no one to date."

- You maintain "friends" of the opposite gender on your Facebook or any other social network account.

- You drive too fast or without a seat belt, and need to be first out of the intersection when the light changes.

- You purchase a car, house or anything else that you hope will impress others.

- You listen to rap or other violent music, or go to adrenaline-pumping movies.

- You have a habit of biting your nails or pulling your hair, skin, nose, etc.

- You get bored easily and need excitement.

◇ **In wedding planning, you are expressing** *pizur hanefesh* **behavior when:**

- You feel an urge to impress others in a manner that places you or others into financial debt.

- You judge love by the size of an engagement ring or cost of a bracelet, cuff links, etc.

- You find yourself in battles over any of the issues related to:
  - The chupah
  - *Sheva brachos*
  - Invitations
  - Seating
  - Menu planning
  - *Kibbudim* (honors)
  - The hall
  - The timing

(It is wise to always have a *Rav* to consult with on each of these issues.)

◇ **You are expressing *menuchas hanefesh* behavior when:**

- You carefully select an appropriate *Rav* to whom you will address all questions and conflicts and whose guidance you plan to follow.

- You show patience and understanding.

- You understand that relationship-building has its challenges and struggles, regardless of your dating partner, *chassan* or *kallah*.

- You do not confuse your possessions with your self.

- You realize that one day you will stand face-to-face with Hashem and give a *cheshbon hanefesh* (spiritual accounting).

- You put your desire to discover your *bashert* above your job, profession and personal interests.

◇ **Strategies to Transform Your *Pizur Hanefesh* Behavior**

+ The most important first step is to understand and appreciate the impact of your *pizur hanefesh* behavior on your relationship with Hashem. Nothing you will ever gain from this behavior will be of ultimate benefit. And if it is severe enough, it will undermine all that is truly precious in your life.

+ When you experience an urge to engage in one of your *pizur hanefesh* behaviors, use the three principles I have discussed as a way of reducing your urge and compulsion to act in a destructive manner.

+ Consult your *Rav* or mentor before acting on your behaviors.

+ Whenever you succeed, even by small victories, congratulate yourself for the courage and strength you are showing.

+ If your behavior is an addiction to cigarettes, gambling, texting or any other addictive behavior, consult with a professional to determine how to overcome the problem.

+ If your behavior is expressed through anxiety and a need to act out, first attempt to use exercises such as Focused Walking, Meditative Walking or the Pulse of Life.

4. ENJOYMENT

The EMBERS Principle: *In a state of menuchas hanefesh, we share enjoyable moments that deepen the foundations of our relationships. In a pizur hanefesh state, enjoyment is self-centered,*

*narcissistic and progressively destructive to our ability to build trust-
ing and close relationships.*

◇ Contemporary Concept of Enjoyment and Pleasure

The word enjoyment conjures images and emotions associated
with our need to be excited and entertained, and to fill every
aspect of our lives with pleasure, fine food, vacations and leisure
hobbies. And the recipient of all these lavish gifts is none other
than "me."

This is why *shidduchim*, dating and engagement have become
such a nightmare for so many. The focus is on the concrete and
superficial needs of the self. Rabbi Paysach Krohn, *shlit"a*, had
a precious insight regarding Apple Computer's naming of its
products, such as the iPad, the iPhone and the iPod, with the
focus of all of our efforts — the "I" — included in their names.
I have come to appreciate that these forms of "enjoyment" are
actually empty expressions of *pizur hanefesh* designed to fill
the vacuum of our deepest feelings of emptiness, unhappiness
and loneliness. There may very well be a correlation between
these electronic gadgets and being unable to maintain and
build relationships that lead to marriage.

The success of these forms of enjoyment is that they profit
by feeding on fantasy and self-centered needs, whether it's a
thrilling movie scene or a fast or luxury car. The same would
apply to an expensive meal at a trendy "fusion steakhouse" —
where the ambience is edgy and electric, filled with other couples, both married and single, who are out to enjoy themselves
in a public environment that generates an excitement and the
feeling of "me" and "now."

In our society, which is so focused on enjoyment and pleasure, there are countless ways that individuals and couples

participate in the "good life." Pursuing this illusion destroys any chance they have of sharing deep and true moments of mutual bonding. The reason is simple. Superficial pleasure and enjoyment are a function of *pizur hanefesh*; they are never fulfilling. They always leave us hungry for more because they emerge from the feeling that "I need to fill my needs." Chazal (*Koheles Rabbah* 1:34) teach that one who has one hundred wants two hundred. There is little meaning or deep emotional bonding in our society's concept of enjoyment because it is driven by narcissism and economics.

◇ **A Parting *Brachah***

Our concept of enjoyment is based on bringing happiness into someone's life, which is illustrated in this story of how a *gadol* guided a *talmid* toward saving his marriage.

"*Samayach tesamach rayim ha'ahuvim* — Gladden the beloved companions ..." This is the fifth of the *sheva brachos*, which are the seven blessings we recite at the wedding ceremony and each day during the week following the wedding. It means that the new couple should share a life dedicated to bringing joy and happiness into each other's lives.

> When Rav Shlomo Freifeld, *zt"l*, was in the final stages of his long illness and was unable to accept visitors, a young man we'll call Ari showed great persistence in attempting to gain a few precious minutes with the Rosh Yeshivah. In the end, he prevailed. Several years later, Ari was asked what had transpired during those moments spent with Rabbi Freifeld. He answered that just a few words from his Rosh Yeshivah changed his life.
>
> Ari and Aviva had been married for a number of years, and life together had been unstable and tumultuous. Ari was looking for guidance to help him understand what

Hashem wanted of him in this marriage.

The Rosh Yeshivah told Ari that the answer can be found in the *sheva brachos*. He directed the young man to consider the *brachah*, "*Samayach tesamach rayim ha'ahuvim*," that in order to create a close and beloved friendship, our focus is always on how to help the person who shares our life to feel *b'simchah* (happy). At that moment, the young man was able to grasp that he could find fulfillment and *shalom bayis* by bringing *simchah* (happiness) to his wife every minute of their lives together.

This is what we need to do help each other feel loving and beloved. This *brachah* is not just meant for the night of the wedding, but is a guiding principle for every second a couple shares in this world. Hashem wants us to learn how to supply each other's lives with *simchah* and enjoyment.

◇ **The *Aishel* of Avraham Avinu**

The Alter of Kelm, *zt"l*, proposed a profound question. The Torah spends just a few sparse sentences describing the *Aishel* of Avraham Avinu. The *Aishel* is the inn where he lavished all visitors with fine food, lodgings and drink, just so they could express their gratitude to Hashem. If Avraham Avinu had spent decades providing this enjoyment to others, why, asks the Alter, does the Torah only deal with it in a few sentences? His answer is that the Torah did not need to elaborate on who came to this *Aishel* or what they received. Its primary message is about how Avraham Avinu cultivated his determination and boundless ability to develop a limitless inner capacity to give to others, without any personal agenda. He did this for the sole purpose of enabling others to enjoy and appreciate the many gifts Hashem bestows upon each of us in our lives. This is what makes us different from others.

As discussed earlier, in the Shabbos Minchah Shemoneh

Esrei we mention the many dimensions of *menuchah* so central to the Shabbos experience. One of the descriptions is *"menuchas ahavah u'nedavah* — the *menuchah* of love and giving." Hashem wants us to experience this on Shabbos through filling our physical and spiritual selves with life's deepest pleasures. Through this experience, we are filled with a deeper sense of love and an ability to give and share. Avraham Avinu was a giver all his life because he cultivated this *menuchas hanefesh* throughout his life. His clarity and purpose enabled him to be the consummate giver, who personified the quality of *chessed*.

Rav Eliyahu Dessler, *zt"l*, a *talmid* of the Alter of Kelm and author of *Michtav M'Eliyahu*, describes how the root of the word to love, *ahavah*, is *hav*, to give. In essence, giving is the primary focus of all our efforts in building a relationship. Building a relationship in dating and engagement is the result of our inner determination to help others experience enjoyment through our many gifts of *chessed*. In giving, we experience an expansion of our selves. This is why Avraham Avinu became the father of our nation. He gave others throughout his life, and his legacy has been firmly imprinted in our spiritual DNA for the past nearly 4,000 years.

Therefore, whenever we share a warm and encouraging thought, affirm someone, are *mevaker choleh* (visit the sick) or do anything that brings happiness, relief, joy or comfort into the life of another, we are expressing this wonderful *middah* of Avraham Avinu. It is this very special quality of giving so others can enjoy that brings our lives together and serves as a central element in EMBERS.

> Menny and Julie had been dating for a few months and Pesach was approaching. Julie had hoped that they would become engaged before the holiday, and then perhaps even spend part of Pesach together as *chassan* and *kallah*.

Menny was self-supporting as his mother was a widow, and his primary form of support was through working part-time for a kashrus organization as a *mashgiach*. While he would not work as a *mashgiach* on Pesach, he did agree to work the month before. Thus, he was out of town and unable to date Julie.

At first, Julie was upset and even wondered whether the engagement would ever occur. Then, after discussing her options with me, we decided that she would send Menny a package that contained a warm letter and some candies to enjoy while he was working.

After receiving the small package, Menny called her to say that the package had come when he was feeling very lonely. It meant a great deal to him and he enjoyed everything she had sent. When he returned, the couple became engaged.

In each act, word or gesture that brings a smile to the face of a dating partner, *chassan* or *kallah*, the relationship is strengthened because we have acted in a manner that reflects our own recognition of how we expand, grow and grow closer when we bring enjoyment into the lives of others. This is the essence of an awareness that emerges from our *menuchas hanefesh*.

Here are a few ways to bring enjoyment into the life of someone you care for:

+ Send a card that says, "You are special."

+ Send a small gift that symbolizes the essence of the relationship. (Teddy bears are great.)

+ Learn to affirm by sharing something you value in your partner.

+ Show appreciation for the way your life is enriched through this relationship.

+ Care about the people your partner cares for.

+ Focus on the exclusiveness of your relationship.

Here are a few things to avoid since they do not bring enjoyment:

+ Avoid constant texting since it creates pressure.

+ Never hurt someone's feelings or criticize.

+ Never express your feelings in a hurtful way.

+ Never look for excitement as a way of generating enjoyment.

+ Never try to be someone you are not.

5. *RUCHNIUS*/SPIRITUALITY AS A BOND

The EMBERS Principle: *Ruchnius is the development of our internal sense of spirituality. Through it, we grow in ways that enable a relationship to thrive with deeply meaningful religious and shared experiences of traditions and mitzvos. The absence of ruchnius creates a spiritual vacuum that is filled by countless expressions of pizur hanefesh that undermine every relationship.*

◇ **Introduction**

Ruchnius is at the heart of our relationships. It serves as the spiritual bond that has always brought our lives together and has enabled couples over four millennia to build lives together that lasted for a lifetime.

A few years ago, this was clarified for me in a very poignant manner when the *rebbetzin* of Rav Avigdor Miller, *zt"l*, passed away. I went to be *menachem* the *aveil*, Rav Shmuel Miller, *shlit"a*, who was sitting *shivah* on Ocean Parkway (in Brooklyn) in the house that his parents had lived in since their move from Canarsie in the 1960s. Rav Shmuel Miller was sharing the significance of the family's move to set up a new home and *kehillah* on Ocean Parkway in Flatbush. In his telling, he revealed a fascinating and compelling piece of information. "In the thirty-four years since establishing the shul here on Ocean Parkway, there was not a single divorce in our *kehillah*."

I was not surprised. The fact that there was not a single divorce in a community for a third of a century is testimony to the strength of leadership of a man of deep vision and commitment to Torah life. Hearing Rav Miller's lectures on *shalom bayis* provided clear and indelible guidelines for how Hashem desires a husband and wife to create their lives within the ever-fulfilling environment of Torah life.

Rav Miller's achievement was clearly based on his ability to guide couples to integrate the *ruchnius* of Torah into their lives. In the same way that our *neshamah* breathes life into our physical beings, *ruchnius* brings depth, meaning and life-giving fulfillment into our relationships, while its absence creates hollowness and a vacuum that leaves a couple dependent on their self-gratifying physical and material needs — which is never really gratifying.

◇ The Illusion of Our Dream Marriage

To illustrate this, I want to describe three marital situations of young couples who believed they were entering into "dream marriages," only to discover how the lack of *ruchnius* left their relationships empty and vacuous.

I attended a wedding one June evening and noticed a young married couple who stood out among the others in their attention-getting mode. I recognized the wife, who had come to see me about two years earlier when she was still single. She was now thinner, wearing a tight skirt and blouse, and her *shaitel* was long and natural-looking. Her look was attention-grabbing, even seductive. She was not at all the way I remembered her when she was single. Her husband was also dressed smartly. As he passed by, I smelled his cologne, mixed with the odor of cigarettes; he was clearly a smoker. He kept looking at his Blackberry, sending and receiving messages. I couldn't help but notice that he was wearing a Rolex watch worth at least $5,000.

The couple had a conspicuously prosperous look. Even more obvious was that while they were together, their focus was on how others saw them. They measured their own value as individuals by the mask of affluence and success they wore.

Later that evening, the *chassan* and *kallah* finally returned from their prolonged photography session. The band began their dramatic countdown, culminating with an ear-splitting blast: "Ladies and gentlemen, for the very first time as husband and wife …" As I heard the brashness of the bandleader and remembered the couple I had observed before, I felt saddened over the loss of *ruchnius* in our lives. We seem unable to comprehend that in this *"goldene medinah"* of America, something very precious has been lost — and we are just too busy celebrating the emptiness to be distressed.

The story doesn't end there. About a month later, I received a call from Judy, the same young woman I saw at the wedding. Judy did not realize that I had seen her at the wedding. She and Shmuel had been married for about a year, and she was fearful that their relationship was not going to last. As we spoke, she shared her initial excitement about finally finding a guy who was *"frum* and successful."

As a *kallah*, she'd looked forward to enjoying the "good life." But all the illusions had long since evaporated.

In their marriage, she felt constant pressure to be someone she was not. "Shmuel wants me to dress like a model, and likes when other men look at me." She seemed embarrassed to share this with me. She also revealed that Shmuel had become friendly with girls in the office, and was part of a group of guys who would impulsively "fly to Vegas for a night." She proceeded to describe their life as a "*frum*" couple that was not only profoundly superficial and empty, but also filled with endless anxiety, hurt and insecurity. For this couple, the *frum* version of Camelot really turned out to be a life of endless hurt and suffering. And now, just a year after their "dream marriage," the persona was falling apart at the seams. It was a marriage of all show and no *ruchnius*.

I would imagine that most of the guests at that wedding who noticed Judy and Shmuel saw them as a couple who really had their "act together." There may have been some who even envied them by falling for their disguise. This is not surprising. In our contemporary world of illusions, a slim, pretty, young wife and her well-groomed husband who oozes success are viewed as a symbol of life's ultimate happiness. At the same time, from an internal perspective, their determined effort to cultivate their "image" reveals a deeper poverty of the spirit. Neither feels secure within themselves or with others. Both have bought into the illusion that happiness is based on satisfying the superficial needs of our lives. They are convinced that achieving "perfection" in the physical sense of looks, possessions and personal enjoyment is the true answer to their shared happiness. But on a deeper level, they always knew the truth resided in a connection that grew from within, and now it is becoming more painfully apparent to them.

This kind of external perfectionism always leads to unhappiness and dissatisfaction with each other because it places the center of self on life's externals: clothing, the car — the image that evokes the envy of others. When this is how we perceive ourselves, we have no way of learning how to share deeper, more caring and closer experiences.

> Pearl and Steve were in their mid-twenties and had been married for three years. Pearl was a teacher and Steve an accountant. They found themselves in constant conflict, particularly when it came to deciding on leisure activities. Both considered themselves solidly "*frum*," but both described themselves as "movie and TV addicts." Yet their tastes in movies were very different. Pearl preferred comedies and romantic movies and TV shows, while Steve enjoyed adventure sagas and sports broadcasts. And given their subscription to the cable networks, there was always a sporting event to watch.
>
> Each viewed the other's disinterest in their movie and TV preferences as a sign of disloyalty. Frequently, their conflicting interests would result in an argument. And while they disagreed on the content, they steadfastly insisted on the legitimacy of their behavior. "Maybe others who are *frum* don't agree, but we think it's normal for us to have an outlet from our work and pressures."

Hearing them talk reminded me of a magazine ad I saw for TV headphones. In the ad, there was a picture of a couple, both wearing headphones and watching their own shows. Underneath the picture was the caption: "These headphones saved our marriage." Clearly there is no marriage, and probably never was one.

Steve and Pearl's values and behavior posed a great challenge for me. The content of these movies was only serving to further divide them as a couple. Yet their investment in these forms of entertainment reflected a profound emptiness in their own sense of *ruchnius*. With each movie and TV show, they continued to numb their sensitivities toward each other, themselves and Hashem. They had both grown up in spiritual deserts, which were *frum* in behavior yet lacked any understanding or appreciation of *ruchnius*. As a result, on one level they truly were "normal," and on another they lacked an appreciation for *ruchnius* as the very essence of human experience. On the surface they were "*frum*." They kept *taharas hamishpachah* (the laws of family purity), observed Shabbos and kept kosher, and Steve attended his regular *shiurim*. Yet on a level beneath their practice, they were the equivalent of being "spiritually challenged." It left a gaping hole in every aspect of their shared and personal lives.

There are also situations in which there is a lack of *ruchnius* even where Torah observance is intense. The absence of this spirituality creates a void of human feelings and sensitivity.

The third and final example was with a young *kollel* couple, still in their first year of marriage. On the surface, all appeared to be ideal. However, beneath this idyllic image, the young *kallah*, Miriam, was experiencing a deep sense of suffering. Her husband, Moshe, came from a family who was very demanding in their precise practice of *mitzvos*, and even more so about cleanliness. Miriam's family was more relaxed and easygoing, and more emotionally expressive and gentle with each other. From the beginning of their marriage, Moshe openly expressed his disappointment over the many areas in which Miriam fell short of his expectations.

During our first session, she was close to tears. "I feel like I'm always on probation, where everything I do is evaluated and scrutinized," she admitted.

When I questioned Moshe about his criticism of Miriam, he was insistent and unyielding in his standards.

"A *frum* home needs to be clean and orderly," he said. "And if you're going to do a *mitzvah*, make sure you do it well."

After understanding the source of the conflict, I asked Moshe, "What do you believe the *Shechinah* requires before It can safely dwell in your home — a spotless floor or a wife who feels loved and cared for?" It took a while before he began to get the message.

Ruchnius is not just religious behavior. It enables us to experience our deeper need for each other and for Hashem. It is based on an understanding of the love that Hashem feels for each of us and our capability to develop love for others. In this way, we learn to feel whole and complete.

When we are passively watching a movie or a baseball game, we have cut off our relationship to our self. And when we are obsessing over cleanliness, here, too, we have lost our awareness of our deeper and more human self.

Ruchnius is our ability to experience the delicate internal awareness of this warm and deeply human self as we perform Hashem's *mitzvos*, learn His Torah, daven and cultivate closeness and human feelings within our growing relationships. Living within *ruchnius* creates a bridge between our own *neshamos* and those closest to us. Without this sensitivity — which is so much a part of *ruchnius* — trust, closeness and caring will always elude us.

With true *talmidei chachamim*, we are always inspired by the level to which they have refined their *ruchnius*, which is reflected in their own lives and experienced by others.

We recently learned of the tragic loss of Rebbetzin Basha Scheinberg, *a"h*, the wife of the *gadol*, Rav Chaim Pinchus Scheinberg, *shlit"a*. Their relationship was legendary. They had been married for almost eighty years without ever arguing.

To many this seems absurd, almost as if they were missing out on something special. But to anyone who cultivates *ruchnius* in his or her life, this is very understandable. *Ruchnius* is the ability to have all of our thoughts, feelings, language and values carefully guided by a deeper sense of Hashem's love for us, and this is apparent in each relationship and *mitzvah*.

> Rav Reuven Feinstein, *shlit"a*, told of his father's (Rav Moshe's) love for him. He shared that when he was growing up, his father would awaken at 4 a.m. On cold winter mornings, his father would place his son's pants on the warm radiator, so that when he woke up later he would feel the warmth against the bitter New York winter cold. Surely he meant the warmth of his father's love as much as the warmth of his clothing.

Ruchnius is not isolation or asceticism; it's living a life that constantly experiences the warmth of Hashem's love, and sharing the beauty of this love with others. This is why it is one of the EMBERS and why it plays such a central role in *shalom bayis*.

How do we gain this sense of *ruchnius*? While it's certainly a quality of our *neshamah*, given the secular and self-absorbed environment in which we live, we cannot use our intuition to cultivate this sensitivity. *Ruchnius* is a direct result of three central elements.

First, it is acquired through emulating and internalizing the gentleness and caring of individuals and couples whose lives thrive in the beauty of Torah life. We cultivate our own sense of *ruchnius* by making these individuals part of our inner circle and emulating their language, behavior and acts of greatness, both overt and covert.

Second, we acquire *ruchnius* by opening our lives to the wisdom of *talmidei chachamim*, the *bais medrash* and the world of Torah. *Ruchnius* means filling our lives with Torah knowledge and *shiurim*, attending learning groups and creating a Torah atmosphere that permeates our lives.

Third, we develop *ruchnius* through learning that we have the power to limit ourselves. We limit our exposure to the influences of the secular world and negate the belief that our happiness is determined by the next indulgence. It is achieved through learning that we can express our thoughts, feelings and needs in harmony with the *retzon Hashem*.

Therefore, when we consider that Rav Miller's *kehillah* went for thirty-four years without a divorce, it was clear that under his guidance, *ruchnius* became an intrinsic and stabilizing dimension of their lives. In contrast, the challenge faced by so many couples today is that their lives are filled with so many empty, personal pursuits — and rarely by shared experiences of *ruchnius* in their marital and family lives.

◇ **Losing the Essence of Life**

Returning to the wedding scene I described at the beginning of this section, I have come to understand how it's so easy for us to see Judy and Shmuel as the epitome of success, based solely on the image of material achievement they show the world. For me, they represent the greatest challenge that exists when building close and loving relationships. There are countless demonstrations of this emptiness when we don't feel fulfilled in marriage. We turn instead to our watches, cars, clothing, gym membership and wireless devices to draw the attention we crave.

The formula is simple. When *shtick*, loud music, fast cars and expensive clothing are viewed as signs of success and happiness, then we have lost all sense of our inner lives. When young yeshivah men are in search of girls with that "look," and so many girls are chasing that empty persona of success, then we have lost our bearings. When a young woman insists that any young man she dates should have already achieved financial success, she may never find someone who is truly her *bashert*. None of these dream machines can ever understand what needs to be done to bring two lives closer together.

◇ **Bilaam's Vision**

When Bilaam, the gentile prophet, gazed down from his mountaintop view, he saw the tents of Israel laid out in front of him in the desert sands. Startled by the unspeakable beauty of Am Yisrael's families, who were living in close yet distinct proximity to each other, he expressed the words that we repeat each morning, even before we daven, "*Mah tovu ohalecha, Yaakov, mishkenosecha, Yisrael* — How beautiful are your tents, Yaakov, your tents, Yisrael" (*Bamidbar* 24:5). Chazal say that he was expressing his awe over how families can be so close yet so respectful of each other's uniqueness and privacy. Each family was careful to look inward into its own home and away from the homes of others. Personal, marital and family fulfillment emerges within the very private boundaries of marital and family bonds. This is the essence of the *ruchnius* that Rav Miller taught his *kehillah* and which has accompanied every intact Torah family since Avraham and Sarah laid the foundations for all our families.

When couples are dating or are engaged, there is a tendency to compare and fantasize over other partners. Our minds so easily accommodate "what ifs" in considering how a dating relationship or an engagement would be so much better if there were another partner. In truth, we all realize the absurdity of this form of *pizur hanefesh* and its very prominent role in destroying relationships, when the "what if" can never be as sweet in the reality as it is in the fantasy. The results are always a deep sense of loss and remorse.

Here are a few guidelines for cultivating *ruchnius* in your dating or engaged relationship:

Ruchnius in Your Relationships

+ Develop a relationship with a *Rav* you respect and trust to guide you through each phase of your dating, engagement and marriage, and select a partner who has a *Rav*, as well.

+ When you are closer to engagement and marriage, select a *Rav* you both trust.

+ Remain focused in your own relationship and not on the external behavior of other relationships.

+ Never look for physical, social or financial "perfection." It never turns out to be perfect. You will only be trapped by your own blindness when this is your goal.

+ The only "perfection" you are looking for is someone who is dedicated to caring for others, without manifesting negative character traits, such as anger or impatience.

+ Never do anything together that violates any halachah; it will always weaken and even destroy your relationship.

Praying from the Inside

+ Learn to daven more slowly, thoughtfully and with feeling. If possible, use a *sefer* such as *Pathways to Prayer* (Feldheim) or *Praying with Fire* (ArtScroll) to enhance your focus and feelings.

+ Learn to be quiet and reflective in shul.

+ Shut off your cell phone and never check your Blackberry while davening. This is your time to spend with Hashem.

Growth through Torah

+ Join a *mussar* or *hashkafah vaad*.

+ Get a *chavrusa* or join a morning or evening *kollel*.

+ Use travel time to listen to Torah material.

Language and Expressions

+ Never use an angry tone or phrase, or profanity of any kind.

Planning Your Home as an Ark

+ Decide to decorate your home with portraits of individuals who personify the essence of *ruchnius*.

+ If you will have an internet connection, plan to use a filter to ensure your safety from the immorality that pervades our society.

+ Be careful about the newspapers, magazines, videos and music you will bring into your home that could possibly promote the destruction of your *ruchnius* and *shalom bayis*.

Choose Your Interests and Relationships Wisely

+ For your future marriage to succeed, you will need to detach yourself from other relationships that dilute your shared sense of closeness. This is particularly true of social networking relationships, membership in clubs and contact with single friends of the opposite gender.

+ Never try to attract attention from the opposite gender through your dress or lifestyle.

Be Proactive about Chessed

+ Develop or participate in a *chessed* project, where caring for others becomes an integral aspect of your personal life.

◇ The Centrality of Shabbos

There are countless areas of our lives where we can internalize this sense of *ruchnius* that enhances *menuchas hanefesh* and your future *shalom bayis*. However, I believe Shabbos may be one of the most important.

Shabbos is central to our *ruchnius* and *menuchas hanefesh* because through it Hashem provides us with the opportunity to be free of the incessant compulsions of our work and stress. It has a power to elevate us beyond the pull of our own primitive needs and habits.

> From my years of smoking, I can vividly remember grabbing that last cigarette before Shabbos. I felt like a prisoner desperately stuffing down his last meal before being taken away, as if I just couldn't get enough of the smoke. Yet once Shabbos set in, for a reason that I could never explain, I experienced no need for a smoke for the next twenty-five hours and experienced no nicotine withdrawal. As I mentioned earlier, this actually defied everything we know about nicotine dependency. And I can still remember, when Shabbos drew to a close, feeling the itch for that column of black tar to seep into my lungs once again.

Since then, I have come to discover that Shabbos serves our lives in many more beautiful ways because it is the primary source of our *menuchah, shalom bayis* and *ruchnius*. Not only did it free a confused adolescent from a noxious addiction, it frees an entire People to learn how to acquire the *menuchah* that serves as the foundation of our inner freedom from all life's compulsions. On

Shabbos, we are free to have a relationship with Hashem, ourselves and all those around us. Perhaps this is why the *brachah* in Minchah Shemoneh Esrei says, "*v'al menuchasam yakdishu es Sh'mecha* — and through the *menuchah* of Shabbos they will sanctify Your Name." Just by experiencing this *menuchah*, we elevate our existence.

Shabbos is not just cessation from work. We can stop working with our bodies, yet our minds can still be spinning with all the worries and pressures we need to leave behind. It's only through the *menuchah* of Shabbos that the veil is lifted on the illusion that it is our efforts and the blind forces of nature that drive our existence and the universe around us. The reality is that it is Hashem Who creates our success and brings life to the world. On Shabbos, our focus is on cultivating our experience of inner quiet and *menuchas hanefesh*.

The *Sifsei Chaim* describes how we can enhance our sense of *menuchas hanefesh* on Shabbos. The Torah says (*Shemos* 20:9) to finish "*kol melachtecha* — all your work." Yet we know that "all your work" is not finished. We all anticipate returning to our work after Shabbos. Rav Friedlander, *zt"l*, tells us to actually believe that our work is finished, and there is nothing more to be done — now and forever. With such an approach, our minds can let go of the compelling influences that create a sense of *pizur hanefesh*. With this, we can train and control our minds to achieve a level of inner calm and belief that are the essence of *ruchnius* and *menuchas hanefesh*.

Through the *menuchah* of Shabbos, we learn to quiet our minds and feel "as if" all our work is done and there is nothing left to do. The illusion that we are the "doer" gives way to the deeper awareness that every moment of our existence, the entire universe is brought into being by Hashem. All our achievements and every stirring in our world are lovingly empowered by Him. And while throughout the week this is no less true, when we achieve *menuchah* on Shabbos, we can actually feel it. With *menuchah*, the veil is lifted on the deepest and quietest secret of the universe.

Why are we compelled to work hard throughout the week? We work hard and are driven to make the effort because this is what Hashem said to Adam Harishon: *"B'zaias apecha tochal lechem* — You will eat bread by the sweat of your brow" (*Bereishis* 3:19). In the words of the Alter of Kelm, we must never lose sight that our *hishtadlus* — our effort — is merely our motions, and it's Hashem Who creates the achievement. The Alter continues by explaining that when we achieve this awareness of the true secret of the universe, it is similar to breaking a wine barrel and discovering that it wasn't the barrel that was keeping the wine within its walls. It was always Hashem. The retaining powers of the walls were just an illusion. It is the same illusion that causes us to believe it is our efforts that create our achievements.

Therefore, when Shabbos enters, we have the ability to quiet our minds that are so busy with completing our work, and accept the reality that our work is truly finished. In this way, Shabbos becomes our portal to *ruchnius*. When we achieve this, we can access the strength to experience *menuchas hanefesh* that has the power to remain within us all week. This is why Chazal refer to a *tzaddik* as Shabbos. When we learn to cultivate this essence of *ruchnius* on Shabbos, we can integrate its countless lessons into the way we live as individuals, as couples and as families.

◇ Bringing *Ruchnius* into Your Shabbos

Here are some guidelines for creating a Shabbos experience with your future partner. Chazal inform us that after the Creation of the world, Hashem understood what was missing. It was *menuchah*, spiritual rest, and with the introduction of Shabbos on the seventh day of Creation, *menuchah* was introduced into our world.

Begin Each Shabbos the Right Way

As Shabbos approaches, attempt to bring it in a few minutes earlier, so you are not harried. Then tell yourself, "I am beginning Shabbos by feeling and believing that all my work is done. Hashem does everything and there is nothing left for me to do. I will cultivate this feeling through the day of Shabbos."

Create a Shabbos Table Filled with Wonderful Thoughts and Inspiring Ideas

I very much like the idea of having a designated *sefer* for the Shabbos table. Rav Shimshon Pincus's thoughts on Shabbos are contained in *Nefesh Shimshon* (Feldheim), from which I try to read each Shabbos at the table.

Learn to Sing Inspiring Zemiros at the Shabbos Table

There was a well-known *gadol* in Eretz Yisrael whose son, while still *frum*, had clearly left the *derech* (path) of his father. When the *gadol* was asked what could have caused this, his response was, "Perhaps because we never sang together at the Shabbos meals."

Bring Guests into Your Shabbos Environment

Chazal tell us that guests at the Shabbos table do more for the hosts than the hosts do for the guests. You will find this is true as guests frequently inspire talk, song and a greater appreciation of the meaning of Shabbos.

Spend Time Together as a Couple

Shabbos is a time for developing closeness in your relationship, where you can share a quiet walk or discussion to appreciate each other's company.

Avoid Anything That Can Lead to an Argument or Anger

Chazal were very sensitive about maintaining the *shalom* of Shabbos. The *Gemara* (Shabbos 23b) asks: If there is only enough money to purchase either Chanukah lights or lights for the Shabbos candles, which is more of an obligation? The answer is that Shabbos candles are more important because without the light of the Shabbos candles, families would have to sit in the dark and this would lead to frayed nerves and arguments.

When Cutting the Challah

Chazal suggest that when preparing to slice the challah, the husband should make an initial indentation before cutting so that the slicing procedure is smoother and quicker. This may seem insignificant. However, if people are hungry and impatient, even a short delay in the slicing of the challah could undermine *shalom bayis.*

Be Gentle and Thoughtful about Teaching the Halachos of Shabbos

A husband told me of his impatience over his wife's habit of preparing for Shabbos at the last moment and not being careful about her preparation of food on Shabbos. This had been going on for more than a decade. But when he learned how to focus on his own *menuchas hanefesh,* he was able to speak to her in a gentle and patient manner.

6. SENSITIVITY

The EMBERS Principle: *In a state of menuchas hanefesh, we develop a sensitivity and understanding of how Hashem has guided our precious individual and shared life journeys. We use this understanding to continuously balance each other in our evolving* *relationship. However, in a state of pizur hanefesh, we lose our understanding of the meaning of our individual life journey and can no longer be sensitive to each other's unique needs that enable us to feel secure.*

◇ Introduction

Hashem has placed each of us in our unique life situations. Whether it's our early family experiences, or our personal, emotional, physical or social challenges, we all invest a good part of our lives learning to overcome life's challenges. Sensitivity is our ability to understand and care for each other's life journey as a significant way of bonding, while learning to care about this deeper dimension of each other's lives. When I meet with dating, engaged and especially married couples, I invariably try to help them develop an insight into the meaning of becoming sensitive to each other's personal history.

The *Chassan* Who Didn't Understand

When Jake and Ruthy came to see me, they had been married for just three months. Both were young and they had dated for five weeks before deciding to get engaged. In the three months since their wedding, their marriage had been a series of ongoing crises, which now threatened to tear them apart.

During our first meeting, Ruthy shared, "For me, dating and engagement had been like a dream. Our relationship was all that I had hoped it would be. I dated a lot of guys. But I was very careful because my parents had a difficult life together; there were many times I felt they would divorce. My father had a terrible temper. I was always fearful that I would marry someone who would treat me the way my father treated my mother. So I always looked for someone who was gentle and sensitive. I thought Jake was everything I had dreamed of in a husband. I even told him how important it was that he was gentle with me. And all through our dating and engagement, I never saw anything in him that made me worry he could be angry or hurtful."

"So when did the problem start?" I asked her.

"I know exactly when it began. It was the first night of *sheva brachos*. We were driving to Jake's family, and he was listening to one of those talk-radio stations. It was close to election time, and everyone was very agitated. The talk-show host was very loud and angry. I'm not used to hearing these things. And on top of everything else, I hadn't slept in two nights. I was very tired and had a headache. So I asked Jake to lower the volume or change the station. He kept on telling me another minute, another minute. My head was aching and I thought it was going to split. So I asked him again. Just then a car came out of nowhere and almost hit us. Jake slammed on the brakes and shouted at me. He said things that I never heard him say before. I was shocked and very hurt. I couldn't believe that this was my *chassan*. I started to cry. He saw how upset I was, but instead of apologizing, he just started driving again and never said a word. I felt more and more hurt. I waited the whole night for him to apologize. It never happened.

"Then I started to notice other things about his behavior toward me. I began to feel more and more upset and depressed. All he ever told me was that I was just too sensitive, and that I was always making a big deal about things. Ever since that time, nothing ever really got better and I'm not sure I want to stay married to him, because there is no way I can go on living with someone who hurts me and doesn't care."

The scenario could have happened to anyone. It was a perfect storm of conditions. The political climate was tense with an upcoming election. Talk-radio hosts, particularly around election time, tend to be loud and abrasive. A young *kallah* feels tired and worn out after weeks of preparation for the wedding. A *chassan* is pulled in by the hype of the hot presidential election and is riveted to every word. Suddenly, a car comes out of nowhere and an accident is just barely averted. Tension escalates, and the *chassan's* temper flares for just a moment. Yet that moment is all it takes. In a second, his *kallah's* dreams are shattered. She's been deeply wounded — in a fight over a loud and abrasive talk-show host. Her *chassan's* behavior triggers her fears of earlier life experiences. And even if these experiences had never occurred, her husband's momentary loss of control creates a breach in her sense of trust and safety that she feels toward the person she committed her life to less than twenty-four hours earlier.

Ruthy's fears do not go away. Where she comes from, angry men continue to be very hurtful. At that moment, she discovered that her new husband is also an angry man. Yet Jake is unaware of her fears about anger and he has never developed the skills to address her hurt. So he hides his embarrassment and remains silent. Jake's attitude is, "I'll be quiet and it will go away." But as anyone who has ever been married will testify, these wounds never really go away. They may go into hiding, but they fester and ferment deep beneath the surface, always fearful of the same event or outburst recurring. Ruthy's wounds will only go away when Jake can truly understand her, when he feels her hurt and can deeply and truly ask her for forgiveness and reassure her that it will never happen again.

◇ The *Kallah* with the Missing Parent

We can contrast the story of Ruthy and Jake with two other couples who learned to appreciate the meaning of sensitivity as the bond in their relationship.

Mordechai was a programmer for a bank, and an amateur musician on the side. He had been dating for about five years and had never been able to get past a third date. After our meeting to discuss his dating experiences, he met Shulamis, a teacher in a local Bais Yaakov. For the first time, Mordechai was able to keep the relationship going to a fifth date. While he felt comfortable with Shulamis, he felt that there was an element missing in their relationship, but couldn't define it.

After hearing about this from the *shadchan,* Shulamis also related that while she felt he was a very sincere young man, she felt a gap in their relationship. It was clear that though they both were willing to continue, the relationship appeared to be stuck on this indefinable sense of "something is missing."

Mordechai and I met once more to discuss the relationship in greater depth. He mentioned that when he'd picked her up, her father was present.

"Where was her mother?" I asked.

"Her mother died earlier this year. She's still in her year of *aveilus* (mourning)."

"Does she have siblings?" was my next question.

"No. She's an only child."

What I was hearing made me incredulous. He had been dating a young woman whose mother had died this past year and was an only child, and all the while he had never related to this profound loss in her life. I developed a series of questions around her mother and her loss that I felt Mordechai should ask Shulamis on their next date. Following the date, Mordechai and I spoke. He had raised the issue of her mother's death and its meaning to her. Shulamis had responded in an open and very heartfelt manner. It clearly made her feel that Mordechai was able to listen to and understand this very profound loss in her life.

A few months later, I attended their wedding and was moved beyond words when I saw Shulamis walk down the aisle with just her father. I said to myself that perhaps Hashem's way of filling the loss in her life was to have that loss serve as the bond that brought this couple over the void that had been separating them.

◇ The Question that Changed Two Lives

Moshe was a yeshivah student who had been dating for a number of years and had seen a significant number of young women. He asked me to help him find his *bashert*. Moshe was a thoughtful and serious young man who invariably found reasons to back out of relationships before they became serious. I noticed that he had an almost imperceptible speech impediment. It was not easy to pick up, and there appeared to be times when it was not evident at all.

After we met, he began dating Tziril. At first, he seemed interested in her and called me following each date with upbeat news. After the seventh or eighth date, he began to pick up her "flaws" on his radar screen, and by the next date he was ready to end the relationship and move on. He felt he was justified — and I felt this was a repeat of the patterns he had demonstrated in the past, and I openly shared my opinion.

"I think you are being unfair to me," he protested. "You cannot expect me to become engaged to someone I feel has basic flaws that would cause us to have an unhappy marriage. I have a date tomorrow night and I want to end it." He was adamant in his position.

Finally, I made a deal with him. "Okay, I agree you can end the relationship tomorrow, but there is one condition."

"What's that?"

"Before you end the relationship, I want you to ask her

if she noticed that you have a slight speech impediment."

"Why in the world would I do that?"

My answer was, "Because I want to see if she is sensitive to who you are."

At first he protested, but then he relented, as it was the only way I would agree for him to end it.

The day after the date he called me.

"Did you end it?" I asked.

"No, we're going out again tonight."

"What happened?"

"I was about to say good-bye and tell her it's over, when I remembered our agreement. So as we sat in my car at about 11:30 p.m., I asked her if she noticed that I had a speech impediment. Her answer was that she realized it from the very first date and even told me when it became more prominent and when it was less noticeable. She began to share many things she saw about me that I never realized she picked up. We spoke for five more hours and finished the date at 4:30 a.m."

Moshe and Tziril dated another few weeks and were then engaged.

When I had committed Moshe to our agreement, I had no idea that such a scenario would ensue. At the same time, it was clear to me that there was a deeper dimension to him that had never emerged in dating. I realized that everyone with even the slightest impediment or challenge struggles in a very personal way to overcome such a challenge, and I felt that by Moshe asking Tziril this question, it could possibly serve as an opening for Moshe to share this struggle. In fact, Tziril had been observing him all along, watching how his slight speech impediment became more and less noticeable and how these changes were connected to other aspects of his life. I could never have realized how sensitive she was, and neither could Moshe.

For the first time in his years of dating, Moshe appreciated the meaning of sensitivity and it spoke to him very deeply. The conversation began at 11:30 p.m. just before he was about to say good-bye; it lasted another five hours, and years later it is still continuing between the two. The deeper truth is very simple. Everyone needs to share his life journey and to have it heard, understood and cared for.

As mentioned, at the heart of our need to experience and share sensitivity is that Hashem creates us with a *neshamah* of silk that serves as the delicate and pure sense of our self. We need these sensitivities to feel that our deepest self can feel safe and trusting with the person with whom we share our life. Sensitivity is our emotional lifeblood. We need it to bring love and warmth into our lives, to bring children into the world — and to raise them to be caring people and *ovdei* Hashem.

◇ Developing Sensitivity in a Relationship

Because we are created with a soul of silk, there can be no true emerging relationship without it. The interface between the sensitivity of self and our *neshamah* is as interwoven and delicate as where the sky meets the horizon. This is why when we do something that is hurtful, the wound to the self also touches the *neshamah* and does not fade with time. Perhaps this is the reason Chazal tell us that when we embarrass someone, our punishment is eternal. This is because until we alleviate the pain of the person we have embarrassed, the pain will not subside. In many situations, I actually encourage dating and engaged couples to learn to become each other's healers.

There are two levels by which we understand this sensitivity. The first is a shared understanding that pertains to all relationships. Even the slightest abrasion mars the gentleness of who we are within. Thus we can never use abrasive or foul language, raise our voice in anger or communicate in any manner that a healthy individual would understand to be hurtful. This first level is common to us all. No one can tolerate hurtful or critical behavior from a friend and perhaps a future life partner. When we feel close to someone and are hurt, we can never defend against its damage.

The second level relates to how each of us struggles through our challenges in life. For example, the Torah tells us that reminding a *baal teshuvah* or a *ger* (convert) about his past is painful because it evokes memories that may be embarrassing. In the same way, we all carry our own memories of painful moments of our childhood and life experiences, which can be triggered by even a suggestion or a gesture. Dating and engaged couples need to be aware of these vulnerabilities and be ever sensitive to the triggers that can cause such penetrating pain.

◇ **Guidelines for Sensitivity**

I would like to present a number of guidelines that can be helpful toward integrating this level of sensitivity into the EMBERS of our relationships.

Gaining Insight into Our Childhood Years

Developing sensitivity requires us to be conscious of how we carry the hurts, wounds and disappointments of our earlier years, particularly childhood, and to understand how these experiences have contributed to our own growth in life.

Developing Insight into the Challenges of Our Partner

Just like we need to understand how our growing-up experiences have impacted our lives, we need to gain insight into how these experiences have affected our partner.

"Just As"

When we feel hurt by our partner, our emerging sensitivity enables us to say "just as":

"Just as I am feeling hurt by the conflict we are experiencing, you, too, are feeling hurt."

"Just as I like to be remembered on my birthday, so do you like to be remembered."

Sharing Our Life Story

The more we share and learn about our growing-up experiences, the more sensitive we can be about each other's deeper selves.

Caring

Caring means learning to be empathic about what your partner has been through and still goes through in life. This requires deep understanding and commitment.

Vulnerability

Sensitivity requires that we become aware of our vulnerabilities. Each of us faces vulnerabilities. They may be related to losses we have suffered, to physical or emotional impairments or to painful life experiences.

Creating a Secure and Safe Environment

Sensitivity means learning to create a safe and comfortable environment for our relationship to grow, through our tone and expressions of caring and concern, as well as through gestures and displays of affection.

Attraction

Know what helps you feel attracted to each other, while not attempting to feel compromised for who you are within. Never attempt to create an attraction that will create jealousy and insecurity by attracting others.

Entertainment

Entertainment should always bring a couple together and never compromise each other's values and sensibilities. The bottom line is that the growing relationship is always about two *neshamos* emerging and recognizing each other above all others in the world. Any entertainment needs to enhance this process and not deaden it.

Significant Personal Events

Always be aware of significant personal events, including:

+ Birthdays
+ Graduations
+ Yahrtzeits

Religious Preferences

Sensitivity means learning to respect and deal with religious differences. This will frequently require a couple to select a mutually acceptable religious authority or *posek* to settle all halachic and *hashkafic* questions.

Maintaining a Level of Caring Contact

Sensitivity means remembering your dating or engaged partner in a caring way. Achieve this by:

+ Agreeing to a mutually acceptable schedule of phone and personal contacts.

+ Never using texting as a way of drawing each other into a dialogue. It always cheapens and trivializes a relationship.

+ Never sharing negative feelings before consulting with

someone who can help you be understood in a manner that will not harm your partner.

✦ Being generous with compliments and other non-intrusive gestures of attention and appreciation.

✦ Providing small ways of saying you care through flowers, candy and other little gifts that are symbolic of your commitment to this growing relationship.

Be Sensitive to Your Changing Moods

Sensitivity means learning to be aware of the quality of your moods. Once you are aware, you can create transformations or share your positive state of mind.

George Pransky provides a useful color chart to own the color of your moods:

✦ Black Moods: Gloom

✦ Gray Moods: Stress

✦ White Moods: Feeling easy

✦ Silver Moods: Feeling enjoyment and appreciation

✦ Golden Moods: Experiencing fulfillment and gratitude

Daily Flow of Life

Sensitivity means learning to engage in dating activities that enable your mutual need for sensitivity to emerge. These include:

✦ Taking walks in botanical gardens, along the shore or in a quiet park

✦ Visiting couples you both respect and who care about your well-being, such as former teachers, *rebbeim* or family members.

✦ Listening to pleasant music when you are driving

together rather than talk-radio — and avoiding using your cell phone for long periods of time.

◇ **EMBERS**
Communication Exercises

EMBERS *Preferences*

Expressions represent a crucial area of marital life. Cultivating a meaningful relationship and engagement means learning to communicate your own EMBERS preferences and learning to understand your partner's preferences, as well. The following communications exercises will guide you to define and share your EMBERS preferences with each other in a safe and coherent manner.

One way to enhance your dating relationship and engagement is through an interactive dialogue that is based on sharing the Five Dimensions of EMBERS.

To use this program, follow these guidelines for each of the EMBERS preferences you wish to communicate:

Define Your Preferences: Select an area of EMBERS and fill out the personal worksheet. (5-10 minutes)

Share Your Preferences: Give each other your worksheet. Study your partner's preferences and write your comments and observations. (5-15 minutes)

Communicate Your Preferences: Communicate your understanding by following these communications guidelines. (20-30 minutes)

+ Study your partner's preferences and select any preference you wish to comment on.

+ Share your understanding of your spouse's preference by saying, "I think you are saying ...," and then share your comment.

- Your partner can either say you are correct and thank you, or he/she can add an additional thought. You will then incorporate this additional thought into your understanding.

- Switch and give your partner a chance.

Some Guiding Principles

- Always listen from your partner's perspective.

- Don't try to resolve anything or answer; just listen quietly and try to understand.

- Your goal is to help your partner feel understood.

- Once you feel your partner has understood you, always express gratitude.

EXPRESSIONS

These are your verbal and non-verbal expressions that enable me to experience a sense of comfort and trust:

- When you speak to me in a quiet and unhurried tone.

_____

_____

_____

_____

_____

_____

_____

_____

_____

These are your verbal and non-verbal expressions that cause me to feel discomfort:

_____

_____

_____

_____

_____

_____

_____

_____

_____

Comments, Insights and Awareness

_____

_____

_____

_____

_____

_____

_____

_____

_____

_____

_____

MOODS

Your mood(s) that enable(s) me to experience a sense of trust and security is/are:

_____

_____

_____

_____

_____

_____

_____

Your mood(s) that has/have an effect on my sense of insecurity is/are:

_____

_____

_____

_____

_____

_____

_____

Comments, Insights and Awareness

_____

_____

_____

_____

_____

_____

_____

_____

_____

_____

BEHAVIOR

Ways you behave that enable me to experience a sense of trust and security are:

_____

_____

_____

_____

_____

_____

_____

_____

Ways you behave that have a negative effect on my sense of insecurity are:

_____

_____

_____

_____

_____

_____

_____

_____

_____

_____

Comments, Insights and Awareness

_____

_____

_____

_____

_____

_____

_____

ENJOYMENT

Things we enjoy together that enable me to feel more fulfilled are:

_____

_____

_____

_____

_____

_____

_____

_____

Comments, Insights and Awareness

_____

_____

_____

_____

_____

_____

_____

RUCHNIUS

The aspects of our religious life that enable me to experience a deeper sense of fulfillment and meaning are:

_____

_____

_____

_____

_____

_____

_____

_____

_____

I feel our lives would be enhanced if we undertook these commitments toward *ruchnius:*

_____

_____

_____

_____

_____

_____

Comments, Insights and Awareness

_____

_____

_____

_____

_____

_____

_____

SENSITIVITY

These are the areas of my personal life that I feel are important for you to be sensitive to:

_____

_____

_____

_____

_____

_____

_____

Comments, Insights and Awareness

_____

_____

_____

_____

_____

◇ **Bringing *Menuchas Hanefesh* into our Homes and Communities**

This book has focused on the centrality of *menuchas hanefesh* in *shidduchim*, dating relationships and engagement. However, this work is only a single part of our vision to promote the integration of this principle into every area of our Torah lives. With this goal in mind, we have established the Menuchah V'Simchah Foundation. The Foundation will concentrate its efforts on educating our Torah community about incorporating this precious gift of *menuchas hanefesh* into the fabric of our individual and communal lives by focusing on seven distinct areas of life:

1. Center for Marital Enhancement

Couples in all stages of their marriage will be provided with services that strengthen existing bonds and teach them skills to heal conflicts and dysfunctional patterns of married life.

2. Curriculum Development for Boys' and Girls' Yeshivos

Programs will be developed for guiding young men and women from high school through *bais medrash* and seminary.

3. *Center for Dating and Relationship-Building Skills*

Singles will be taught skills to enhance their ability to successfully date and marry.

4. *Center for Divorce Intervention*

Couples in the midst of divorce proceedings will be provided with the means to consider healthier and more productive options based on their growth in *menuchas hanefesh*.

5. *Parent and Child Programs*

+ Children will be guided to achieve emotional and relational maturity.
+ Pathways for healthy parent and child communications will be developed.

+ Children will be taught to navigate the challenges of contemporary society from a Torah perspective.

6. Professional Training Center for:

+ Mental Health Practitioners
+ Rabbis
+ Teachers
+ Yeshivah *Rebbeim*
+ Volunteers
+ *Shadchanim*

7. Center for Healthy Living

Services will be provided for:

+ Emotional well-being
+ Stress and anxiety in the home and workplace
+ Contemporary addictions

Glossary

Adam — the first man

Adam gadol — a great Torah personage

Aharon Hakohen — Aaron the High Priest, brother of Moshe

Ahavah — love

Am Yisrael — the Jewish nation

Aron Hakodesh — the Holy Ark

Askanim — community activists

Av — the tenth month of the Jewish year

Aveil — a mourner

Avodah Zarah — tractate of the Talmud that focuses primarily on sins of idolatry

Avodas Hakodesh — holy work

Avodas Hashem — service of Hashem

Avos — our forefathers, Abraham, Isaac and Jacob

Avraham Avinu — Abraham our forefather

Baal teshuvah — a Jew who has returned to religious observance

Baalei emunah — people who possess faith

Bachur, bachurim — young, unmarried yeshivah student(s)

Bachuros — young, unmarried women

Bais din — a Jewish court

Bais Hamikdash — the Holy Temple in Jerusalem

Bais medrash — house of Torah study

Bar mitzvah — thirteen, the age at which a Jewish male becomes obligated to observe the Torah commandments

Baruch Hashem — thank Hashem

Bas kol — a form of Divine communication that is on a level lower than actual prophecy

Bas mitzvah — twelve, the age at which a Jewish female becomes obligated to observe the Torah commandments

Bashert — one's Divinely chosen mate

Bayis ne'eman b'Yisrael — a faithful Jewish home

Bechirah, Bechirah chafshis — choice, free choice

Ben Torah — a Torah-educated person

Bereishis — the Book of Genesis

B'ezras Hashem — with Hashem's help

B'tzelem Elokim — in the Divine image

Bitachon — trust in Hashem

B'nei Yisrael — the Children of Israel, the Jewish people

Brachah, brachos — blessing(s)

Brachos — tractate of the Talmud that primarily focuses on the laws of blessings

Bubby — grandmother

Bris — circumcision

Chachmah — wisdom

Chag, chagim — holiday(s)

Challah — traditional bread (usually braided) used at Sabbath and holiday meals

Chanukah — festival that commemorates the victory of the Jews over the Syrian Greeks and the restoration of the Holy Temple

Chas v'shalom — Heaven forbid

Chassan, chassanim — groom(s)

Chassidic — pertaining to Chassidus, a branch of Orthodox Judaism promoting spirituality and joy, which arose in eastern Europe and Russia in the latter half of the eighteenth century

Chasunah — wedding

Chavah — Eve, the first woman

Chavrusa — Torah study partner

Chazal — acronym for "the Sages, may their memory be blessed"

Chessed — kindness

Cheshbon hanefesh — spiritual accounting

Chiddush — renewal; novel Torah insight

Chinuch — education

Chizuk — encouragement

Chol Hamoed Pesach — the intermediate days of Passover

Chovos Halevavos — *Duties of the Heart*, a classic Jewish work by Rabbeinu Bachya ibn Pakuda

Chumash — the Five Books of Moses

Chupah — wedding canopy; figuratively, marriage

Chutzpah — audacity

Da'as Torah — the insights and opinions of a true Torah personality, which are assumed to be in consonance with Torah ideals

Daf yomi — the daily study of a page of Talmud

Dan l'chaf z'chus — judging a person favorably

Daven (Yidd.) — pray

Dayan — judge

Dovid Hamelech —David the King, founder of the Davidic dynasty and forebear of the future Messiah

Eisav — Esau, brother of Jacob

Eliyahu Hanavi — Elijah the Prophet

Eretz Yisrael — the Land of Israel

Erev Shabbos — Friday

Esrog — the citron fruit, taken as one of the Four Species, which are a Torah commandment on the holiday of Sukkos

Frum — religiously observant

Frumkeit — religious observance

Gadol, gadol hador — Torah leader of a generation

Gan Aden — the Garden of Eden

Gaon — Torah genius

Gashmius — materialism, physicality

Gedolim — Torah giants

Gemara — Talmud

Hakaras hatov — gratitude

Halachah, halachos — Torah law(s)

Har Sinai — Mount Sinai

Harav — the Rabbi

Hashem — the Almighty

Hashkafah, hashkafos — Torah-based outlook(s)

Hashra'as haShechinah beineichem — the Divine presence resting among you

Imahos — our foremothers, Sarah, Rivkah, Rachel and Leah

Kallah — bride

Kavanah — intention, focus

Kedushah — holiness

Kehillah — community

Keruvim — the angelic statues on top of the Holy Ark

Ki Sisa — one of the weekly Torah portions in the Book of Deuteronomy

Kiddush Levanah — blessing over the New Moon

Klal Yisrael — the Jewish people as a whole

Kohen Gadol — the High Priest

Kollel — institution of higher learning for intensive Torah study, the members of which are usually married men

Kosel — the Western Wall

Kotzer ruach — shortness of breath; impatience

Krias Shema — recitation of the Shema, the traditional Jewish prayer that proclaims the absolute unity of Hashem

L'chaim — lit., "to life!"; a traditional Jewish toast

Leviim — Levites

Maariv — the evening prayer

Mashgiach — spiritual supervisor or guide, responsible for the non-academic areas of yeshivah students' lives; supervisor of kosher standards

Matzos — unleavened bread eaten on Passover

Mayim amukim — deep waters

Mazal tov — good luck

Mechilah — forgiveness

Menorah — the Candelabra in the Tabernacle, and later in the Holy Temple

Menuchah — tranquility

Menuchas hanefesh — tranquility of spirit

Meraglim — the Spies who spoke badly of the Land of Israel and caused the Jews to be punished with forty years of wandering in the desert

Mesader kiddushin — rabbi who officiates at a wedding ceremony

Metziah — discovery; a found item

Middos — characteristics

Midrash — homiletic interpretation of Scripture

Minchah — the afternoon prayer

Mishkan — the Tabernacle; the mind as a sanctuary

Mishlei — the Book of Proverbs

Mishloach manos — gifts of food to fellow Jews, one of the commandments on the holiday of Purim

Mitzrayim — Egypt

Mitzvah, mitzvos — Torah commandment(s)

Moshe Rabbeinu — Moses our Teacher

Motza'ei Shabbos — Saturday night

Mussar vaadim — small study groups focused on character improvement

Nachas — satisfaction

Ne'ilah — the final prayer on Yom Kippur

Neshamah, neshamos — soul(s)

Niggun — Jewish melody

Nissan — the seventh month of the Jewish year

Ovdei Hashem — servants of Hashem

Parashah, parashas — the weekly Torah portion (of)

Pasuk — verse

Pesach — Passover

Pizur hanefesh — lit., "scattering of spirit," the feeling of being fragmented, troubled, hurt and alone

Posek — halachic decisor

Purim — holiday that commemorates the salvation of the Jews from destruction at the hands of the wicked Haman in the days of the Persian-Medean empire

Ratzon — will

Ratzon Hashem — Divine will

Rav — rabbi

Re'eh — one of the weekly Torah portions in the Book of Deuteronomy

Rebbe — leader of a Chassidic group

Rebbetzin — rabbi's wife

Rebbi, rebbeim — Torah teacher(s)

Retzon Hashem — the will of Hashem

Rosh Hashanah — the Jewish New Year

Rosh Yeshivah — head of a yeshiva

Ruach — spirit

Ruchnius — spirituality

Satan — the angelic force that tempts a person to sin and acts as the accuser in Divine judgment

Seder — Torah learning session

Sefer, sefarim — Torah book(s)

Seudah — festive meal

Shadchan, shadchanim — matchmakers

Shaitel — wig

Shalom — peace

Shalom bayis — domestic peace

Shanah rishonah — the first year of marriage

Shanah tovah — Good Year

Shechinah — the Divine presence

Shema Yisrael — traditional Jewish prayer that proclaims the absolute unity of Hashem

Shemoneh Esrei — the Silent Devotion, the central prayer recited every morning, afternoon and evening

Sheva brachos — meals of celebration during the seven days following a Jewish wedding

Shidduch, shidduchim — marital match(es)

Shiluach hakan — the Torah commandment of sending away the mother bird before taking her eggs or chicks

Shiur, shiurim — Torah class(es)

Shivah — seven-day period of mourning following the death and burial of an immediate family member

Shlita — acronym for *"sheyiz-keh l'chayim tovim v'aruchim,"* he should merit a good, long life

Shlomo Hamelech — King Solomon, son of King David; builder of the first Temple in Jerusalem

Shtick — gimmick

Simchah, smachos — celebration(s)

Simchas chassan — gladdening a groom and bride

Sukkah — temporary dwelling occupied by Jews on the hioliday of Sukkos

Taharas hamishpachah — the laws of family purity

Tallis — prayer shawl

Talmid chacham, talmidei chachamim — Torah scolar(s)

Talmid, talmidim — Torah student(s)

Tanach — Scriptures

Tanna — Sage of the Mishnaic era

Tefillah, tefillos — prayer(s)

Tefillin — phylacteries, small

black boxes containing scrolls with specific Torah portions, worn by adult Jewish males during morning prayers

Tehillim — Psalms

Tishah b'Av — the ninth of the month of Av, the national day of mourning for the destruction of the First and Second Temples in Jerusalem, as well as for the numerous national Jewish tragedies throughout the millennia

Tzaddik — righteous man

Tzedakah — charity

Tzelem Elokim — the Divine image

Tzomet — crossroads

Vaad — group

Vayechi — one of the weekly Torah portions, last in the Book of Genesis

V'ahavta es Hashem Elokecha — and you shall love Hashem your G-d

Vort — engagement party

Yaakov Avinu — Jacob our forefather

Yahrtzeit — anniversary of someone's death

Yarmulke — skullcap

Yerushalayim — Jerusalem

Yeshivah — Torah school

Yiddishkeit — Judaism

Yitzchak Avinu — Isaac our forefather

Yom Kippur — the Day of Atonement

Yom tov, yamim tovim — holiday(s)

Yosef Hatzaddik — Joseph the Righteous

Zaidy — grandfather

Zemiros — traditional Jewish songs sung on the Sabbath

Zt"l — acronym for "*zecher tzaddik livrachah*," may the memory of the righteous be for a blessing